W9-BPO-329

ASSASSINATION
AND
Commemoration

ASSASSINATION
A N D
Commemoration

JFK, Dallas, and The Sixth Floor Museum at Dealey Plaza

Stephen Fagin

Foreword by Conover Hunt
Preface by Edward T. Linenthal

UNIVERSITY OF OKLAHOMA PRESS : NORMAN

Library of Congress Cataloging-in-Publication Data

Fagin, Stephen, 1979–
  Assassination and commemoration : JFK, Dallas, and The
Sixth Floor Museum at Dealey Plaza / Stephen Fagin.
     pages cm
  Includes bibliographical references and index.
  ISBN 978-0-8061-4358-3 (hardcover : alk.
paper) 1. Kennedy, John F. (John Fitzgerald), 1917–1963—
Assassination. 2. Sixth Floor Museum at Dealey Plaza.
I. Title.
  E842.9.F34 2013
  973.922092—dc23

                        2012050643

The paper in this book meets the guidelines for permanence
and durability of the Committee on Production Guidelines for
Book Longevity of the Council on Library Resources, Inc. ∞

Book design and composition: David Alcorn, Alcorn Publication Design

For my parents,
Steve and Debra Fagin

And all of the other schoolchildren who were
changed forever on November 22, 1963

CONTENTS

List of Illustrations   IX

Foreword, by Conover Hunt   XIII

Preface, by Edward T. Linenthal   XVII

Acknowledgments   XXI

Introduction   XXIII

1. A Site of Tragedy   3
2. A Site of Shame   44
3. A Site of Reflection   59
4. A Site of Conflict   89
5. A Site of History   123

Conclusion   165

Epilogue   170

Notes   175

Bibliography   219

Index   229

ILLUSTRATIONS

Figures

1. Author standing alongside UN ambassador William vanden Heuvel during the fortieth anniversary of the assassination in 2003   xxix

2. Lee Harvey Oswald is escorted by homicide detectives Richard Sims and Elmer Boyd   5

3. The presidential limousine departs Love Field for a motorcade through downtown Dallas   8

4. The motorcade makes its fateful turn from Houston Street to Elm Street   9

5. A man walks along Commerce Street in downtown Dallas on the evening of November 22, 1963   11

6. The Texas Theatre in Oak Cliff, where suspect Lee Harvey Oswald was arrested   12

7. Dallas Police and other law enforcement officials surround the Texas School Book Depository   14

8. Dallas Police crime scene photograph of the "sniper's perch" on the sixth floor of the Depository   15

9. Dallas Police crime scene photograph looking down into the sniper's perch   16

10. Right-wing protesters stand outside Memorial Auditorium on UN Day, October 24, 1963   24

11. Jack Ruby converses with his attorneys Joe Tonahill and Melvin Belli in 1964   28

12. The news media surround Dallas district attorney
    Henry Wade after the guilty verdict in the Ruby trial
    (March 14, 1964)   30
13. The John F. Kennedy Memorial near Dealey Plaza, 2009   34
14. Aubrey Mayhew purchased the Texas School Book Depository in
    1970 to create a museum and research center   39
15. A view of the empty sixth floor by restoration architect
    Eugene George   66
16. Dallas County public works director Judson Shook stands alongside
    the Texas Historical Marker (March 29, 1981)   74
17. John Sissom's privately owned John F. Kennedy Museum across
    Houston Street from the Depository building   76
18. The Sixth Floor exhibit, conceptual design (October 1982)   82
19. The Sixth Floor exhibit, conceptual design (June 1983)   86
20. Dallas County judge Lee F. Jackson (2002)   99
21. The Visitors Center and elevator shaft under construction
    in 1988   109
22. The Sixth Floor Exhibit, as opened in 1989   132
23. Looking toward the "Assassination" section of The Sixth Floor
    exhibit   134
24. The "Legacy" section of The Sixth Floor exhibit in 1989   141
25. During exhibit construction, a worker repairs damage to the
    southeast corner window   144
26. The reconstructed "sniper's perch" in The Sixth Floor exhibit
    (1989)   145
27. Publicity image of Conover Hunt and Lindalyn Adams
    (February 1989)   147
28. The completed Visitors Center and elevator shaft (1989)   149
29. Bob Hays and a TV news crew surprise the exhibit's one millionth
    visitor in June 1992   156

Plates

1. Enthusiastic crowds greet President Kennedy at Dallas Love Field on November 22, 1963   115
2. The assassination of President Kennedy as captured in the home movie of Abraham Zapruder   116
3. Mourners transform Dealey Plaza into a shrine   117
4. Dealey Plaza in the decade following the assassination   118
5. The exhibit planners at work in May 1988   119
6. Documentary filmmakers Allen and Cynthia Mondell share ideas (February 1988)   119
7. A close-up view inside the model of The Sixth Floor exhibit   120
8. Sketch showing the exterior elevator shaft and Visitors Center   121
9. The former Texas School Book Depository building, 2009   122
10. Dealey Plaza, 2009   122

FOREWORD

I am honored to write the foreword for this publication, the first that exhaustively chronicles the creation of The Sixth Floor Museum at Dealey Plaza, which opened in February 1989 and welcomed 6 million visitors in its first twenty years of operation. As the original project director and the museum's chief curator and later historian, I was one of many now known as "the founders." Although I am assigned a significant role in Fagin's narrative, the original exhibition on the sixth floor of the former Texas School Book Depository in Dallas owed its success to the efforts of many people. Lindalyn Adams led a team of eye and ear witnesses, elected officials, community leaders, museum exhibition and film professionals, architects, historians, government investigators, and assassination researchers, all of whom contributed time, money, talent, heart, and sometimes stubborn determination to provide people the opportunity to visit a tragic site and determine for themselves the meaning of JFK's life, times, death, and legacy for their own lives.

I salute those who are gone and honor those founders who have survived. I speak for all of us in applauding the outstanding work performed by the talented staff of the museum in the decades since our early work in establishing what is today a nationally respected educational institution. Certainly I applaud the museum's leadership for encouraging Stephen Fagin to advance his education and for giving him the time to research and write this penetrating behind-the-scenes analysis of the creation of a new cultural organization. Fagin is an excellent writer and a thorough researcher, and he has admirably captured the temper of the times and the spirit of the project team.

When the museum opened, the majority of the audience had actually lived the events of 1963. With only one exception, the project team for The Sixth Floor consisted of men and women who had experienced firsthand the overwhelming shock of JFK's death. Stephen Fagin and many of the other professionals at the museum today have inherited memory, learned from their families, the media, books, films, and their own visits to the assassination site. Two-thirds of the current visitors to the museum are of his or a younger generation.

Now Fagin has written a history directed toward this audience. His book accurately portrays the founders' individual and collective roles with honesty and a respect that is quite flattering, providing compelling proof of the technical and emotional difficulties that we encountered on our long journey to telling this terrible story in a truthful and meaningful way. Stephen's own peak moment in memory is the *Challenger* explosion. Mine will always remain the afternoon of Friday, November 22, 1963, when Prentis Gandy, a friend at Hampton High School in Virginia, heard a bulletin on his transistor radio and yelled down the hallway, "Kennedy's been shot!" I can see him as clearly now as I saw him then. Prentis died in his early twenties, but he lives on in my mind. Unfortunately, future tragedies will create new peak moments that become cemented in the collective memory. For those who experience them, the strongest moments will not only produce shock and fear but also engender keen awareness of personal loss and a sense of stolen innocence.

When The Sixth Floor opened in 1989, the local media reported that Dallasites had come together to serve the needs of an international audience of visitors who came to Dealey Plaza in search of information about a troubling world event. The national media reported that the opening symbolized Dallas's ability finally to come to grips with its painful past. Both interpretations were correct. Yet Dallasites did not generally visit the museum for years after 1989; the pain was still too raw, the fear too great. More of the local community came to Dealey Plaza in 1993 when the entire assassination site was dedicated as a National Historic Landmark. In a very real way, those dignified ceremonies represented the passing of the baton from memory to history. Oliver Stone's film *JFK* was upsetting to many Dallasites, but it empowered young people all over the country to demand that all remaining documents about the assassination be released to the public. I heard that Chuck Briggs, who served on the project team after retiring as staff director at the Central Intelligence Agency (CIA), had been brought out of retirement to declassify the same materials that he had classified decades earlier.

In my view, credit for the creation of The Sixth Floor Museum should always include the people of Dallas. Willing to put their trust in the always gracious but very determined Lindalyn Adams and her outstanding leadership board, they put aside a hideous collective memory to allow and eventually to support a controversial project to its completion. In the decades since 1989 the museum has been successful in its efforts to increase community involvement, while it continues serving the education needs of a global audience. The original project team and its leaders created a highly successful museum experience, but Dallas had to approve of the effort and live with its results. That took guts. Dallasites raised the funds, led the communications efforts, and supplied much of the content in the museum. Dallas is the only city I know of that has ever been accused, however unfairly, of killing a president. When we talk about the meaning of courage, Dallas earns my vote.

Conover Hunt
Hampton, Virginia

PREFACE

I vividly recall my visit to The Sixth Floor Museum several years ago on the anniversary of the assassination of President John F. Kennedy. As I moved through the exhibition, I was transported in time, becoming once again a junior at University High School in Ann Arbor, Michigan, where I first heard the news that JFK had been murdered. I saw yet again the familiar images of the President and First Lady greeting an enthusiastic crowd at Dallas's Love Field, the all-too-familiar limousine taking them on this last journey, and Walter Cronkite struggling to contain his emotions as he notified his television audience that the President had died.

The reserved, articulate, heart-breaking exhibition, housed in the Texas School Book Depository, was even more resonant on the anniversary. The enduring deadliness of the sniper's perch—enclosed in glass and painstakingly reconstructed to appear as it was on that fateful day—mocked my wish to travel back in time and do something, anything, to change history: Don't go to Dallas, Mr. President! Don't travel with the top down! Don't turn on Elm Street! Bend over before the shots come!

I recently found myself rooting for Jake Epping, the protagonist of Stephen King's novel *11/22/63*, who travels back in time to change history. On one of his time trips, well before the assassination, Epping visits the Texas School Book Depository and feels a "palpable sense of wrongness about the building," a "sense of sentient menace." He adds: "And I remembered feeling that something was in there. Something alive. Something that *wanted* me to walk into it." Much later, but still before he changes history, the iconic windows on the sixth floor speak to him as he sits outside the building: "*We know a secret,* they said. *We're going to be famous, and you can't stop us.*"

The building did not speak to me as I walked around Dealey Plaza that anniversary morning. I expected, foolishly, as it turned out, to experience moments of quiet reverence, as the everyday quality of the busy street, plaza, and underpass was transformed into reverential space from which to bump up against a past moment indelibly imprinted in our collective memories. But the plaza was anything but quiet. While it was often filled with vendors eager to share with visitors the "real" story of November 22, 1963, on this anniversary morning it was bustling with curious tourists and energized by the fervor of conspiracy advocates, many wearing name tags apparently from a popular conference on the assassination. They walked the small plaza, carefully remapping it in their imagination, populating the grassy knoll and other sites with the alleged other—or additional—assassins. For them, it seemed to me, the day was about the never-ending search for hidden truths. Reverence was to be measured not in profound silence but in a hunger for a final resolution, a yearning for a completed puzzle that would for all time answer the enduring questions that haunt so many.

There was no break in activity on the plaza that day at the exact time of the assassination. As that moment approached, a dark blue Lincoln stretch limousine appeared on Elm Street carrying passengers who had paid for the opportunity to "experience" the moment in a historically "authentic" vehicle. I was told that in the car the sound effect of shots would ring out at the exact dramatic moment. Even today in the midst of this busy street an X marks approximately where the President was killed. When a red light stops traffic, people frequently run to the spot to have their picture taken. Once, I was told, a mother placed her baby on the spot, rushed back to the pavement, and took a photograph. Such is the often bizarre life of this iconic site.

The Sixth Floor Museum does not, of course, control what goes on in Dealey Plaza or on Elm Street. And the volatile space of the plaza provides a challenging context for a museum housed in a building that still, at least for me, expresses Jake Epping's "sentient menace." Could a museum exist successfully in a building that JFK never set foot in, on the very floor that houses the sniper's perch, offering visitors the visual perspective of the alleged assassin? Could it flourish in a city that was stained by the assassination unlike any other city burdened by the murder of a President and remained ambivalent about intense processes of remembrance for decades after the event? Could such a museum remain aloof from the gritty, often tasteless, sometimes bizarre expressions that so often erupted on the plaza? Could its permanent exhibition tell a story that brought visitors into the drama and heartbreak of that day, move out from it to engage the complex legacies of JFK, and forthrightly acknowledge the still bitterly contested motive for the assassination and the identity of the assassin(s)?

Stephen Fagin's compelling book painstakingly details how a group of committed individuals struggled for several decades with these and so many other "razor's edge" issues. They worked against formidable odds to preserve the building against those who wanted to tear it down, to house the museum in the building, and to create an exhibition that would stand the test of time. This biography takes readers into the labors involved in the creation of a volatile historic site. One of its many virtues is how effectively Fagin demonstrates how often the most important work is not in the "grand decision" but in the day-by-day work of civic culture: cultivating influential individuals and convincing members of boards and committees of the importance of preservation and interpretation. This is the art of democracy at work. Fagin, director of the museum's oral history program, is well aware that the ongoing life of the museum will eventually call for a second edition of his book. For this dynamic site will evolve as it is continually challenged to introduce future generations to the enduring legacies of this most painful event.

Edward T. Linenthal
Bloomington, Indiana

ACKNOWLEDGMENTS

This book began life as my master's thesis, inspired by my career at The Sixth Floor Museum at Dealey Plaza, which was the result of a lifelong interest in the assassination of President Kennedy. Therefore it is impossible for me to recognize each and every person who has touched, inspired, or assisted me in the totality of this undertaking. For the sake of time and space, here I will briefly acknowledge those whose specific contributions helped to bring about this institutional and cultural history.

From the University of Oklahoma Press, I would like to thank Editor Kathleen A. Kelly, Editor-in-Chief Charles E. Rankin, Managing Editor Steven Baker, freelance copy editor Kathy Lewis, and especially Director B. Byron Price, my onetime thesis advisor, who envisioned this work as a publication on the basis of my initial thesis proposal. I would also like to thank Dr. Michael A. Mares and Professor Gail Kana Anderson from the University of Oklahoma, who kindly served on my thesis committee in 2009. Thanks also to Drs. Edward Linenthal and Dennis M. Simon for reviewing the manuscript and offering valuable advice.

I owe a debt of thanks to Executive Director Nicola Longford of The Sixth Floor Museum at Dealey Plaza, who provided sage advice and encouragement as a mentor and invaluable leader; and Megan Bryant, Director of Collections and Intellectual Property, who facilitated my access to the museum's institutional archives and has been a longtime colleague, friend, and supervisor. Thanks also to Curator Gary Mack, my once and future hero, who provided firsthand stories, recommendations, and, above all, invaluable friendship during this process; and to Curator of Collections Lindsey Richardson and Collections Coordinator Amanda Brekhus for assistance in reviewing text and preparing visuals for this book.

In my opinion, three extraordinary individuals ultimately deserve credit for saving the Texas School Book Depository from demolition in the 1970s. First, I would like to acknowledge the late Aubrey Mayhew, who purchased the building but was unable to fulfill his bold vision for a museum. I am grateful to his son, Parris Mayhew, for granting me permission to include a photograph of his father in this book. Second, I would like to acknowledge the efforts of Dallas's Mayor Wes Wise at the city level and the late C. Judson Shook at the county level for recognizing the historical significance of the Depository and taking active steps to ensure its continued safety. In addition to these individuals, I want to thank the museum founders and consultants who shared stories for the museum's Oral History Project over the years, including Lindalyn Adams, Allen and Cynthia Mondell, Lee Jackson, the late Glenn Linden, and many others. I particularly want to acknowledge Conover Hunt for her extraordinary contribution to history and her willingness to answer many questions without complaint.

Ultimately, none of this would have been possible without the unwavering support of my family. My wife, Jessica, has been my rock for over a decade, while my daughter, Deanna, has grown and matured as this thesis morphed into a book. My second daughter, Melody, was born during the final editing of this manuscript. My brother, and best friend, Christopher has dutifully served as my technical advisor, providing formatting and citation guidance. Finally, I want to thank my parents, Steve and Debra Fagin (both elementary school students in the Dallas area at the time of the assassination), who instilled in me a passion for history and this subject matter in particular. All my academic and professional achievements are the result of my family's support.

INTRODUCTION

And that's the oddity of this place, that it seems so banal. The concrete pergola from a WPA project, the curve downhill toward the freeway, the railroad overpass, the Depository building—all of these totally banal city structures, in the crucible of this event, gain a kind of symbolic significance. . . . It all happened here, and yet all one has here is banality. Concrete, grass, bricks.

JOSIAH THOMPSON, author and assassination researcher

On Saturday, November 22, 2003—the fortieth anniversary of the assassination of President John F. Kennedy—a collective silence enveloped Dealey Plaza in downtown Dallas, Texas. I found myself standing at the site of that shooting, surrounded by a crowd estimated at over five thousand people. Like many of those around me, I did not have firsthand memories of the death of President Kennedy, and I instinctively turned my thoughts to the first national tragedy on my personal timeline—the 1986 explosion of the space shuttle *Challenger*. On a wave of emotion caused in part by the electricity of the day's activities, I relived snapshot images from my childhood: watching the *Challenger* crew on the news the evening before the disaster, seeing my mother's tears when she relayed the day's events to me as we sat by the mailbox in front of our house, hanging up my coat at the back of my first-grade classroom while the school principal called for a moment of silence the following morning, and listening to news anchor Peter Jennings explain how this horrific event could have happened in America. Like many of the individuals standing alongside me in that crowded city park, I shed a few tears in that quiet moment, crying not so much for the memory of John F. Kennedy as for my own memories of collective tragedy and lost innocence. I suppose that this is the power that a place of pilgrimage such as Dealey Plaza can have on any individual, regardless of age, gender, or country of origin. It remains one of those rare sites, often called "sacred ground," where we can literally point to a specific geographic location and say with some certainty that this is where world history changed.[1]

The moment of silence observed at 12:30 P.M. marked the precise minute when shots were fired at President Kennedy's limousine as he concluded his parade through downtown Dallas in 1963, four decades earlier. For me, it was the culmination of several months of work as an employee at The Sixth Floor Museum, overlooking Dealey Plaza. Occupying the top two floors of the former Texas School Book Depository building, where significant evidentiary material was discovered shortly after the shooting, the museum is tasked with chronicling the death and legacy of President Kennedy.

That anniversary weekend the museum opened a new exhibition called *Remembering Jack: Intimate and Unseen Photographs of the Kennedys,* a retrospective of images by the family's personal photographer, the late Jacques Lowe. On Friday the museum hosted a three-hour symposium on the President's life and legacy. This invitation-only event, moderated by Dr. Douglas Brinkley and Jeff West, the museum's executive director, featured a diverse panel, including former *Time* magazine White House correspondent Hugh Sidey; filmmaker George Stevens, Jr., who produced the U.S. Information Service's documentary tribute, *John F. Kennedy: Years of Lightning, Day of Drums;* and former U.N. ambassador William vanden Heuvel, an assistant to U.S. attorney general Robert Kennedy in 1963. Using video excerpts from Stevens's celebrated documentary, the symposium explored significant programs and achievements of the Kennedy administration, from the Peace Corps and the Alliance for Progress to Kennedy's personal commitment to land a man on the moon before 1970 and the immediate impact of Kennedy's untimely death.

On Saturday evening the museum partnered with the Dallas Symphony Orchestra to present a special sold-out performance of Leonard Bernstein's *Mass: A Theater Piece for Singers, Players and Dancers.* Jacqueline Kennedy Onassis had commissioned the work for the 1971 opening of the John F. Kennedy Center for the Performing Arts in Washington, D.C. The performance held at the Morton H. Meyerson Symphony Center in Dallas featured the symphony's chorus, the Children's Chorus of Greater Dallas, and a group of dancers from the Booker T. Washington High School for the Performing Arts. The event was a remarkable tribute to the memory of President Kennedy by some of the finest artists in Dallas. To commemorate the occasion, the museum mounted a special lobby exhibit at the Meyerson on the history of the Kennedy Center; a more detailed installation was also opened in the museum's lobby and remained for a year. The impressive collection of exhibits and programs and the response of the Dallas community marking the fortieth anniversary of the Kennedy assassination are even more remarkable when we consider the shame and guilt that Dallas endured in the aftermath of the shooting and the troubled history that led to the opening of The Sixth Floor Museum at Dealey Plaza.[2]

John F. Kennedy was not the only victim in Dealey Plaza on November 22, 1963. The stigma associated with the killing of the U.S. president haunted the City of Dallas for years. Evoking the moodiness of novelist J. R. R. Tolkien, Dallas businessman Glen Gatlin, who watched the Kennedy motorcade from his office window, later reflected that "a dark spirit had descended on the community."[3] Kennedy's murder troubled and disheartened many city leaders, one of whom is said to have contemplated suicide in the wake of the assassination. Embarrassed and traumatized by the shooting, Dallas residents traveling out of state were often reluctant to reveal their hometown for fear of criticism or worse reprisals.[4]

Standing as a perpetual reminder of the assassination, and the city's most popular tourist destination literally from the day of the shooting, was the Texas School Book Depository building at 411 Elm Street. After the textbook distribution company vacated the building in 1970, persistent questions regarding its fate graced the pages of local—and occasionally national—newspapers for almost a decade. For many, the building was a physical representation of evil, civic shame, and personal mortification. An early effort to establish a state-run museum inside the building was quickly quashed, as was a private attempt to create a historical display and research center. Many Dallas residents wanted the building torn down. The heated debate on the fate of the structure finally ended in 1978 when Dallas County purchased the building and converted it into an administration building and the seat of county government.[5]

Another eleven years passed before an exhibit opened on the building's infamous sixth floor, where a rifle and empty shells were discovered by investigators following the assassination. The remarkable team of historians, scholars, amateur researchers, designers, politicians, community leaders, architects, and filmmakers charged with creating a tasteful interpretive experience on the sixth floor faced a myriad of hurdles. In addition to producing an exhibition that tackled the myth and reality of the Kennedy assassination—and installing it into a 9,000-square-foot warehouse space constructed in 1901—the development team also faced community ambivalence and wariness and battled outside forces, from historical organizations to the Dallas Area Rapid Transit (DART).

Missing its intended opening date on the twenty-fifth anniversary of the assassination, The Sixth Floor exhibit opened on President's Day 1989, to nearly universal praise. The development team succeeded in addressing the darkest moment in the city's history, providing a place of exploration and remembrance—if not at first for cautious local residents, then at least for the tourists who could often be seen wandering about Dealey Plaza, listening to dubious assassination interpretation from a colorful subculture of street vendors. The exhibit did not officially become a museum, however, until 1994. By this time Oliver Stone's film *JFK* had made the assassination relevant to a new generation, and the museum's presence no longer seemed threatening to Dallas residents.

Dealey Plaza and the Texas School Book Depository building remain sacred spaces for many around the world and are part of an important tradition of transforming sites of pain and turmoil among America's violent landscapes into experiences of reflection and renewal in the face of adversity. When visiting the site in 2003 for the first time since being part of the Kennedy motorcade forty years earlier, Lyndon Johnson advisor Jack Valenti remarked: "I can see how people would want to visit this place because—other than two wars—the most horrific event of the 20th century took place here. And as I see it, all these memories come flooding back. . . . And some 400,000 people a year visit this Museum. I think they ought to—to see how our president was murdered and where it happened. And I think Dallas, to its credit, has come to grips with this."[6]

It took nearly one hundred years for Ford's Theatre to embrace its history as site of the Abraham Lincoln assassination in 1865. Used as War Department offices, an Army Medical Museum, and a warehouse for decades, the building finally became a museum in 1932. After President Dwight D. Eisenhower signed a congressional act to restore the historic building in 1954, it became a National Parks Service museum and working theater in 1968.

Twenty-one years after the Japanese attack on Pearl Harbor, the U.S.S. *Arizona* Memorial was dedicated during the Kennedy presidency in 1962. The Lorraine Motel in Memphis, Tennessee, where Dr. Martin Luther King, Jr. was shot on April 4, 1968, opened as the National Civil Rights Museum in 1991. The site of the Alfred P. Murrah Federal Building in Oklahoma City, where a devastating truck bomb killed 168 on April 19, 1995, was transformed into the Oklahoma City National Memorial exactly five years after the tragedy.

In each of these examples, the larger meaning and lasting impact of a violent act are remembered as a significant turning point and part of a process of national renewal in the face of deep tragedy. Emerging from the immediate impulse to hide, deny, or even destroy sites of violence comes the human need to commemorate, and we have come a long way since Ford's Theatre in our societal recognition of loss and renewal. One of the features of modern memorialization is a compression of time between event and memorial. Within this ever-shrinking window, television commentators began speculating on the possibility of a memorial or museum at the site of the World Trade Center less than twenty-four hours after the terrorist attacks of September 11, 2001. The Sixth Floor Museum at Dealey Plaza found itself in a unique position on that day as journalists sought insight into a previous national tragedy in an effort to contextualize and make sense of yet another moment in which "everything had changed," at least within the immediate popular mind-set. My own memories of 9/11 find me in the museum's collections storage room combing through the yellow newspaper pages of November 1963, dutifully listing business closures and event cancellations in the wake of the Kennedy assassination, for potential use as sound bites by the news media in interpreting current chaos within the context of the nation's collective history of tragedy and grief.

In the handwritten Memory Books at The Sixth Floor Museum at Dealey Plaza in the days following the Oklahoma City bombing, visitors made unprompted connections between the tragic events and found a strange sense of solace. One wrote of "a similar feeling" and immediately expressed a desire for renewal: "My hope is the spirits of Americans will continue to lift us forever." In a Memory Book entry on September 11, 2001, a visitor wrote, "On this tragic day it is encouraging to be reminded that JFK stood for courage and freedom, and that our nation is resilient and will overcome the cowardly acts committed today, just as it did in 1963."[7]

These connections are part of the historical record as well. Standing at the podium at the Dallas Trade Mart luncheon on November 22, 1963, community leader J. Erik Jonsson prefaced his announcement of the President's shooting with the lament: "I feel a little bit like the fellow on Pearl Harbor day."[8] Likewise, in a sermon four days after the bombing of the Murrah building, Oklahoma City pastor William Simms told his congregation: "We know that it is possible for a man to sneak beyond the guard of the Secret Service and take the life of President John Kennedy. . . . We know that a man can take the life of Martin Luther King, Jr., while he was on a motel balcony. We know that a man with a truck bomb can take the lives of many folks in Oklahoma City. But no one can sneak beyond the protective arm of God and take the soul of one of God's children."[9] And cultural comparisons between tragedies abounded in the immediate aftermath of the September 11 attacks. Lewis Eisenberg, chair of the Port Authority of New York and New Jersey, noted that "in many respects this is significantly worse than Pearl Harbor." An eyewitness to the towers falling said: "I feel like I've seen the Kennedy assassination or the *Challenger* explosion, or witnessed World War II. We don't even know where we go from here."[10]

With sites such as Dealey Plaza and Ford's Theatre standing as physical reminders of dark moments of the past, individuals are compelled to make connections between these cultural touchstones and build bridges of understanding between generations. Such experiences offer individuals the opportunity to exercise a societal duty to do justice to tragic events by remembering them properly. With this integrity of memory, a site such as Dealey Plaza can offer visitors some sense of healing while also serving its larger audience as a place of education and historical discovery. As a part of this history of violence in the United States, The Sixth Floor Museum at Dealey Plaza is both a careful study in community reflection and apprehension in directly confronting tragedy and a trailblazer in exploring and preserving modern memory.

In the twenty years since its opening, The Sixth Floor, perhaps more than any other institution, event, or individual, has helped heal the painful wounds of the assassination for Dallas, Texas. It has emerged as a site of changing exhibits that place the death of President Kennedy in its historic context, a place of educational outreach, and, perhaps most surprising of all, a venue for community gathering and interaction. The activities surrounding the fortieth anniversary in 2003 remain just one example of this evolution. The story of the museum's development is intrinsically linked to the collective memory of Dallas, reflecting through the prism of history the pain, frustration, wariness, denial, and renewal experienced by those who lived through the events of November 22, 1963. At the same time, it captures the sense of skepticism, mystery, and cultural significance felt by those who do not remember the tragedy firsthand but who view the assassination as a historical jigsaw puzzle and JFK as the heroic but flawed leader of a mythical Camelot.

If we choose to believe in the Camelot legend as it relates to President Kennedy's administration, then Dealey Plaza perhaps serves as a kind of Avalon—the place where Arthur went to die but may actually have lived on in some form, haunting its hallowed ground. The estimated 1 million people who visit the plaza each year come for different reasons. It is a must-see tourist destination, the most popular historic site in north Texas, but it is also a place of quiet reflection, ongoing investigation, social activism, and memorial services. An impromptu shrine covered with wreaths and flowers during the weekend of the assassination, the plaza remains a beacon for the curious, mournful, and thoughtful on each anniversary.

Lost as I was in the crowd of thousands on November 22, 2003, I had a few moments to reflect briefly upon this remarkable journey of both a museum and its city. At exactly 12:30 P.M. that day, unbeknownst to me, a co-worker snapped a photograph that, in retrospect, captures not just the atmosphere of that day but the true spirit of Dealey Plaza. This freeze-frame image shows former U.N. ambassador William vanden Heuvel, one of the museum's symposium panelists, staring pensively toward the spot on Elm Street where the President was cut down. Hands clasped behind his back, he is perhaps remembering John F. Kennedy, whom he knew personally, and considering the impact of his death. Behind him, the museum's curator, Gary Mack, is captured mid-sentence, fingers raised in gesture, as he offers a small group of listeners a nuanced sense of various conspiracy theories. A man standing nearby, arms folded, looks skeptical. Among those listening intently is Gayle Newman, one of the closest eyewitnesses to the President's assassination. Like many of the surviving eyewitnesses, police officers, and other key players, she visits the site for significant events, remembering, engaging in discussions, and perhaps to a degree enjoying the celebrity status that comes with being a participant. Next to her, at the center of this particular photograph, I am standing with my hands in my pockets, eyes closed, head bowed, lost in the middle of Dealey Plaza. I'm thinking about the *Challenger.*

FIG. 1

On November 22, 2003, I stand alongside U.N. ambassador William vanden Heuvel during the moment of silence that marked the fortieth anniversary of the Kennedy assassination. Curator Gary Mack and eyewitness Gayle Newman (back turned to camera) stand behind us.

INSTITUTIONAL ARCHIVES/THE SIXTH FLOOR MUSEUM AT DEALEY PLAZA

ASSASSINATION
AND
Commemoration

Chapter 1

A SITE OF TRAGEDY

B uell Wesley Frazier remembered the morning of Friday, November 22, 1963, as overcast with "a little fine, real pinpoint-type mist in the air."[1] The nineteen-year-old had been employed at the Texas School Book Depository Company warehouse at 411 Elm Street in downtown Dallas since September of that year. Building manager Roy Truly hired Frazier to fill orders for textbooks at $1.25 per hour. One of Frazier's coworkers at that time was a twenty-four-year-old native of New Orleans named Lee Harvey Oswald.[2]

Oswald owed his job at the Depository in part to Frazier, who lived in Irving, Texas, with his sister. Their neighbor, Ruth Paine, a Quaker and student of Russian, had befriended Oswald's young wife, Marina, and taken her in when the Oswalds had separated in September 1963. When Paine mentioned during an afternoon gathering of neighbors that Marina's husband was in need of work, Frazier's sister said that her brother had recently found a job at the Texas School Book Depository.[3] Paine called Roy Truly on October 14, 1963, to ask about a job opening, describing Oswald as "a fine young man . . . [whose] wife is expecting a [second] baby . . . in a few days, and he needs work desperately."[4]

Lee Harvey Oswald, living at that time in a boardinghouse in the Oak Cliff section of Dallas, visited his pregnant wife and daughter in Irving on week-ends and was still in search of work when he learned of the job opening. He went to the Depository the following day to meet with Truly. They discussed Oswald's service in the Marine Corps, and Oswald falsely indicated that he had never "had any trouble with the police." Recognizing that Oswald's employment would likely be temporary, Truly hired the "quiet and well mannered" young man on the spot. "He looked like a nice fellow to me," Truly told the Warren Commission in 1964. "He used the word 'sir,' you know, which a lot of them don't do at this time."[5] Oswald reported to work the following day, filling book orders in the sixth floor storage area and moving them to the ground floor for shipment.[6]

On Oswald's first day, Depository manager Bill Shelley assigned Buell Frazier the task of training the new employee. Frazier remembered Oswald as a quiet intellectual, always interested in solving problems. To his coworkers, Oswald seemed primarily focused on his work. According to one, Oswald's rare attempts to "fit in" with his peers invariably failed and unintentionally triggered laughter on occasion. Oswald, who was closer to Frazier than to any of his other coworkers, once asked him why the other employees laughed at him. Frazier replied that the newcomer expressed himself "on a little bit higher level," adding, "It's very easy to make fun of someone when you don't really understand what they're saying."[7]

Upon learning that Oswald visited his estranged wife and daughter in Irving, Frazier offered Oswald a ride whenever he wanted. This first occurred on Friday, October 18, two days before the Oswalds' second daughter was born.[8] Thereafter, Frazier routinely provided Oswald with a lift to Irving every Friday and drove him back to work the following Monday. Oswald deviated from this schedule during the week of President John F. Kennedy's scheduled visit to Dallas. Explaining that he needed to pick up some curtain rods for his rooming house, Oswald rode with Frazier to the Paine residence on Thursday, November 21, instead. That evening he unsuccessfully tried to convince Marina to move back in with him. When he went to work the following morning, he inexplicably left his wedding ring and $170 in cash on a bureau at the Paine home. Oswald accompanied Frazier to the Texas School Book Depository on Friday, November 22, 1963, with a package wrapped in brown paper that Oswald said contained curtain rods. Walking briskly into the building that morning, Lee Harvey Oswald "was, in that moment, a quiet young man in his 24th year, in the midst of a disintegrating marriage, a menial job and a confused political ideology."[9]

Born on October 18, 1939, two months after the death of his father, Oswald endured a nomadic existence during his earliest years, including spending over a year in an orphanage, when his mother could not financially care for him. He attended six different elementary schools between the first and fourth grades.[10] A 1953 psychiatric evaluation of thirteen-year-old Oswald in New York City, prompted by truancy charges, found him to be "seriously withdrawn, detached and emotionally isolated." Social worker Evelyn Strickman, however, noted "a rather pleasant, appealing quality" about the quiet youth.[11] Overprotected by his mother, Marguerite, to whom he was both devoted and abusive, Oswald seldom made friends and spent much of his time reading at home. Around 1955, while living with his mother in New Orleans, Oswald began reading Communist literature obtained from the local public library. The political philosophy of Karl

FIG. 2

Texas School Book Depository employee Lee Harvey Oswald is escorted down the third-floor hallway of Dallas Police Headquarters by homicide detectives Richard Sims (*left*) and Elmer Boyd (*right*) after his first interrogation by Captain Will Fritz.

Marx would fascinate him for the rest of his brief life. Dorothy Bush, one of Oswald's teachers at Beauregard Junior High School, later described him as a poor but typical student who once had to be moved for talking excessively and failing to follow instructions on an important assignment.[12]

One week after his seventeenth birthday, Lee Harvey Oswald joined the U.S. Marine Corps. During basic training, he qualified as a sharpshooter. As a private first class at Keesler Air Force Base in Biloxi, Mississippi, he earned a "confidential" security clearance. Oswald was assigned to the Atsugi Air Base near

Tokyo, Japan, where some researchers and theorists suggest—though no con-vincing evidence supports this claim—that Oswald may have been "recruited by the CIA for covert intelligence work."[13] Court-martialed twice while in Japan, Oswald suffered a nervous breakdown that prompted another psychiatric eval-uation. By the time he returned to the United States in 1958, he was "blatantly demonstrat[ing] his devotion to communism by studying the Russian language, playing Russian music and addressing fellow Marines as 'comrades.'"[14]

The following year Oswald defected to the Soviet Union, after having requested a dependency discharge from the Marines, ostensibly to care for his mother, who had injured herself in a work-related accident. Arriving in Moscow on October 16, two days shy of his twentieth birthday, Oswald expressed his desire to become a Soviet citizen. When his formal request was rejected, he attempted suicide. Still eager to prove himself to the Russians, Oswald tried for-mally to renounce his citizenship at the U.S. Embassy but never completed the process. Soviet officials permitted him temporary residence and provided him with a comfortable apartment and a factory job in the industrial city of Minsk. After a brief period of celebrity as an American defector, Oswald became disen-chanted with life in the Soviet Union, angered by the inequities in the lifestyles of the working and ruling classes and perpetual food shortages.[15]

By early 1961 Oswald had indicated to the U.S. Embassy that he wanted to return home. Before doing so, however, he met and married Marina Prusakova, the niece of a Russian colonel, after a courtship of a little over one month. After a year of "running Soviet and U.S. bureaucratic hurdles," Lee and Marina Oswald left Russia and settled in Fort Worth, Texas, two weeks prior to the birth of their first daughter.[16]

Married life proved difficult for the Oswalds. Lee, now twenty-three, became reclusive and irritable. Marina later told the Warren Commission that her hus-band's attitude changed drastically after their arrival in the United States. Adding to Oswald's frustrations were two probing interviews with Federal Bureau of Investigation (FBI) agents following his return—standard procedure for return-ing defectors. According to Marina, Oswald struck her on several occasions and refused to teach her English. She found solace in the local Russian com-munity, which Lee generally resented. The dislike was mutual, and some mem-bers of the community helped Marina through the couple's separations and reconciliations.[17]

Oswald worked briefly as a sheet metal worker in Fort Worth and later at an advertising photography firm in Dallas after moving there in October 1962. Although he scored high on a Texas Employment Commission aptitude test, Oswald rarely got along with fellow employees, was often inefficient, and continued to tout his interest in Russia. In 1963, under the alias "A. Hidell," Oswald purchased a .38 revolver and a 6.5mm Mannlicher-Carcano rifle. He explained to his wife that they were for hunting, though he posed with the guns and two Communist newspapers for a series of photographs in the backyard of the couple's apartment house.[18]

On April 10, 1963, Oswald allegedly fired a rifle shot into the home of Maj. Gen. Edwin A. Walker, a right-wing extremist, who was slightly wounded. At his wife's behest, ostensibly to prevent another attempt on Walker's life, Oswald moved to New Orleans shortly thereafter. Though briefly employed lubricating machinery at a coffee factory, he spent much of his time reading gun magazines and launching an unofficial chapter of the Fair Play for Cuba Committee, with himself as the only member. While passing out "Hands Off Cuba" leaflets, Oswald got into a street brawl with a trio of Cuban exiles, was arrested, and spent a night in jail. His activities in Louisiana during the summer of 1963 have long interested researchers seeking to tie him to the local intelligence community, including two individuals later implicated in the Kennedy assassination by New Orleans district attorney Jim Garrison. Former FBI agent Guy Bannister was allegedly involved with Cuban exiles training to overthrow Fidel Castro, and businessman Clay Shaw was a rumored CIA operative.[19]

Oswald traveled to Mexico City in September in an unsuccessful attempt to get a visa to visit Cuba before returning to the Soviet Union. According to Marina, he had long regretted leaving Russia and periodically talked about wanting to return. Dejected, Oswald returned to Dallas by bus, arriving on October 3, 1963. He frequently saw but was separated from Marina and their daughter June, who were living with Ruth Paine in Irving. Such was the personal history and mind-set of Lee Harvey Oswald when Paine informed him of a potential job at the Texas School Book Depository.[20]

President John F. Kennedy visited Dallas on Friday, November 22, 1963, as part of a political tour of the state. Shortly after the Kennedys arrived at Love Field at 11:37 A.M., a presidential parade made its way through downtown en route to a bipartisan luncheon at the Dallas Trade Mart. Shots were fired at the motorcade at 12:30 P.M., just after the limousine carrying President and Mrs. Kennedy and Texas governor John B. Connally and his wife, Nellie, turned from Houston Street to Elm Street, passing by the front door of the Texas School Book Depository. According to a federal investigation of the incident conducted by the Warren Commission, one shot missed the limousine. Another struck Kennedy in the back of the neck, exited the front, and traveled forward, severely wounding Governor Connally, who was seated in front of the president.[21] After a third shot

FIG. 3
The presidential limousine departs Love Field for a motorcade through downtown Dallas.
Tom Dillard Collection, *Dallas Morning News*/The Sixth Floor Museum at Dealey Plaza

fatally struck Kennedy in the head, his limousine sped to Parkland Memorial Hospital. Despite efforts at resuscitation, physicians pronounced the President dead at 1:00 P.M. That afternoon Secret Service agents escorted Mrs. Kennedy and the late President's remains to Love Field for the return trip to Washington, D.C. The new President, Lyndon B. Johnson, took the oath of office aboard Air Force One prior to takeoff.[22]

President Kennedy's funeral on Monday, a national day of mourning, involved seven thousand members of the military. More than one hundred foreign leaders and dignitaries attended to pay their respects to the late president. Grief over the Kennedy assassination galvanized the nation and the world in a manner not witnessed again until the events of September 11, 2001.[23] The *Sunday Times* in London commented that there had "never [before] been such intense world-wide grief," and the *New York Times* called the Kennedy assassination "another day of infamy which the American people will never forget."[24] Psychologist Therese Rando later wrote that the nation endured "a grieving process quite similar to what an individual experiences when [a family member] dies."[25]

FIG. 4

The motorcade makes its fateful turn from Houston Street to Elm Street. The decorative latticework of the Texas School Book Depository is visible in the background.

PHIL WILLIS COLLECTION/THE SIXTH FLOOR MUSEUM AT DEALEY PLAZA

Millions of Americans collectively experienced that weekend through unprecedented news coverage, as most commercial programming was suspended. Events were canceled across the United States, and some stores, movie theaters, and restaurants closed for part of the weekend. Disneyland experienced its first unscheduled closing and did not do so again until the terrorist attacks in 2001. In Dallas a Saturday balloon parade and various social events were canceled, most theaters and nightclubs closed, and many downtown office buildings were shuttered by 3:00 P.M. on Friday.[26]

The evening of the assassination, a Canadian colleague asked Vivian Castleberry, *Dallas Times Herald* women's news editor, to write a story on the city's mood. Castleberry's experiences during a stroll in downtown Dallas reflected the sudden impact that the tragedy had on the city on a usually busy Friday evening:

> The wind was gusting. There probably were not more than four cars that I met [and] they were traveling very, very slowly. Everything was closed. The Crystal Charity Ball had been canceled, which was the

biggest charity ball that we have—was and still is—in Dallas. The opera had been canceled. All of the nightclubs were closed. All the restaurants were closed. Dallas had come to a screeching standstill. Nothing was going on. And the story that I wired that night to Canada led with the idea that Dallas is a ghost town.[27]

At football commissioner Pete Rozelle's discretion, the Dallas Cowboys played the Browns at Cleveland on Sunday before a crowd of 55,000. Many in the crowd booed the Cowboys as they took to the field, in what coach Tom Landry felt was a clear acknowledgment that his team hailed from the city where Kennedy had been shot. The Columbia Broadcasting System (CBS) canceled all television sports and entertainment programming in memory of the fallen President, so the game was not televised.[28]

World attention was divided that weekend between Washington, D.C., where preparations for President Kennedy's funeral were underway, and Dallas, the site of the ongoing investigation into the assassination. Following the shooting of Lee Harvey Oswald while in police custody on Sunday morning, November 24, President Lyndon Johnson launched an official government investigation into the Kennedy assassination, headed by Earl Warren, Chief Justice of the U.S. Supreme Court. The Warren Commission concluded the following year that three shots, fired by lone gunman Lee Harvey Oswald, originated from the southeast corner window on the sixth floor of the Texas School Book Depository. The commission's twenty-six volumes of hearings, testimony, and exhibits explored Oswald's background in detail and traced his movements immediately before and after the shooting in Dealey Plaza.

Thirty-five minutes before the shots were fired, Charles Givens, a Texas School Book Depository employee, observed Oswald. Carrying the clipboard that he used to fill book orders, he was "walking from the southeast corner of the sixth floor toward the elevator."[29] Between ninety seconds and two minutes after the assassination, Dallas motorcycle policeman Marion Baker, the first law enforcement official to enter the Depository, encountered Oswald in the second-floor lunchroom. He released Oswald when Roy Truly identified him as a fellow employee. Oswald allegedly walked out of the Depository's front entrance at 12:33 p.m.[30] Police arrested him eighty minutes later at the Texas Theatre in the Oak Cliff section of Dallas after Oswald allegedly shot and killed patrolman J. D. Tippit near the corner of Tenth and Patton Streets. According to eyewitness accounts, he also attempted to shoot officer M. N. McDonald in the movie theater. A trio of cops wrestled Oswald to the ground. McDonald and Oswald had traded punches to the face, and the police officer recalled that Oswald yelled

FIG. 5

A man walks along Commerce Street in downtown Dallas on the quiet evening of Friday, November 22, 1963.

WILLIAM BEAL, PHOTOGRAPHER, *DALLAS TIMES HERALD* COLLECTION/THE SIXTH FLOOR MUSEUM AT DEALEY PLAZA

FIG. 6

Many restaurants, clubs, and businesses around Dallas closed early on Friday, and many remained closed throughout the assassination weekend. Among them was the Texas Theatre in Oak Cliff (seen here), where suspect Lee Harvey Oswald was arrested by Dallas Police. JIM WALKER COLLECTION/THE SIXTH FLOOR MUSEUM AT DEALEY PLAZA

"police brutality" and "don't hit me anymore."[31] The scuffle left a bruise under his left eye and a slight cut above his right, leading reporters to speculate that officers may have abused him while he was in custody.[32]

Shortly after Oswald arrived at Dallas Police Department headquarters at 2:00 P.M., authorities recognized that he was the missing employee from the Texas School Book Depository. He was interrogated and appeared in several police lineups prior to being charged at 7:40 P.M. with the murder of officer Tippit and shortly after 1:30 on Saturday morning with the murder of President Kennedy.[33]

During the last forty-eight hours of his life, Oswald maintained his innocence, denying involvement in the deaths of Tippit and Kennedy and demanding his civil rights. During a routine prisoner transfer from the city jail to the county jail on Sunday, November 24, local nightclub operator Jack Ruby, a law enforcement enthusiast who had spent time in the hallways at headquarters that weekend, fatally shot Oswald in the basement parking garage—the first murder broadcast live on American television.[34]

Lee Harvey Oswald died at 1:07 P.M. at Parkland Memorial Hospital. By then the Dallas Police Department felt that it had a good case against him for the murder of the President. On Saturday homicide captain Will Fritz told reporters that "this case is cinched. . . . [Oswald] killed the president."[35] Crucial pieces of evidence in the case, a Mannlicher-Carcano rifle traced to Oswald and three empty bullet shells, were recovered from the sixth floor of the Texas School Book Depository, the focal point of the local investigation.

"Three Loud, Reverberating Explosions"

The name "Texas School Book Depository" appeared in news broadcasts within moments of the shooting. Some reporters in Dealey Plaza in the immediate aftermath of the incident, including Robert MacNeil, the assistant White House correspondent for the National Broadcasting Company (NBC), sought to use the telephones inside the building.[36] Pierce Allman, a reporter for the Dallas American Broadcasting Company (ABC) affiliate WFAA, is believed to have encountered Lee Harvey Oswald when inquiring about a phone. Within minutes of the assassination, Allman phoned in a live report to WFAA Radio, mentioning the building three times by name. In this breathless live report, Allman said that as the presidential limousine passed "by the Texas School Book Depository, headed for the triple underpass, there were three loud, reverberating explosions. . . . There are two witnesses . . . who say that shots were fired—from which upper window, we do not know."[37] Another Dallas radio station, KLIF, however, repeatedly identified the Depository as the Sexton building, its name before the John Sexton Company moved out in November 1961.[38]

The seven-story warehouse at 411 Elm Street, later known around the world as the Texas School Book Depository, was constructed in 1901 atop the 1898 foundation of another building that had burned down. The new structure served as a warehouse and showroom for the Rock Island Plow Company of Illinois until 1909, when ownership went to the Dallas-based Southern Rock Island Plow Company, which used the building for the same purpose. The Carraway-Byrd Corporation of Dallas owned the building between 1937 and 1939, when Col. D. Harold Byrd, an oil tycoon and co-founder of the Civil Air Patrol, purchased it outright at public auction.[39] Byrd's first tenant, the John Sexton Company, a national grocery wholesaler, occupied the space beginning on January 1, 1941. After twenty years the Sexton Company moved to a larger, single-story facility better equipped to store frozen food.[40]

By 1963 the Texas School Book Depository, a privately owned textbook distribution company incorporated in 1927, had moved into the former

FIG. 7

Dallas Police and other law enforcement officials surround the Texas School Book
Depository in the aftermath of the President's shooting.

WILLIAM ALLEN, PHOTOGRAPHER, *DALLAS TIMES HERALD* COLLECTION/THE SIXTH FLOOR
MUSEUM AT DEALEY PLAZA

Sexton building. The new occupant stored its stock on the building's fifth
through seventh floors; the bottom four floors contained offices for the distribution company and several regional textbook publishers.[41] A wooden loading
dock was located on the north side of the building. After occupying the warehouse, Depository building manager Roy Truly installed new plywood on the
upper floors so that oil left over from the Sexton occupation could not "penetrate
the cardboard of the Depository's book cartons." Building employees were laying
the new flooring on the west side of the sixth floor on the day of the Kennedy
assassination; as a result, book boxes were moved and "piled unusually high."[42]

Dallas County deputy sheriff Luke Mooney discovered the "sniper's
perch"—a barricade of book boxes arranged around the southeast corner of the
sixth floor—and three empty cartridge cases shortly after 1:00 P.M. Ten minutes later investigators found a bolt-action Mannlicher-Carcano rifle with a tele-
scopic sight between two rows of boxes near the northwest corner stairwell of
the sixth floor. In the interim the Dallas Police Crime Scene Search Unit began
to photograph the crime scene and dust for fingerprints. Word of President

FIG. 8

This Dallas Police crime scene photograph from November 22, 1963, looks toward the barricade of boxes surrounding the "sniper's perch" in the southeast corner of the sixth floor of the Depository. This image would later introduce visitors to The Sixth Floor exhibit.

R. W. RUSTY LIVINGSTON COLLECTION, DALLAS POLICE DEPARTMENT PHOTOGRAPH/THE SIXTH FLOOR MUSEUM AT DEALEY PLAZA

Kennedy's death and the shooting of officer J. D. Tippit soon reached investigators. According to Deputy Mooney, the atmosphere on the sixth floor was silent but emotionally charged. "You could have heard a pin drop," he remembered, "and I pointed [to] a carton of books torn open and on the book laying there [was] a picture of Jesus, and it said, 'Christ leads the way.'"[43]

Tom Alyea, a newsreel photographer for Dallas ABC affiliate WFAA-TV, accompanied investigators to the sixth floor and filmed the crime scene. Unable to leave the Depository, Alyea dropped reels of film out the window to assistant news director Bert Shipp, who rushed them back to the station so that viewers around the country could get their first glimpse inside the building.[44]

Broadcast repeatedly during weekend news coverage, the black-and-white images of the dusty warehouse illuminated by the windows overlooking the assassination site lingered in the national consciousness. This haunting scene

FIG. 9

This Dallas Police crime scene photograph from November 22, 1963, looks down into the sniper's perch in the southeast corner of the sixth floor of the Depository. Three cartridge shells are noticeable on the wooden floor.

R. W. Rusty Livingston Collection, Dallas Police Department Photograph/The Sixth Floor Museum at Dealey Plaza was soon joined by other images: Lee Harvey Oswald in police custody, crowds of reporters jockeying for position on the third floor of Dallas police headquarters, the blur of movement as Jack Ruby shot Oswald on Sunday, and John F. Kennedy, Jr., on his third birthday, saluting his father's casket.

Anger accompanied sorrow following the assassination. In the aftermath of the Oswald shooting, much of it was directed at Dallas. The *New York Times* blamed the death of the alleged assassin on "the electrically emotional atmosphere of a city angered by the president's assassination and not too many decades removed from the vigilante tradition of the old frontier."[45] In an editorial titled "The Shame of Dallas, Texas," the *Saturday Evening Post* belittled the Dallas Police Department for treating Oswald "as if he were a celebrity or a participant in some extravaganza planned and executed for the convenience of television and the press."[46] Even some Dallasites responded negatively to their own police department, perhaps out of embarrassment. One officer later recalled that citizens cursed at him on the street, calling the police a "sorry bunch of people [who] let the president get killed."[47] Another officer, responding to a domestic disturbance in south Dallas a few days after the shooting, remembered an abusive husband taunting his wife: "How in the hell are they going to protect you when they couldn't protect Kennedy?"[48]

Within twenty-four hours of the Kennedy assassination more than three hundred representatives of the national and international news media descended upon Dallas. The Dallas Police Department, allegedly under orders from city officials fearful of the city's reputation, actively assisted the press in news-gathering, including a brief midnight showing of Oswald before the suspect had been charged with the President's murder. While local reporters had long enjoyed a friendly, even casual relationship with the police (including witnessing documents, riding on patrol with officers, and even typing up confessions), outsiders were not long in taking advantage of the cooperative atmosphere.[49] French journalist François Pelou likened Dallas police headquarters to a "marketplace [where] you could do anything you wanted."[50]

Out-of-town reporters took advantage of the city's two major newspapers as well, in some cases destroying portions of their archives in the pursuit of local color. *Dallas Times Herald* publisher James F. Chambers said that the negative news stories written by visiting journalists "killed us as a city," adding that he was ashamed of his profession that weekend. He later described the news coverage as "totally irresponsible," noting that many pundits traded on rumor rather than fact.[51] His managing editor, Felix McKnight, described the blatantly negative assassination coverage as "one of the great disappointments of my journalistic life."[52] Although not all of the news stories written in the aftermath of the

Kennedy assassination directly criticized the City of Dallas, those that did and those that chronicled the city's recent political history cemented its reputation as the nation's most conservative town, a "city of hate" as some called it. The stigma of such charges took years—arguably decades—to shed fully.[53] In one of several stories that unflinchingly besmirched Dallas, the *London Evening Standard* warned its readers "not [to] bring your children to this city."[54]

Letters to Dallas's Mayor Earle Cabell, who received death threats that weekend prompting police protection, were openly hostile. One called Dallas "a blemish on the complexion of human civilization." Another demanded that residents hang their "heads in shame at the terrible crime that was allowed to happen."[55] More remarkable were numerous personal examples of aggression directed at local residents. Dallasites were sometimes refused service in restaurants when traveling and were disconnected by angry long-distance telephone operators. *Times Herald* publisher James Chambers found himself standing in Detroit snow when a cab driver ordered him out after learning his hometown.[56] One young resident vividly remembered receiving a letter from an East Coast relative addressed "Shame on You, Texas."[57]

On a 1964 business trip to Washington, D.C., Dallas insurance executive George Jefferies was heckled about the assassination by a gas station attendant. In reply Jefferies shot back, "Yes, and you're from Washington. Isn't this where Abraham Lincoln was shot?"[58] This retort actually went to the root of the community soul-searching at the time and in the years since, particularly after the 1968 assassinations of Dr. Martin Luther King, Jr., and Robert F. Kennedy. Why single out Dallas for blame and not other cities where political shootings had taken place? The answer lay at least in part in the city's national reputation as a politically conservative community. A few headline-grabbing events in the early 1960s had made much of this. Incessant parroting of the idea by national news media after Kennedy's death associated Dallas with political assassination in ways that Memphis and Los Angeles later avoided. Though the Warren Commission concluded that a left-leaning, lone assassin with a Marxist background murdered the president, many people considered Dallas a haven of right-wing extremism, "a logical place for something unpleasant and embarrassing to happen."[59]

"What Kind of City Have We Become?"

Although Texas remained a largely Democratic state, the City of Dallas consistently voted Republican in the years prior to President Kennedy's visit. The city twice rallied around Dwight D. Eisenhower for president, as did the majority of Texans. Although the state went Democratic in the 1960 presidential election,

Dallasites supported Republican Richard Nixon over Kennedy by the largest margin of any city in the United States. In the three years that followed, eight of the county's nine seats in the state legislature were won by Republicans. The city's political leanings were recognized nationwide.[60] Real estate developer Tom Russell took his family to visit the Harry S. Truman Library in Independence, Missouri, a few years before the Kennedy assassination. He secured a private audience with Truman after telling the former president's secretary: "Lady, you've got a long line, but you haven't got any Democrats from Dallas, Texas. There ain't many of us."[61] While mainstream conservatism had long been the city's reality, however, the highly publicized activities of fringe extremists "dominated the political image of the city" in the early 1960s.[62]

Although pockets of vocal extremists brought unwanted attention to Dallas, the city's civic leaders, largely mainstream conservatives, did not "seek to disown or to discourage these groups."[63] Instead Dallas became, as one author observed, "a Camelot of the right."[64] Its accommodating atmosphere lent extremism "a respectability . . . granted in few other places" and soon gave rise to more than one radical organization and a series of larger-than-life ultraconservative personalities.[65] *Dallas Morning News* publisher Joe Dealey said in 1963 that Dallas was home to "some extremely articulate" right-wing activists.[66] A liberal business executive lamented that these individuals made Dallas "a city of hate, a city of vitriolic tenor."[67]

Established in 1958, the John Birch Society, a religiously motivated, deeply conservative political organization, operated a regional headquarters and a bookstore in Dallas. With some seven hundred local members, the society was popular among not only the "oil-rich" but also lawyers, doctors, business executives, and housewives. Its most outspoken Dallas member was retired major general Edwin A. Walker.[68] While stationed in Germany in 1961, the Texas native came under investigation for distributing right-wing propaganda to his troops. After a reprimand from the U.S. Army, Walker resigned in protest and immediately "embarked upon a career devoted to speaking out against communism" around the United States. When Walker protested the enrollment of African American student James Meredith at the University of Mississippi, U.S. attorney general Robert Kennedy charged him with "seditious conspiracy, insurrection, and rebellion" and had him arrested and jailed for five days.[69]

Drawn to the pro-conservative climate of Dallas, the retired officer bought a home on prestigious Turtle Creek Boulevard, where he frequently flew the American flag upside down as a distress signal that the nation was in danger from a potential Communist takeover. A local celebrity and "the darling of the far right," even after finishing last among six candidates in the race for governor of Texas in 1962, Walker remained an outspoken critic of communism and the Kennedy administration.[70] The following year Walker was slightly wounded on the arm during an assassination attempt at his home. Lee Harvey Oswald, who considered Walker a "dangerous fascist" who needed to be stopped before he gained too much power, allegedly fired the shot.[71] His arm still bleeding, Walker excused himself from reporters that April 10 evening, quipping that he needed to finish his income taxes or else Robert Kennedy might throw him in jail again.[72] Despite Walker's following among ultraconservatives, at least some Dallasites, including longtime Southern Methodist University (SMU) professor Marshall Terry, considered him to be "a true nut." Terry, who occasionally encountered the retired general on campus, recalled hearing Walker give a speech about Freddy Squirrel and Jonny Redbird in which the allegorical redbird, representing communism, stole all of the squirrel's nuts.[73]

Among the other well-known conservative personalities in Dallas was oil tycoon H. L. Hunt, who sponsored right-wing organizations, including the Facts Forum and the Lifeline radio commentary program. He also authored pamphlets with such inflammatory titles as "Hitler Was a Liberal" and "We Must Abolish the United Nations." Hunt's son Nelson Bunker Hunt was a prominent member of the John Birch Society.[74] The Reverend W. A. Criswell, the influential and archconservative pastor of the First Baptist Church of Dallas, endorsed Richard Nixon in one of his 1960 sermons, indicating that a Kennedy victory "would mean the end of religious liberty in America."[75]

Dallas resident Frank McGehee founded the National Indignation Convention to protest congressionally approved military aide to Communists. Although a mere 100 people turned out for one of its earliest meetings in 1961, the organization soon had chapters across the United States. A crowd of 1,400 attended an October 1963 rally where Texas rancher and conservative activist J. Evetts Haley's call for the hanging of Supreme Court Justice Earl Warren "won loud applause."[76]

In 1954 Dallas native Bruce Alger became the first Texas Republican congressman since Reconstruction and went on to serve for the next decade. Known during his tenure as "one of the most conservative Congressmen in the nation," Alger decried socialism and communism, sponsored a bill for the United States to withdraw from the United Nations, and earned national headlines as the only member of the U.S. House of Representatives to oppose a federally funded school lunch program.[77] Alger proclaimed that his party was "unafraid to point out the sound, the right, and the moral way."[78]

Supporters rallied around the congressman, hoping that he might single-handedly usher in a two-party system in the Democratic South. A local executive later remarked that Alger represented the view that Dallas could, in effect, politically function as an island independent of either Austin or Washington, D.C.[79] The handsome and charismatic Alger remained popular in Dallas, with a particularly loyal following among politically active socialites, sometimes dubbed "the rabble in mink."[80] "During the Kennedy Administration, an expressed admiration for the President could literally ruin a dinner party," one observer later recalled. "So could any objection to the policies and conduct of Republican congressman Bruce Alger."[81]

Both major Dallas newspapers were conservative, though in varying degrees. The afternoon *Times Herald* prided itself on being if not "more or less liberal" then at least "a little more flexible" in its political viewpoint.[82] Both papers backed Nixon against Kennedy in 1960, though *Times Herald* publisher James Chambers, a Kennedy supporter, maintained that his paper never tied itself directly to a political party but always backed the best candidate.[83] Under the leadership of publisher E. M. "Ted" Dealey, the *Dallas Morning News* grew increasingly conservative, strongly criticizing the civil rights movement and what it viewed as President Kennedy's "socialistic tendencies."[84] Before the 1960 election, Dealey editorialized that Kennedy, a Catholic, would be "beholden to the bishops and pope in Rome" if elected.[85] The publisher openly criticized Kennedy at a White House luncheon in October 1961, insisting that the country needed "a man on horseback" rather than someone "riding Caroline's tricycle."[86] *Times Herald* publisher Chambers, at the same luncheon, immediately apologized to Kennedy on behalf of Dallas, stressing that Dealey did not represent the views of everyone.

This awkward confrontation at the White House instigated a battle of words between the Dallas newspapers that exposed the city's political divisions in the early 1960s. Chambers later explained that citizens wrote to both newspapers "either agreeing with what had been done or disagreeing." He added: "And most of the letters I got supported me and my attitude and what I had said to the president, and most of the letters he got supported him and what he had said to the president—but it went on for weeks."[87]

Beyond Ted Dealey's public criticism of President Kennedy, two other incidents exemplify the power of the city's vocal ultraconservative minority to seize the national spotlight to the detriment of Dallas's reputation. The first occurred on November 4, 1960, designated by city Republicans as "Tag Day," four days before the presidential election. Crowds of young women distributed pro-Nixon tags and flyers and solicited funds on the downtown streets. Republicans waving signs reading "Lyndon Go Home" and "Let's Ground Lady Bird" were also on hand at the Adolphus Hotel, where Democratic vice presidential candidate Lyndon Johnson appeared at a campaign luncheon.[88]

Lyndon and Lady Bird Johnson arrived by motorcade to find 400 hecklers at the intersection of Commerce and Akard Streets. As the Johnsons retreated into the Baker Hotel across from the Adolphus in order to freshen up, a young woman grabbed Mrs. Johnson's gloves and tossed them into the gutter. By this time the crowd had grown to include "riff-raff from the [nearby] beer parlors and some of the lower class restaurants."[89] After refusing both police protection and recommendations that he and his wife enter the Adolphus via a side door, Johnson's party made their way across the street. The fifty-yard trek took thirty minutes.[90]

Among the hostile crowd, Congressman Bruce Alger, later deemed "the man primarily responsible for the demonstration," brandished a sign that read "LBJ Sold Out to Yankee Socialists."[91] Though Alger later claimed that he was not present for any of the pushing or shoving that ensued, he did tell the jubilant crowd that he wanted to demonstrate that the Senate majority leader was unwelcome in the City of Dallas. Alger's supporters "hissed at and spat upon" the Johnsons as they pushed their way across the street.[92] One of the senator's supporters later said that she was kicked, hit, stuck by pins, and cursed at by the angry protesters.[93] The following day the *Dallas Morning News* described the scene as "45 minutes of Republican bedlam that was the nearest thing to an uncontrollable mob Dallas [had] witnessed since the wilder days of the Texas-Oklahoma football games."[94]

Inside the Adolphus Hotel's Grand Ballroom, a crowd of 2,000 cheering supporters greeted the Johnsons. Texas attorney general Will Wilson introduced the candidate by emphasizing that the raucous demonstration outside "did not reflect 'the true spirit of Dallas.'" Johnson referred to the incident in his prepared remarks, saying that he refused a police escort simply to find out "if the time had come when [he] couldn't walk with [his] lady through the corridors of the hotels of Dallas."[95] In a televised interview in Houston the following day and for the remainder of the campaign, Johnson continued to recall the incident, lamenting that it felt like being in another country. By this time Democrats were circulating handbills with a photograph of Alger at the demonstration captioned "Dallas—Not Venezuela."[96]

By some accounts, Johnson and the Democrats exaggerated the ferocity of the mob for political advantage.[97] Will Wilson said that although the crowd exhibited "the poorest sportsmanship . . . maybe it is for the good—it is going to get us votes."[98] Whether intentional or not, the Johnson campaign's frequent references to the incident reinforced the impression that Dallas was angry and inhospitable. Within two days the *Dallas Morning News* received over a hundred telegrams about the incident, and many newspapers devoted editorials to the event.[99]

According to one reporter "considerable . . . anti-Dallas sentiment" persisted around the country in the aftermath of the election.[100]

Three years later, less than a month before the Kennedy assassination, a second political protest embarrassed the city. To mark United Nations Day on October 24, 1963, the Dallas Council on World Affairs invited U.N. ambassador and two-time Democratic presidential nominee Adlai Stevenson to speak at Memorial Auditorium. In protest, Frank McGehee of the National Indignation Convention dubbed the day before Stevenson's appearance "U.S. Day" and arranged an event at the same auditorium with Edwin Walker as the keynote speaker. Texas governor John Connally, duped by the innocuous name of the rival event, issued an official proclamation recognizing "U.S. Day," and 1,400 listened enthusiastically while Walker exposed the United Nations as "a part of the world-wide communist movement."[101]

A larger crowd turned out at Memorial Auditorium the next evening for Stevenson's appearance. Among them, however, were a number of right-wing protesters determined to derail the program, which was locally broadcast on the Dallas CBS affiliate KRLD-TV. During the speech, Frank McGehee shouted questions at Stevenson through a bullhorn until police escorted him from the auditorium. Other hecklers, which by one account equaled the number of UN supporters, waved flags and placards, shouted, laughed, coughed, and repeatedly used mechanical noisemakers to disrupt the program.[102] Making matters worse, the cloth "Welcome Adlai" banner hung near the stage had been sabotaged; in the middle of the program a protester negotiated the auditorium's catwalk and turned it over to display the message "U.N. Red Front."[103]

After the speech, approximately one hundred demonstrators confronted Stevenson outside Memorial Auditorium with shouts of "traitor" and "Communist." Briefly leaving his police escort, the ambassador approached one particularly agitated woman to try to calm her down. At that moment, photographed and captured on film, another woman struck Stevenson in the head with a placard while a male college student spat on him. Both were arrested, but the ambassador declined to press charges.[104] One of Stevenson's hosts, Stanley Marcus, chair of the board of luxury retailer Neiman Marcus, vividly recalled protesters shaking his car so violently that it nearly tipped over. "We were surrounded," said Marcus, "and I think we were in imminent danger of being manhandled."[105]

The image of the placard striking Stevenson taken by *Dallas Times Herald* photographer William Beal and the KRLD-TV film of the Thursday night incident were quickly broadcast and published throughout the nation. The *Today Show, CBS Evening News,* and *Time* magazine were among those who ran the story.[106] Recalling the Johnson incident, a front page editorial in the *Dallas Times*

FIG. 10

Right-wing protesters stand outside Memorial Auditorium in Dallas on UN Day, October 24, 1963. UN Ambassador Adlai Stevenson was accosted leaving the theater following his speech.

BILL WINFREY COLLECTION/THE SIXTH FLOOR MUSEUM AT DEALEY PLAZA

Herald wondered, "Must our city gain the reputation around the world of being a place where a guest is physically endangered if he expresses an idea of which a belligerent, minority mob disapproves?"[107]

Less than a day after the incident, the Dallas Chamber of Commerce issued an apologetic telegram to Stevenson signed by one hundred Dallas business and civic leaders. Bruce Alger quickly and publicly denounced it, adding fuel to the fire.[108] Within a week the Dallas City Council passed an anti-harassment ordinance that specifically protected visiting speakers. Though a direct response to the attack on Ambassador Stevenson, the measure also anticipated the impending visit of President Kennedy the following month. On UN Day, however, right-wing handbills bearing a mug-shot image of the President titled "Wanted for

Treason" were distributed around Dallas. The flyers, which contained a list of Kennedy's alleged "treasonous activities against the United States," resurfaced the morning of the assassination.[109]

President Kennedy's 1963 trip to Texas—traveling to San Antonio, Houston, Fort Worth, and Dallas, with a scheduled final stop in Austin canceled by the assassination—was both a fund-raiser in preparation for the 1964 presidential campaign and a peace mission to heal a rift in the Texas Democratic Party between conservatives led by Governor John Connally and liberals represented by Senator Ralph Yarborough.

Dallas went to great lengths to welcome the President and ensure that nothing marred the visit or the city's reputation. The influential Citizens Council, a non-political though predominantly conservative organization of business executives that oversaw civic projects, co-sponsored the President's luncheon at the Dallas Trade Mart and promoted a peaceful reception.[110] Cooperative news media saturated the city with scripted statements from community leaders and law enforcement officials, including Sheriff Bill Decker and Police Chief Jesse Curry. Helen Holmes, an executive with the public relations firm that coordinated the presidential visit—the same company that had worked with the Citizens Council to promote peaceful school integration—recalled that the "messages were very simple and clear . . . please put aside your personal party affiliations and help welcome your president."[111] On alert for potential agitators, the Dallas Police Department assigned more than two hundred officers to the presidential luncheon site. Dallas churches, at the behest of the Citizens Council, urged their congregations to exhibit friendliness during Kennedy's visit.[112]

On the morning of the assassination a full-page advertisement with a funereal black border ran in the *Dallas Morning News*, "welcoming" the President to Dallas and posing twelve rhetorical questions, most of which accused Kennedy of being soft on communism.[113] A trio of ultraconservatives, including H. R. "Bum" Bright, the future owner of the Dallas Cowboys, paid for the advertisement, signing it "The American Fact-Finding Committee." Ted Dealey allegedly approved publishing the ad, later saying that it "merely represented what the *News* had been saying editorially." President Kennedy saw the advertisement before Air Force One touched down in Dallas, reportedly telling his wife that morning that they were headed into "nut country."[114] Fort Worth congressman Jim Wright, who sat with Kennedy during the short flight from Fort Worth to Dallas, remembered that Kennedy wondered aloud how to approach the newspaper in friendship.[115]

The President's initial reception was overwhelmingly positive. Nearly four thousand people greeted the Kennedys at Love Field. Signs and banners welcoming the President to Dallas and promoting his 1964 reelection dwarfed the few negative signs in evidence. Eager to maintain the decorum of the occasion, a local chair of the Republican Party stood on top of a protester's sign while shaking hands with the President and First Lady as they made their way down the fence line.[116]

An estimated crowd of two hundred thousand in downtown Dallas cheered the President's motorcade, and by all accounts the visit was shaping up to be a stunning success. Even the weather had cooperated, with bright sunshine and a cool breeze replacing the morning drizzle, prompting a spectator to remark: "I believe God is on the president's side today."[117] By the time the motorcade reached Dealey Plaza—the official end of the parade—many in the entourage expressed relief that nothing untoward had occurred. *Dallas Morning News* chief photographer Tom Dillard relaxed for the first time that day, telling his companions in the motorcade press car: "Boy, it went great . . . no problems. Thank God."[118] Nellie Connally, the First Lady of Texas, spoke the final words that President Kennedy heard that day: "Mr. President, you certainly can't say that Dallas doesn't love you!"[119] A few seconds later shots rang out.

"The spirit of assassination has been with us for some time, not manifest in bullets, but in spitting mouths and political invectives," preached the Reverend William A. Holmes at Northaven Methodist Church in Dallas on the Sunday following Kennedy's death. "In the name of God, what kind of city have we become?"[120] Holmes was not the only resident to criticize the City of Dallas in the wake of the assassination, but his controversial sermon gained international notoriety after portions of it appeared on the *CBS Evening News*. The minister recounted recent right-wing extremist activity and revealed that a class of fourth graders in Dallas had cheered upon learning that the President had been shot. The latter assertion prompted an investigation by the city's school superintendent and led to a teacher suspension immediately protested by the American Civil Liberties Union. Several other Dallas teachers reported similar incidents in their schools.[121]

The Reverend Holmes received a flood of telephone calls and over four hundred letters from all over the world in response to his sermon. The vast majority from outside Dallas praised his honesty and his assertion that the city was partly to blame for allowing such a politically charged atmosphere to exist. Holmes recalled that "most of the negative reactions came from Dallas citizens who, while acknowledging that what I said about the city was true, were outraged that I would publicly express it." The minister also received several death and bomb threats. On the advice of the police, he moved his family out of their home for several days to stay with friends under police protection. Both Dallas newspapers, Holmes noted, declined to carry stories about the threats against his family, fearing the negative publicity.[122]

The Friday after his sermon Holmes met with seventy-five other local ministers to contemplate a citywide religious response to the Kennedy assassination. The end result was a campaign calling for "A Hundred Days of Love," during which the clergy agreed to preach on the beauty of love and promote the writing of love letters. Holmes lent his support but lamented that the city had substituted "pious platitudes and sentimental phrases" for more positive action.[123] The already fragile reputation of Dallas following the shooting of the President was completely shattered by the murder of his alleged assassin, a shocking event that confirmed to many the city's violent nature and the incompetence of law enforcement officials. Holmes and others of his ilk knew that it would take more than one hundred days of love to restore a positive image to the place now known as "the city of hate."[124]

"The City That Works"

The murder of President Kennedy followed by the sudden shooting of his alleged assassin Lee Harvey Oswald on national television were not the last incidents to embarrass the City of Dallas. Its global reputation was further sullied in early 1964 during the widely publicized trial of Jack Ruby, the local nightclub owner who fatally shot Oswald in the basement of Dallas Police Department headquarters on November 24, 1963. The "trial of the century" pitted Dallas's folksy and respected district attorney Henry Wade and his assistant Bill Alexander against Ruby's defense team, consisting of Melvin Belli, a flamboyant tort lawyer from San Francisco, and Texas attorneys Joe Tonahill and Phil Burleson. Judge Joe B. Brown of Criminal District Court Number 3 tried the high-profile case.[125]

The courtroom proceedings began with bond hearings in December 1963 and January 1964; Ruby had been held without bail at the Dallas County Jail in Dealey Plaza since the shooting. Defense attorney Belli argued that his client could not receive a fair trial in Dallas due to the excessive media coverage and asked for a change of venue.[126] Prior to a hearing on the motion, Belli told the Associated Press that Dallas needed "a sacrifice in order to cleanse" itself of guilt over the President's assassination.[127] Among the forty-two defense witnesses who took the stand during the February change-of-venue hearing were clothier Stanley Marcus, who recalled the Adlai Stevenson incident, and the Reverend William A. Holmes, whose recent sermon about the atmosphere in Dallas earned him international prominence. Although many observers assumed that the trial

FIG. 11

Jack Ruby (*center*), the local nightclub owner who killed alleged assassin Lee Harvey Oswald, converses with his attorneys Joe Tonahill (*left*) and Melvin Belli (*right*) at the Dallas County Criminal Courts building in 1964.

BILL WINFREY COLLECTION/THE SIXTH FLOOR MUSEUM AT DEALEY PLAZA

would be moved to another Texas city, Judge Brown ultimately denied Belli's request, concluding that millions of television viewers had witnessed Ruby shoot Oswald, so "getting a fair jury was going to be difficult anywhere."[128]

Nearly four hundred journalists covered the Ruby trial, prompting Judge Brown to hire the same public relations firm that had managed President Kennedy's visit as his personal press advisor during the trial. Although not permitted inside the courtroom, cameras and recording equipment lined the hallway outside.[129]

Following two weeks of jury selection, testimony began on March 4, 1964, with closing arguments nine days later. A Dallas County jailbreak in full view of the media on the third day of the trial brought further criticism of Dallas law enforcement and ridicule of the city. Although the seven escapees were all apprehended by the following day, the damage had been done. The front page of the *New York Daily News* read simply: "Oh, Dallas!"[130] Helen Holmes, Judge Brown's public relations director, later recalled, "We'd been the 'city of hate,' and then we became the 'city of clowns.'"[131]

During Ruby's trial, Belli argued that his client suffered from a rare condition called psychomotor epilepsy and was not aware of his actions. Unconvinced, the jury found the defendant guilty of murder with malice after two hours of deliberations and gave him the death penalty on March 14, 1964. The verdict was broadcast live on television before an audience of millions by one pool camera set up by CBS. Before the jury left the courtroom, Melvin Belli jumped to his feet and shouted, "May I thank this jury for a victory for bigotry and injustice!"[132] At that moment all decorum inside the courtroom broke down live on national television as a mad scramble of reporters and cameramen rushed to record the scene, some standing on furniture. Watching the action unfold on her television, Judge Brown's girlfriend called him to say, "They're making your courtroom look like a clown's room!"[133]

Surrounded by reporters, cameramen, and the chaos of the courtroom, Belli bitterly proclaimed:

> I hope the people of Dallas are proud of this jury that was shoved down our throats. . . . Every Texas jurist knows this thing was the greatest railroading kangaroo court disgrace in the history of American law. . . . Why in a civilized country in the heart of darkest Africa you wouldn't argue a man's life starting at twelve o'clock in the morning. When I think that we're coming into holy week and Good Friday, to have a sacrifice like this, I think we're back 2,000 years. And the blight that's on Dallas with those twelve people who announced the death penalty in this case, they'll make this a city of shame forevermore.[134]

Belli directed much of his wrath toward Dallas power brokers, whom he called the "oligarchy." The defense attorney claimed that leaders "in whatever passes for the Kremlin of Dallas could figuratively press a button and, as if it had signaled transistors in their brains, direct [people's] thinking."[135] Ruby and his family fired Belli less than one week after his tirade, and the State Bar of Texas unsuccessfully tried to disbar the California attorney from practicing law

FIG. 12

Members of the news media surround Dallas district attorney Henry Wade (*center*) on the steps of the Dallas County Criminal Courts building after the guilty verdict is announced in the Jack Ruby trial on March 14, 1964.

BILL WINFREY COLLECTION/THE SIXTH FLOOR MUSEUM AT DEALEY PLAZA

in the Lone Star state because of his courtroom remarks.[136] But the damage had been done.

Belli's account of the trial, *Dallas Justice,* was published before the end of 1964. He claimed that the book was "written in a spirit of constructive and sympathetic criticism of Dallas . . . whose deficiencies were brought into glaring focus by the tragic events of last November and the Ruby trial that followed." Belli laid the blame for right-wing activities in Dallas in the early 1960s at the feet of the powerful Citizens Council, who selfishly advanced their own motives, eliminated democracy, offered respectability to fanatics because communism threatened private property, and facilitated the peaceful integration of the Dallas Independent School District only because "violence would [have been] bad for the Dallas dollar." The San Francisco attorney hoped that his critical assessment might help the city "face up to its failures."[137] It also helped solidify negative public opinion of Dallas and made the city's road toward recovery all the more difficult.

Belli was not the only person to criticize the community's power structure. An opponent of a Citizens Council–approved incumbent in a local election complained that his line of credit was canceled at Republic National Bank, whose president sat on the council. The term "oligarchy" was used so frequently in the aftermath of the assassination that council member Bob Cullum shortened the word to "garch" and jokingly used it to salute fellow Citizens Council members on city streets.[138]

The majority of Dallasites acknowledged the considerable influence wielded by Dallas business executives but felt that it was in the city's best interest at least in part because, as one writer put it in 1964, "they are all able to commit their companies to civic expenditures."[139] A local businessman acquainted with many on the council added that "most cities that have made progress have had people of substance, people of vision that helped make things happen [and] bring in big projects."[140] Editor Bert Holmes of the *Dallas Times Herald* agreed that the city's "oligarchy made some good decisions, and the great populace seemed . . . satisfied with them." The news media were supportive of the Citizens Council as well, never publicly challenging decisions or printing negative stories about their activities.[141]

Although small but powerful elites controlled other American cities, the way in which the Dallas Citizens Council conducted business in such a public and well-organized manner surprised many observers.[142] Dallas historian Darwin Payne explained that the Citizens Council's "overriding influence dominated municipal politics, public schools, bond issues, industrial development, housing projects, and civic endeavors." All members of the council "were required by charter to be the chief executives of their organizations."[143]

Not surprisingly perhaps, members of the Citizens Council took charge of the rehabilitation of Dallas's image in the wake of the assassination, beginning with council president J. Erik Jonsson, co-founder of the electronics firm Texas Instruments, who attended the President's funeral in Washington, D.C.[144] With the cessation of media coverage of Dallas's now disfavored right-wing community, city leaders determined that Congressman Bruce Alger needed to be replaced by "a more moderate candidate" and supported the candidacy of

Mayor Earle Cabell, a moderate conservative, in the 1964 congressional race.[145] Cabell, who decried extremism, won the election by a wide majority and served until 1972. At the behest of the Citizens Council, the Dallas City Council drafted J. Erik Jonsson to fill Cabell's term as mayor, a maneuver later described as "an example of the power structure working at its most efficient—and also most exclusive—level."[146]

As mayor from 1964 to 1971, Jonsson helped to reshape the image of Dallas. From the outset, the mayor saw the need actively to involve residents in rehabilitating their city's image.[147] The result of his vision was the ambitious Goals for Dallas program, announced in November 1964, one year after Kennedy's death. Jonsson's plan brought together thousands of local residents to articulate a series of goals relating to "local government, design of the city, transportation, health and welfare, education, cultural activities, recreation, and public safety," with the ultimate desire of creating "the best city in the United States." A series of books published by the Goals for Dallas staff listed timetables and priorities. While the city's power structure still largely shaped civic development, over one hundred thousand Dallasites contributed ideas in the program's first five years.[148]

Among the accomplishments credited to Goals for Dallas within seven years was the opening of the Dallas/Fort Worth International Airport, a new city hall, plaza, and parking garage complex, an expanded Dallas Public Library System, the introduction of kindergarten classes for Dallas public schools, air conditioning of public school facilities, and the launch of a public television station.[149] Dr. Bryghte Godbold, executive director of the Goals for Dallas program, disagreed with those who believed that the program's sole intent was to improve the city's reputation after the assassination, arguing that the objectives of those involved were much broader.[150] The program earned Dallas the designation of "All-America City" by *Look* magazine in 1970, while *Newsweek* proclaimed it "the city that works."[151]

Despite economic growth and prosperity and a renewed sense of purpose, Dallas remained haunted by the Kennedy assassination. Local death rates by suicide, murder, and heart disease briefly increased following the President's shooting, prompting a psychologist to conclude that the community's collective guilt and frustration had impacted its physical and mental well-being.[152] An executive who no doubt reflected the feelings of many of his fellow citizens described the assassination's aftermath as "a scary and unusual time" in a "city of darkness."[153] A history professor at Southern Methodist University touring Europe more than five years after Kennedy's death recalled the shame he endured over frequent remarks about his "terrible city . . . where they kill presidents."[154]

Goals for Dallas never directly addressed the Kennedy assassination, and many residents felt the need to respond to the tragedy with a monument or memorial to the late President. Such a suggestion by Judge Lew Sterrett two days after the assassination led to the establishment of the John F. Kennedy Citizens Memorial Committee in December 1963, organized by the Dallas County judge and Mayor Earle Cabell. Composed of two dozen prominent Dallas residents, the group called for memorial suggestions from around the world, and 260 ideas poured in within a week. By February 1964 the number of suggestions totaled 700.[155]

The notion of memorializing President John F. Kennedy was controversial from the beginning. R. L. Thornton, a respected former mayor, vocally opposed such a monument. Others joined him in rejecting a physical reminder of what had quickly become the city's darkest memory. Nearly 200 letters addressed to the committee called instead for a "living memorial," such as a scholarship, education grant, or monetary contribution to the arts. Those in support of a physical memorial debated whether Dallas or Washington, D.C., was more appropriate as a locale.[156]

After consulting with Kennedy family member Stephen Smith, who suggested "something very simple," the committee announced that a modest memorial—initially described as a wall of marble—would be installed near Dealey Plaza. In April 1964, while donations for a memorial were being solicited, the Dallas County Commissioners Court designated a site for the installation across from the city's new courthouse and some two hundred yards from where the assassination took place. Over a year later, with $225,000 in contributions in hand, the committee invited noted American architect Philip Johnson, an acquaintance of the Kennedys, to design the memorial. The construction of an underground parking garage at the site, however, delayed the project for more than six years.[157]

Dedicated on June 24, 1970, Philip Johnson's memorial to John F. Kennedy consisted of a roofless room, thirty feet tall and fifty feet square. Composed of seventy-two white concrete columns, most of which appeared to float above the ground, the memorial's walls were supported by eight pillars, two in each corner. A pair of "narrow axial openings" on either side permitted access to this cenotaph (open tomb), and in the center was a black granite slab bearing the President's name in gold letters.[158] Architect Johnson envisioned "something very humble and spartan . . . a memorial for one whose remains lie elsewhere."[159]

Perhaps because of its simplicity, the Kennedy Memorial was frequently misunderstood by tourists expecting to find a Kennedy bust or statue inside the structure instead of a plain granite slab. Dallas historian Darwin Payne thought

FIG. 13
The John F. Kennedy Memorial near Dealey Plaza, 2009.
Institutional Archives/The Sixth Floor Museum at Dealey Plaza

its lack of public appeal stemmed from the fact that few people understood the concept of a cenotaph.[160] A *Dallas Morning News* reporter once described it as "a stark and ugly monument," while a less tactful local resident wrote that it resembled "a European public lavatory."[161]

Additional Dallas memorials to President Kennedy, though on a much smaller scale, emerged in the 1960s, including the John F. Kennedy Memorial Book Fund to provide volumes written about or by Kennedy to public libraries. Ironically, Dealey Plaza—the city's number one tourist destination—was not publicly acknowledged as the site of the assassination with a marker for nearly three years. In the summer of 1965, however, Richardson resident Martina Langley launched such an effort, almost single-handedly, to convince the City of Dallas to recognize the Kennedy assassination at the actual site. Since the event, Langley had visited Dealey Plaza more than one hundred times to pay her respects. She made note of the frequent tourist complaints that Dallas had not yet installed a tribute to the late President. Unhappy that Philip Johnson's delayed John F. Kennedy Memorial would not be constructed in the plaza, she joined a dozen other individuals in organizing the awkwardly titled Committee for Kennedy Assassination Site Memorial. Langley and her associates passed out leaflets and talked with tourists in the plaza daily. She argued that Dealey Plaza was as historically significant as Ford's Theater in Washington, D.C., site of the Lincoln assassination.[162]

The committee's efforts led the Dallas Park Board to propose a multipaneled bronze marker mounted on marble supports near the statue of George Bannerman Dealey, where a similar bronze display honoring Dealey was already installed. As originally designed, the new plaques only briefly explained the President's shooting beneath eight detailed paragraphs about the city's early history. Though the park board twice approved the wording of the $8,500 marker, Langley protested that the Dallas historical information was extraneous and appealed the matter before the city council in March 1966.[163]

The council agreed. The twin 500-pound bronze plaques installed in November 1966 acknowledged only the Kennedy assassination. One displayed a map of Dealey Plaza, identifying the motorcade route and the approximate location where the assassination took place. The second plaque described the shooting in a straightforward manner, primarily providing directional information. A reference to alleged assassin Lee Harvey Oswald was deleted during final review, though the plaque did acknowledge the findings of the Warren Commission.[164]

On November 22, 1966, the third anniversary of the assassination, Langley led several hundred people in a memorial service in front of the plaques. Her children placed a large floral display bearing the message "Lest We Forget."[165] Looming above the newly installed marker one block away was an infamous structure soon to be at the heart of a two-decade-long community struggle to come to terms with its place in history—the Texas School Book Depository.

"Some Kind of Shrine or Memorial"

The transformation of Dealey Plaza into a site of memorial and pilgrimage was instantaneous, with the Texas School Book Depository building at the center of the experience. "A drab, weathered building on the corner of Houston and Elm," wrote *Dallas Morning News* reporter Carlos Conde two days after the assassination, "was turned into a shrine Saturday."[166] That weekend, floral arrangements, handwritten notes, and memorial cards were placed on both sides of Elm Street—a few at first. Then the grass of the plaza was covered with tributes, with a perpetual stream of spectators walking through what one reporter called "this field of memories."[167] The curious and the respectful came to remember President Kennedy, accept the reality of the situation by seeing the site in person, and trace his final moments. Many of the first visitors that weekend referred to newspapers to pinpoint the location of the presidential limousine during the shooting. A Richardson resident who came to the plaza the day after the assassination said that he came to pay his respects, noting that it was difficult "for an ordinary citizen like me to pay tribute in any other way."[168] Dallas real estate developer Tom Russell paid for one of the largest, most ornate displays in Dealey Plaza. "I called my florist," he later recalled. "I said, 'I want a permanent memorial to Kennedy, and I want you to spare no expense.'"[169] In addition to an oversized memorial cross, Russell personally insisted on a small replica of Kennedy's eternal flame, authorizing the florist to take as much money as necessary out of his account to keep it lit indefinitely. Though Russell's controversial display was soon removed from the plaza, he kept it on public display in front of his Dallas home for the next year.[170]

On the Monday following the assassination, the day President Kennedy was buried at Arlington National Cemetery, Ike Pappas, a radio reporter for station WNEW in New York City, went to Dealey Plaza to record a "mood piece" about the atmosphere at the site of the murder. He was surprised by the number of wreaths and cards that had been left there, and his reading of some of the cards served as his radio report. "I picked one up and it was from a Boy Scout," recalled Pappas in 1993, "and it said . . . 'To my president, we know you're now with God and happy. From Billy.' And the other said, 'You were our father, and we love you, President Kennedy.' Well, I was overcome by this . . . and it was a very emotional, kind of wonderful, sad [radio] piece."[171] The *Dallas Morning News* added that "the heart of Dallas [was] in these little cards attached to the wreaths dropped on patches of green grass on either side of" Elm Street.[172] Several of the handwritten cards apologized and asked for forgiveness.[173]

Much of the public fascination was focused on the Depository building, where individuals were often seen pointing toward the sixth floor.[174] This curiosity was not lost on the Depository's staff; the building was soon "swarmed" by individuals wanting to see the interior and the alleged "sniper's perch." Management, however, barred all visitors from the premises and placed a large sign proclaiming "NO ADMITTANCE Except on Official Business" next to the main entrance.[175] According to Bill Holt, the Depository's credit manager, the front door was often kept locked for the first few years after the assassination.

As late as 1970 Holt remembered being caught in tourist photographs "several thousand times coming in and out of the building at lunch."[176] While tourists may have been banned from the building, investigators—including members of the Warren Commission—continued to have open access to the sixth floor crime scene throughout the following year. During a September 1964 visit, Senator Richard Russell of the commission startled plaza tourists by aiming a rifle out of the sixth floor window.[177]

Transformed overnight into perhaps the most famous warehouse in the world, the Texas School Book Depository retained a grisly fascination for all except perhaps the citizens of Dallas, who continued to feel guilty about what had happened in their community and to suffer negativity beyond the city limits as well. Yet so long as the Depository company occupied the structure, there was no noticeable public outcry to tear down the building. An inkling of the controversy that would follow, however, came when Louis Toppel, a Democratic candidate for the Texas Senate, advocated the removal of the Hertz Rent-a-Car sign atop the building, calling the advertisement "a 'tumorous growth' of the past."[178] The sign remained for another decade before it was determined that it was damaging the building's structural integrity.

In 1969 the Texas School Book Depository Company stopped actively storing books on the building's top three floors and had constructed a new warehouse space on Ambassador Row in Dallas by March 1970.[179] While the company's growth was cited as the main reason for relocating, some believed that the Kennedy assassination likely influenced this decision.[180] The following month Col. D. Harold Byrd, who had been privately offered as much as $1.5 million for the Depository after the assassination, put the "valuable business property" up for public auction, hoping to sell it to downtown developers.[181] His initial announcement about the auction did not mention the Kennedy assassination.[182]

Five days before the sale, the *Dallas Morning News* ran a lengthy story on the notorious building, again "the focus of worldwide attention." G. C. Walters, whose firm handled the transaction for Byrd, told the paper that he had received numerous calls about the building and expected as many as one thousand people to turn out for the auction. Like Byrd, Walters downplayed the building's connection to the assassination, noting that it was a matter of "simply liquidating properties." Among the prospective buyers was a Tennessee book publisher who wanted to retain the building's warehouse function and an individual from Pennsylvania interested in tearing down the building to sell $1 souvenir bricks.[183]

Enter Aubrey Mayhew, a country music publisher and promoter from Nashville, Tennessee. A conservative Republican who nevertheless greatly admired John F. Kennedy, Mayhew bought the building for only $650,000—much less than Byrd's hopeful estimate of $1 million.[184] "I read in the Nashville papers that the building was going up for auction," Mayhew recalled in 1971. "I planned to just come down to observe . . .[but] I found most of the people involved in the thing were just kind of making a joke of it."[185] The only other serious bidder, Mayhew explained, wanted to demolish the building and commercially develop the site; Mayhew, however, saw the historic value of the Depository and decided to save it.[186] Declaring at the time of purchase that he had no idea what he would do with the warehouse, Mayhew nevertheless told the *Dallas Morning News* that "he would never sell it." The only hint as to the new owner's intentions was his revelation to the press that he was co-owner of the John F. Kennedy Memorial Center in Nashville, which opened in September 1969. But he did make a series of promises—not to tear down the building, turn it "into something gaudy," or establish "some kind of shrine or memorial."[187]

Over a year passed before Aubrey Mayhew finally announced his plans for the building. In the interim the mysterious Mayhew had dropped out of the public eye, prompting considerable speculation among Dallasites as to his intentions.[188] He routinely canceled interviews and press conferences. Mayhew's few interviews took place only when eager reporters tracked him down and "persuaded" him "to talk on the spot."[189] The picture of Mayhew that emerged in the press was that of an obsessive collector of Kennedy memorabilia. He was in Houston at the time of the assassination. Armed with a portable tape recorder, he immediately captured the Kennedy speeches and memorials as they were broadcast. Within thirty-six hours he had edited the material at a studio in New Orleans and produced a memorial album for Pickwick Records entitled *John Fitzgerald Kennedy: The Presidential Years 1960–1963*, which, according to Mayhew, sold several million copies. By 1966, as the owner of Little Darlin' Records in Nashville, Mayhew's growing Kennedy collection included magazines, coins, medals, autographed books, rough drafts of Kennedy speeches, and even the presidential seal that topped Kennedy's 1961 inaugural ball cake. "Nothing was too big or too small," he later said.[190] Despite the project's historical overtones and emphasis on original artifacts, some prominent Dallas residents feared that Mayhew "would turn [the Depository] into a honky-tonk tourist trap."[191]

In July 1971, having closed his short-lived Nashville memorial center, Mayhew expressed his plans to move the center's contents to the Depository building to form a John F. Kennedy museum. An associate told the *Morning News* that Mayhew's "first-rate, 'historically significant' national museum" would chronicle the late President's life on the first five floors, while the sixth floor would remain "dramatically vacant."[192] The estimated cost for his museum was $2 million.[193]

FIG. 14
Nashville music promoter Aubrey Mayhew purchased the Texas School Book Depository
in 1970 with a grand vision to create a museum and research center.

Mayhew soon contacted Dallas architect James L. Hendricks, among others, to discuss and submit work for his ambitious project. When the pair met, Mayhew told Hendricks that he wanted to display several large pieces, including one or more Kennedy-owned limousines and thousands of smaller artifacts. Mayhew's audacious vision for the building included a personal apartment on the seventh floor and a multifloor experience for visitors.[194] In his plan, visitors would conclude their tour of the first floor by walking outside onto the loading dock to see the shell of a PT (Personal Transportation) boat permanently moored there. Indeed, Mayhew had acquired motor torpedo boat *PT-59*, which John F. Kennedy had commanded during World War II. In July 1971 he expressed his intention to fund an expedition to locate Kennedy's first command—the more famous *PT-109*, which sank in 1943—and add it to his collection.[195]

In announcing his plans to open a private museum, Mayhew emphasized his personal "interest in history—not money."[196] By April 1972 his plans called for the purchase of ten acres of land adjoining the Depository to provide space for a public park, an office building, and a library named for Robert F. Kennedy. The estimated cost of the proposed Memorial Center, which now included a theater and research facilities, had risen to $18 million and was to include some 200,000 artifacts.[197]

Less than three months after announcing this bold vision, however, Mayhew's dreams began to crumble. In short, he had no financial backers who could provide the operating capital needed to develop his plans.[198] One potential Dallas investor declined to assist, emphasizing the Nashville entrepreneur's lack of credentials: "I'm interested in the project . . . but not in the way Mr. Mayhew wants to do it."[199] The lack of support in Dallas surprised Mayhew, who admitted in a 1997 interview with Gary Mack that his music background probably triggered unfair comparisons to "kind of a carnival barker."[200]

While persistently insisting that his museum would not be a "tourist trap," Mayhew solicited funds by opening the lobby of the Depository to sell Kennedy souvenirs and "symbolic square inch[es] of the property" for $1 each.[201] He refrained from charging tourists to tour the empty sixth floor, however, so as not to "taint" his project by making it "a commercial enterprise."[202]

Despite embarking on a nationwide tour to raise money for the stalled project, Mayhew, six months behind on his $6,000 per month payments to D. Harold Byrd, found himself in danger of foreclosure by Republic National Bank.[203] For many fearful of exploitation at the site, Mayhew's travails were no doubt greeted with relief; even the architect initially consulted on the project reflected, "Thank goodness all that fell through."[204]

With foreclosure imminent by July 1972, Mayhew vowed that he would go down fighting and publicly blamed the lack of local interest in his project on the guilty feelings still prevalent in the Dallas community. "If the people of Dallas feel that they killed Kennedy," he told the *Dallas Morning News* on July 17, "then they are committing a much greater crime by not preserving this historic site."[205]

Three days later fifty firefighters responded to a two-alarm blaze at the Texas School Book Depository. The fire, which took only minutes to extinguish, damaged two floors, although not the infamous sixth floor. Investigators found twenty cans of gasoline scattered throughout the building and concluded that the fire would have been much worse had the sprinkler system been deactivated. In the end, most of the $5,000 worth of damage was caused by water rather than by fire.[206]

Within a week of the fire, which garnered significant media attention, Win Anderson, the building's twenty-five-year-old caretaker, was arrested on arson charges; he himself had called in the fire.[207] After an arraignment, Anderson was incarcerated in the Dallas County jail because he was unable to pay the $10,000 bond.[208]

Even if he had wanted to help his employee, Aubrey Mayhew had problems of his own. Back in Nashville, he had been arrested for allegedly selling a Steinway piano that turned out to be a fake for $1,200.[209] Released on bond, Mayhew threatened to file federal charges against the Dallas Fire Department for "illegally taking possession" of the building by stationing "round-the-clock guards" on-site during the investigation.[210] To ward off any further attempts at arson, fire officials had also padlocked the sprinkler system so that it could not be turned off.[211]

Mayhew's federal lawsuit, however, proved to be an empty threat. His Dallas attorney, John J. Solon, who had personally filed for bankruptcy in February and was now moonlighting as a mechanic, spent the following days attempting to stop foreclosure of the building by Republic National Bank. Solon's petition for a temporary restraining order was denied by U.S. District judge Robert M. Hill, ostensibly because Mayhew's attorney could not pay the $250 cash deposit needed for a $2,500 court bond.[212]

On August 1, 1972, Aubrey Mayhew lost the Texas School Book Depository. At a foreclosure sale held on the steps of the Dallas County Courthouse, the building's previous owner, Col. D. Harold Byrd—the only bidder—secured the Depository for $471,958.77. In reality, no money changed hands: Byrd's bid was simply the exact amount that Mayhew still owed. Byrd seemed pleased to reclaim ownership of the building that he had first purchased at public auction in 1939 and vowed to "sell it on a first come, first serve basis." He claimed that a potential buyer had already offered $1.1 million for the building. A federal court denied Mayhew's appeal to void the transaction.[213]

The question of whether or not Mayhew may have been involved in the arson attempt remained a mystery contemplated by many in the aftermath. Investigators were never able to tie him to the crime. Win Anderson pled no contest to the arson charge and received a sentence of five years' probation.[214] Conover Hunt, who spent years researching the Dealey Plaza area as The Sixth Floor exhibit's project director, noted that a month after the fire "the case . . . virtually disappear[ed]."[215] With the passage of time, however, suspicions persisted that Mayhew may have played some role in the fire. One former Depository building manager felt "without a doubt" that Mayhew was involved in the arson attempt.[216] The county's public works director, Judson Shook, opined: "I think it had to do with an unprofitable building that somebody wanted to maybe collect insurance on."[217] Until his death in 2009, Mayhew always denied any involvement. Likewise, Win Anderson never implicated his former boss, revealing in 1976 that the fire was the result of his being left "high and dry" on the failed museum project.[218]

Although it rapidly slipped from the Dallas newspaper headlines, the symbolic impact of the arson attempt—and Aubrey Mayhew's brief ownership of the building—was not soon forgotten by the Dallas community: it had "poignantly dramatized the troublesome fate of what [had] become the city's biggest tourist attraction."[219] For Mayhew, the experience was one of great personal tragedy. Gary Mack said that "Aubrey was very bitter about the whole experience. He explained to me, 'Gary, buying that building was one of the worst things I have ever done. It cost me my personal fortune. It cost me my marriage, and it took years to recover.'"[220]

Even if his intentions for a museum were meant as a respectful tribute to the memory of President Kennedy, Aubrey Mayhew's association with the Texas School Book Depository likely prompted even stronger resentment toward the building from Dallasites than any other event following the Kennedy assassination. For the first time, the community worried about commercial exploitation of the site. With the tenth anniversary of the assassination rapidly approaching in November 1973, many felt that the time had come to remove the Depository from the collective memory of Dallas. Others, however, recognized the historical significance of the structure and—perhaps more importantly to them—the possible ramifications for Dallas if a developer came forward to demolish the key component of such an internationally recognized murder site.

Both ideologies were represented on the Dallas City Council. Not long after the building's ownership reverted to Byrd, Dallas city councilman Garry Weber presented a resolution "calling for the city building inspector to permit no alterations to the building"—in essence, ensuring that the Depository would not be torn down for the time being. It also called for the city manager's office "to apply for federal funds to purchase the structure." Weber, however, faced an uphill challenge on his second point. In order for the building even to qualify for federal funding, under the National Historic Preservation Act of 1966, it would first need to be listed on the National Register of Historic Places and "become part of the state's historical preservation plan."[221] Although ardent efforts to interest the state in the fate of the Texas School Book Depository had been made by state senator Mike McKool as far back as 1968, thus far he had not been successful.[222]

Councilman Weber's bold move, coming so soon after Mayhew's controversial ownership of the building, prompted a fervent response from the Dallas community. Many people, as it turned out, were interested in the fate of the Texas School Book Depository. With a passion not publicly demonstrated since the aftermath of the Kennedy assassination, the *Dallas Morning News* published letters expressly suggesting that the building be demolished. "Get rid of the ugly thing and the memories," wrote one resident who could not fathom why the city might want to renovate the Depository, "so Dallas can say 'a president was murdered here.'"[223] Another Dallasite suggested "wrecking the old building," challenging the city instead to "dream beautiful, big dreams."[224]

On September 5, 1972, the Dallas City Council voted nine to two to "block demolition or alteration" of the Texas School Book Depository while the city applied for historic site status. Only councilmen Fred M. Zeder and Russell Smith, advocates for tearing down the building, adamantly opposed Weber's proposal. Zeder told the *Morning News* after the vote that Dallas should not "immortalize that day of infamy."[225]

Despite opposition from some quarters, the council's historic vote was still a victory for those in the community who saw the historic value in the Depository. It marked the first time that city officials openly addressed Dallas's most infamous structure—with preventative action—and, by extension, the darkest and most painful chapter in its recent history. This was also, as Conover Hunt pointed out, "the first pro-active move on behalf of the community to acknowledge a longer term responsibility to preservation of an historic site." Moreover, the council's decision clearly demonstrated that the city discouraged and would actively oppose future commercial use of the structure.[226] The battle over the building was far from over, but emerging in September 1972 were the parameters of the war that would be fought publicly for the next seventeen years. It was a struggle between the public fascination with the site of the Kennedy assassination and a sensitive community's desire to promote civic progress and emerge from the long dark shadow of history.

Chapter **2**
A SITE OF SHAME

A crumbling, condemned, ugly, [seven]-story memorial to what? To the
fanatic foul deed of a sick little man? . . . Surely, this building can never
be a memorial to John Kennedy, who never set foot in it, who never knew
it existed."[1] So spoke Dallas city councilman Fred M. Zeder, who quickly mar-
shaled opposition to the council's vote to save the Texas School Book Depository
from demolition. Just as one angry Dallas resident encouraged the city to get
rid of the building *and* the memories, Zeder argued that saving the Depository
from destruction was tantamount to "immortaliz[ing] that libelous legend . . .
'City of Hate.'"[2]

Zeder and fellow council dissenter Russell Smith asked the council to reconsider its decision, hoping that "private enterprise" would submit proposals for
the site.[3] In the interim, on September 11, 1972, Zeder helped organize a group
of interested citizens called Dallas Onward who called for nothing less than the
demolition of the Depository building, which they felt "continue[d] to give Dallas
a black eye."[4] Challenging the city's legal right to block demolition and blasting
the council's steadfast ruling as not representing the mind-set of the community,
Zeder encouraged Dallas Onward to "challenge the action of the City Council
in placing restrictions on building permits on private property." Zeder received
lukewarm agreement from city attorney Alex Bickley, who said that Zeder was
likely correct about the illegality of the council's resolution, though he ruled that
neither Zeder nor Russell Smith could move to overturn the controversial resolution because both had previously voted against it.[5]

In the face of mounting opposition, Garry Weber clarified his position,
noting that his resolution did not in any way guarantee that the building would
be preserved. The National Historical Sites Commission, he said, "may well
decide to raze it and make some other fitting use of the site." Weber stressed
to the *Morning News* that he simply wanted to put an end to ten years of controversy surrounding the site and avoid another situation in which the build-

ing might be used "for purposes detrimental to Dallas, or to the memory of President Kennedy."[6]

In reality the Dallas Onward organization consisted of fewer than twelve individuals, mostly Dallas businessmen. But by the time the City Council reconvened to discuss the fate of the Depository building, the group had pledges of $100,000 to buy the building and tear it down.[7] Their spokesman was Thomas B. Rhodes, the senior vice president and general counsel of Sedco, Incorporated, a Dallas-based oil drilling company.[8] Dallas Onward proposed a series of alternative uses for the site, including a public park, a school, or even a museum dedicated to local history—presumably excluding the Kennedy assassination— that would reflect "the true background of Dallas."[9] The City Council, however, refused to back down from its position, with the full support of Mayor Wes Wise.

Wise, formerly a television news and sports broadcaster who had helped cover the assassination story for CBS affiliate KRLD-TV, was strongly opposed to tearing down the building.[10] "I didn't think it was a blight on the city of Dallas because we didn't have the responsibility of shooting the president," he recalled in 2005. "Number two, I felt that it would always be an historic building."[11] Wise found an ally in Judson Shook, the director of public works for Dallas County, who had become interested in preserving the building in 1969 when day after day from his office window he observed hundreds of tourists gazing up at the empty structure.[12] Wise and Shook—who shortly became the building's most vocal public champion—garnered support to save the structure, though Wise later admitted that no one else on the City Council wanted to become embroiled in the controversy.[13]

"There were a lot of political shenanigans going on there," remembered Mayor Wise, who personally felt that prominent Republicans did not want to memorialize a site associated with the murder of a Democratic president.[14] More prevalent, however, were concerns that Dallas would embarrass itself by preserving the building that represented the President's assassination. "I shared those same fears," said Judson Shook. "I did not share their ideas [about the building's fate] . . . because I felt that if it was ever torn down, that a good many people would see that as verification that [Dallas was] trying to hide something."[15]

Many in the community agreed with Shook and the mayor. One Dallas resident suggested sarcastically that, if the building embodied the Kennedy assassination, then perhaps Dallas should "narrow the hateful item not to the building, but to the [infamous corner] window . . . or maybe the screws" on the window's handle. "All this," he wrote, "is to point out how ridiculous it is to condemn an object because of an unpleasant act."[16]

Undeterred, opponents of preserving the Depository building replied with the now familiar argument that the building not only perpetuated the tragedy of the Kennedy assassination but held no historic value, "but for the fleeting presence of a murderer."[17] To others, the Kennedy Memorial near Dealey Plaza was "reminder enough" of November 22, 1963.[18]

"A Monument to an Assassin"

The question remained: if the building was preserved, what would become of it? The Dallas city attorney quipped that the building could simply be condemned, ensuring that it remained vacant.[19] Historian Conover Hunt distilled the debate down to two overarching questions: "Do we have an obligation to preserve this building—certainly Dallas' most unpopular building—and how do we really feel about commercial efforts at this site?"[20]

Councilman Fred Zeder grounded his argument in favor of the building's demolition in the history of assassination sites. In a passionate editorial that he authored in the *Dallas Times Herald* in September 1972, Zeder discussed the fates of the Memphis, Tennessee, rooming house from which James Earl Ray allegedly fired the shot that killed civil rights leader Dr. Martin Luther King, Jr.; the Ambassador Hotel kitchen in Los Angeles where Robert Kennedy was shot; and the University of Texas tower in Austin where gunman Charles Whitman fired at passing students. In each instance, Zeder noted, no city official stepped up to recommend a memorial, shrine, or bronze plaque because "none of these places made a contribution to history." Ford's Theatre in Washington, the site of Abraham Lincoln's 1865 assassination, was the only exception; it bore a legacy of its own in the history of American theater. Zeder wondered how a rundown "architectural monstrosity" could ever house a tribute "to the youthful, zestful ideas of John Kennedy?" It could not, he concluded, which would force any future memorial or museum created within the Texas School Book Depository to be recognized as a shrine to the alleged assassin, Lee Harvey Oswald.[21] This powerful argument would be repeated in later years as the museum exhibit team sought support in the community.

Meanwhile, the City of Dallas submitted an application to the Texas Historical Commission in hopes that the State Board of Review would recommend the Texas School Book Depository for the National Register of Historic Places. But even before the board agreed to review the proposal in early 1972, there were serious doubts that it would be successful. Aubrey Mayhew's similar 1971 application had been unanimously rejected.[22] Nevertheless, those interested in preserving the building found a glimmer of hope in a concurrent effort (separate from that of the Dallas City Council) that had begun in Dallas four years earlier, in December 1968.

State senator Mike McKool was ahead of his time when, one month after winning his seat on November 9, 1968, he promised to introduce legislation for the state to turn the Texas School Book Depository into "one of the greatest museums in the world."[23] During his campaign for the sixteenth district seat, the liberal Democrat sharply criticized the city's conservative establishment.[24] There is no evidence that McKool ever mentioned the Depository during the campaign, though he held a press conference before the end of the year outside of the building to disclose his plan to introduce legislation to form a John F. Kennedy Memorial Commission tasked with acquiring the structure. The Texas School Book Depository company still occupied the site. McKool, believing that the state could acquire the property through eminent domain, apparently did not bother to brief owner D. Harold Byrd before making his public announcement.[25]

McKool's statement triggered predictable responses from naysayers. "Mike McKool has to be kidding," wrote one. Another thought the proposal a poor use of state funds.[26] Perhaps most telling was the comment that Senator McKool's proposal "seem[ed] to be admitting to the world our collective civic guilt."[27] McKool, however, believed that there was a genuine need for a museum in Dealey Plaza about the Kennedy assassination and that the Depository was the key; his press conference acknowledged the area's persistent tourist presence.[28]

McKool's rough sketch in 1968 of what a museum inside the Depository should be remains markedly similar to the end result that opened twenty-one years later on the sixth floor. He thought that large photographic displays, supplemented by the written reports found in newspapers and magazines, should guide visitors through the events of the day. The results of the Warren Commission's investigation should be included, as should information and material relating to the shooting of Lee Harvey Oswald and the 1964 trial of Jack Ruby.[29] Original artifacts should also be displayed, including "clothing worn by some of the principals."[30]

This vision was not the first time that Mike McKool sought to memorialize John F. Kennedy. On December 2, 1963, just over one week after the assassination, McKool, then a Dallas attorney, appealed to the City Council for "a structural monument to President Kennedy" to symbolize the community's "real love and deep grief" in the aftermath of the assassination.[31] In addition, his wife, as a member of the Democratic Women of Dallas County, headed up the John F. Kennedy Memorial Book Fund project in early 1964.[32]

The proposed legislation to acquire the Depository was doomed from the start. Although the bill won approval in the Senate State Affairs Committee on March 5, 1969, all references to a proposed museum inside the Depository were omitted.[33] As amended, the bill simply sought to establish a nine-member John F. Kennedy Memorial Commission, appointed by the Texas governor, tasked with creating a memorial "financed solely through private contributions" rather than with $55,000 in state funds as McKool had originally suggested.[34] This proposal sounded similar to the Dallas-based John F. Kennedy Citizens Memorial Committee, which had already been established in 1963. Its work had resulted in the Philip Johnson–designed John F. Kennedy Memorial near Dealey Plaza, dedicated on June 24, 1970.[35]

Even after the most controversial element of his bill had been removed, however, McKool faced further opposition in the state senate.[36] The provision that empowered the commission with eminent domain authority was swiftly eliminated, thwarting all hope that the Depository could be appropriated for use as a state memorial or museum. One vocal opponent, Senator Ralph Hall of Rockwall, read aloud on the senate floor a letter that he had received from former Kennedy aide Ted Sorensen, who opposed locating anything inside the Depository building that would serve "to glorify the crime more than the victim." Two other senators threatened to filibuster the bill, prompting a week-long delay. One of the opponents, Jack Strong of Longview, believed that the senate "would set a dangerous precedent" by creating a state agency to memorialize a single person. He also tried, unsuccessfully, to add an amendment forcing the governor to appoint only Dallas residents to the proposed commission.[37]

On March 25 the senate passed McKool's largely decimated bill, after adding one final concession limiting the commission's existence to six years.[38] The Texas House of Representatives approved the measure on May 16, 1969, and it was signed into law shortly thereafter.[39] A year passed, however, before Governor Preston Smith appointed the nine-member panel. Three of them were Dallas residents, including chair Raymond D. Nasher, a real estate developer and civic leader.[40]

The legislature's failure to fund the operation of the commission became painfully clear during the first meeting of the new body on September 15, 1970. United Press International reported that "members were told legislative appropriations . . . included no funds to cover costs of hearings or even to pay for clerical help for the commission, much less finance the actual memorial."[41]

From the start, the commission that Mike McKool had hoped would transform the Texas School Book Depository into a museum instead favored a "living and continuing memorial" in the form of student scholarships, a John F.

Kennedy graduate school in Dallas, or a day of mourning.[42] Commission secretary Bernard Rapoport proclaimed that any meaningful artifacts relating to President Kennedy had "already been grabbed up by somebody else."[43] In fact, not until after Aubrey Mayhew announced his plans for a private John F. Kennedy Memorial Center did the commission suddenly become interested in the Depository.[44] Two days after Mayhew announced his intentions, McKool appealed to the commission to reconsider the Depository, noting that his prediction that private enterprise would step in if the state failed to act had come true. He argued that the Texas School Book Depository "should be owned by the people of Texas."[45] The commission agreed.

In August of 1971 the John F. Kennedy Memorial Commission officially petitioned the Texas Legislature for the power of eminent domain. The goal was to pay Mayhew a fair market price, resorting to eminent domain only if the price got "out of reason."[46] McKool seized on this moment once more to vocalize his support for a state-run museum inside the Depository, emphasizing that it would be more respectful and dignified than any commercial effort. Neither he nor the commission, however, met with Aubrey Mayhew regarding his plans for a privately operated memorial center.[47]

Mayhew called the proposal for the state to take over the building "ridiculous," dismissing any criticism of his ownership as blind prejudice because Mayhew hailed from Tennessee rather than Texas.[48] Meanwhile, McKool reassured those in the community who were wary of taxpayer money being used to fund a state project at the Depository: while acquiring the building and creating a museum might cost as much as $2 million, the state eventually would be reimbursed by admission fees. He compared the approach to the building and operation of a state-owned toll road.[49]

Public reaction to McKool's proposal was mixed. One Dallas resident called the plan "the lesser of two evils," saying that it was better than having an individual—namely Aubrey Mayhew—profit from the tragedy.[50] Ironically, the commission itself did not fully embrace McKool's vision; chair Raymond Nasher quickly put the brakes on, preferring to secure the building first, before deciding what it would contain. By November, however, Nasher appeared to support demolishing or at least gutting the building, which was in poor condition. Instead of a museum, he suggested developing the site into a living memorial along the lines already suggested by the commission.[51]

The commission anxiously awaited a decision on the question of eminent domain. Although state representative Joe Golman agreed to introduce such a bill in January 1973, he did not do so. After ownership of the Depository reverted to Col. D. Harold Byrd, the City of Dallas blocked all demolition permits and launched efforts for the building's recognition as a historic site.[52] In the end, the John F. Kennedy Memorial Commission dissolved at the end of its six-year term, before McKool's goal of establishing a state museum inside the Texas School Book Depository could be realized.[53] It appeared that any effort to save the Depository would have to begin at the local level.

On March 23, 1973, the state committee that reviewed the application by the City of Dallas to add the Depository to the National Register of Historic Places unanimously rejected the proposal. In February city officials had presented plans that included the Depository as part of a downtown historical preservation district. Several Dallas residents opposed to the project had also appeared before the committee. Chair D. B. Alexander justified the committee's decision by saying that "it would be rather embarrassing if new evidence" later surfaced indicating that shots were not fired from the building. Alexander likewise stated that the City of Dallas had no definite plans for the building and was unwilling to commit city tax money to preserve and maintain the structure.[54] This decision, from the same committee that unanimously rejected Mayhew's application in 1971, sent a clear message to the Dallas community: federal funding would not save this building. A decade after the Kennedy assassination, the Depository apparently was still too controversial for official historic recognition.

Despite this setback, Dallas mayor Wes Wise was "still hopeful that the depository [could] be preserved."[55] The building's owner, D. Harold Byrd, expressed similar sentiments but was not moved to donate the building or maintain ownership until funds could be raised.[56] In March 1972 he renewed his efforts to find a buyer or a tenant, calling the Depository a "Famous Historic Dallas Landmark" in an advertisement in the *Dallas Morning News*.[57]

Such ads continued to appear in Dallas newspapers at least through September 1975, leaving observers to speculate on the fate of the city's most famous structure.[58] In an April 1973 commentary, *Dallas Morning News* writer Dave McNeely articulated one poignant scenario. McNeely posed a fictionalized future in which, though the Depository was indeed torn down, a dedicated street vendor continued to sell souvenir photographs of the building to the crowds of tourists who flocked to the site. "Somebody's got to do it," said the fictional vendor. "How else will people know what it looked like?" The article also described the imaginary sale of $20 souvenir bricks from the demolished Depository and how the Hertz Rent-a-Car sign was donated to the Smithsonian Institution. When asked if anyone still cared about historic preservation, the author, again speaking through the street vendor, replied: "Not many in Dallas. Some folks figured it served as a monument to an assassin instead of a historic place. So they figured they'd just tear it down so that no one could profiteer from people's morbid curiosity."[59]

"A Useful Part of Our Community"

Judson Shook, as director of public works for Dallas County, took a personal interest in the Texas School Book Depository in the spring of 1969. From his office window in the nearby Records Annex building, Shook had an unobstructed view of the controversial Depository and noticed that "there were people every day in large numbers, taking pictures and pointing up at the building, trying to figure out which of those windows up there the shots were fired from." Many, he witnessed, mistakenly assumed that a painted red circle—actually a Dallas Fire Department indicator noting where to access the building from a ladder truck—marked the infamous window.[60] Tourists were largely unobservant: for decades all downtown buildings had sported similar red circles on upper floor windows.[61]

Shook heard many tourists wondering aloud about the window and "some saying that they wanted [to go] up in the building." As one who had seen the Kennedy motorcade in person on November 22, 1963, he adamantly disagreed with Dallas residents and political leaders who wanted to tear down the building. At the same time, he did not support Aubrey Mayhew's approach, believing that from a purely economic standpoint it would be impossible to create a tasteful museum without the benefit of government support.[62] Shook carefully followed the 1972 debate within the Dallas City Council and soon developed a cordial friendship with Mayor Wise, who felt much the same way he did. When the state commission stalled and the city's application for landmark status was rejected, Shook quietly went to work on a plan to have Dallas County purchase the building—even as D. Harold Byrd again tried to sell it through ads in local and national newspapers such as the *Wall Street Journal.*[63]

"I felt it was my role really to run up trial balloons," recalled Shook in 1992, "to see how many shots were fired at it and where those shots were coming from." At that moment, he was perhaps the most effective champion that the Texas School Book Depository could have. He was a high-ranking Dallas County official yet not a politician who had to avoid controversy for fear of losing reelection.[64]

As Dallas marked the tenth anniversary of the Kennedy assassination on November 22, 1973, the fate of the Depository was still in question. Media focus remained on the "mood" in Dallas, with some stories reflecting on preassassination extremist activity. Media inquiries poured into Dallas City Hall beginning the first week of November. Wes Wise, the former television news and sports broadcaster who had spoken with Jack Ruby in Dealey Plaza the day following the assassination, now found himself in the unenviable position of representing the community as mayor.[65]

After giving approximately one dozen interviews to national and international reporters, Wise concluded that many had "the same preconceived notions about Dallas that they had 10 years ago."[66] Whenever possible, Wise defended his community and lauded its civic achievements, which included the All-America City Award from the National Civic League in 1970.[67]

The mayor publicly encouraged a large number to come to the city's official memorial service (held at the John F. Kennedy Memorial, not in Dealey Plaza), noting that Dallas had suffered media criticism "for the relatively small showing" on previous anniversaries.[68] Approximately five hundred attendees watched him place a wreath inside the memorial and, in a brief statement, declare that a decade had "not diminished the memory."[69]

During a cocktail reception at a national conference of mayors earlier that year, one of Wise's Midwestern counterparts had asked him in front of a group how it felt "to be mayor of the city that killed the president." The Dallas chief executive refrained from commenting, and the offending mayor apologized the following day after "catching hell" from those within earshot. Although the incident reflected the deep-rooted animosity that persisted a decade after the assassination, neither the opinions of others nor the probing media diminished Wise's interest in saving the Texas School Book Depository. If anything, such incidents probably strengthened his resolve. At one point Wise even consulted with former Texas governor John B. Connally—the other motorcade victim on November 22, 1963—about the building's fate. Though he made no known public statement, Connally thought that demolishing the building was a terrible idea and privately encouraged the Dallas mayor that he should not "let that building go down the tubes."[70]

Another state official involved in President Kennedy's 1963 visit who harbored strong feelings about the building was U.S. congressman Jim Wright. Wright had helped host the president in his hometown of Fort Worth, Texas, and during the short flight to Dallas on the day of the assassination. Though he never publicly commented on the Depository, he later indicated that his opinion at the time would have been: "Yes, tear it down. Expunge it from the face of the Earth. Get rid of it. Leave no recollection of so foul a deed."[71] Whether it was expressed openly or not, Judson Shook faced considerable resistance among the political and civic leaders who had been involved in President Kennedy's ill-fated visit to Texas. As early as March 1964, for example, Earle Cabell, the mayor of Dallas at the time of the assassination, told a local rotary club that creating a "monstrous monument" or even "converting the Texas School Book Depository into a mausoleum" was not the right way for the city to respond to the tragedy.[72]

Wary of potential opponents, Shook took a diplomatic approach in interesting Dallas County in the Depository. The growth of both the city and the county and an associated need for office and storage space aided him in his effort.[73] Dallas was undergoing a period of "robust expansionism."[74] A new city hall designed by I. M. Pei opened in 1978, and a $42.7 million Dallas Public Library building soon followed across the street. A successful 1979 bond election provided $27 million for a new art museum and concert hall to serve as the foundation for the Dallas Arts District.[75] The construction of a new sports and concert arena, the development of the Dallas Area Rapid Transit, and, most significantly, the 1974 opening of Dallas–Fort Worth International Airport all contributed to the city's new reputation as a "hustling boomtown."[76] By 1975 Dallas County was "busting at the seams," according to one commissioner, and desperately needed additional office space.[77]

Amid the rapid growth and development, many Dallas residents also began contemplating historic preservation of some of the city's oldest—and potentially endangered—structures. Although the 1901 Texas School Book Depository was rarely cited in arguments for local preservation, practical considerations no doubt helped in part to spare the infamous structure before Dallas County decided to act. In the early 1970s an effort began to transform the city's old warehouse district near Dealey Plaza into a large shopping and dining venue aimed at tourists, similar to Underground Atlanta and San Francisco's Ghirardelli Square. Entered into the National Register of Historic Places in 1978, the West End Historic District covered a total of fifty-five acres and included the Texas School Book Depository. For the first time, the Depository building was publicly acknowledged as a historically significant structure in terms of its turn-of-the-century function as a warehouse and its relationship to the nearby railroad.[78]

A local architectural firm headed by James L. Hendricks was contacted by Judson Shook as the county ramped up its efforts in the mid-1970s to acquire the Depository and possibly other buildings in downtown Dallas for adaptive reuse. By that time Shook felt that the Depository could serve as the seat of county government, with a new Dallas County Commissioners Courtroom on the ground floor. Hendricks, Burson, and Walls, one of the top firms in the city at that time, had gained local prominence in 1970 for its conversion of the Cumberland School—one of the oldest brick buildings in the Dallas Independent School District—into the administrative offices of Sedco, Incorporated. The project, one of six recognized by the Texas Society of Architects, won the top award in Dallas Architecture in 1971. Hendricks's ideas about adaptive reuse meshed perfectly with what Judson Shook had envisioned for the Texas School Book Depository. Shook asked Hendricks's engaging partner, Rodger Burson, to make a presentation before the Dallas County Commissioners about the Depository. Burson agreed to plead with the commissioners to preserve the historic structure.[79]

Burson's outstanding presentation convinced the commissioners to lend their support to Shook's endeavor. In addition to providing the county with seven stories of space at a bargain price, it was an innovative means, in James Hendricks's view, of rescuing an attractive brick structure.[80] "At that time," Hendricks later reflected, "the words 'adaptive reuse' and 'recycling' . . . [were] completely new. In fact, nationally that direction was kind of 'high-tech.'"[81]

Dallas County made its interest in the Depository public on September 16, 1975. Stressing the need for additional office and storage space, commissioner David Pickett told the *Morning News* that the Depository—and at least one more downtown building—might be purchased or leased by the county. Less than two weeks later the county sought a ninety-day option on the Depository while it conducted a structural analysis.[82]

When one newspaper reported that the commissioners were considering "keeping the sixth floor vacant as a possible museum or shrine," Judson Shook, quick to quell fears about exploitation at the site, emphasized that city fire codes forbade any public gatherings inside the building.[83] County officials also soon acknowledged that the "historically tainted" sixth floor was unfit to function as office space.[84] Their first goal, however, was simply to secure the building.

The county's initial efforts to acquire the Depository were short-lived, however: the owner rejected the county's offer of $250,000, demanding instead no less than $400,000. For five months Shook explored other downtown buildings before announcing that the Depository was among eleven possible structures for county purchase. After further negotiations, the county met owner D. Harold Byrd's terms and signed a new purchase option on the 80,000-square-foot building on April 20, 1976.[85]

In the days following this significant announcement, a number of different perspectives on the property emerged from the Dallas County Commissioners Court. As city and county officials tried to agree on building code restrictions that would permit the county to renovate the seventy-five-year-old space, Judge John Whittington announced that Dallas County would seek both state and federal funding to assist in the purchase of the Depository. Whittington envisioned a joint venture between the State of Texas and the federal government, which, he believed, had a "responsibility" to provide matching funds for the purchase. Whittington felt that the county should not purchase the Depository without this aid, even though he considered the building to be of "extreme historical significance."[86] Surprisingly, just as the county announced that it intended to reuse the building for office space, the judge told the *Morning News* that the Depository "should be used '100 per cent for historical value and 0 per cent for utility value.'"[87] He later clarified that the building could be used for "light storage," but he remained steadfast that it should house a county-owned historical museum.[88]

Two county commissioners, Roy Orr and Jim Tyson, agreed with Judge Whittington that at least a portion of the building should be devoted to a museum or shrine, but they argued that the remainder should house county offices as Judson Shook had initially proposed. Only commissioner Jim Jackson opposed the county's desire to purchase the Depository. Unlike the active and passionate campaigning by Dallas city councilmen a few years earlier, however, Jackson quietly accepted the court's majority vote. Nonetheless, he continued to oppose a museum inside the building.[89] In the end the commissioners reached a consensus: while the first five floors should be fully converted into county offices, the top two floors of the Texas School Book Depository should remain vacant and unchanged until "a historical perspective [was] achieved."[90]

While commissioners openly discussed their personal thoughts on the building at meetings and with reporters, public works director Shook spent his time in the spotlight carefully emphasizing that the Depository project would be handled "with class and taste." His focus centered on the functional use of the space for county business and proposed that any renovation emphasize the Depository's 1901 origins.[91] Shook's position received support from several in the community, including Dallas architect Bill Benson and Lindalyn Adams, then chair of the Dallas County Historical Commission. Both voiced their support of the Depository purchase at a Commissioners Court session on May 20, 1976.[92] An editorial in the *Dallas Morning News* called the county's proposal "laudable," dismissing the possibility of demolishing the building as "a regrettable waste of a potential resource."[93]

By the end of May 1976 Dallas County had identified two downtown buildings—the Depository and the nearby Purse Building at Elm and Record Streets—to provide a total of 180,000 square feet of potential space, which would theoretically support the needs of Dallas County into the next millennium. The cost to purchase and renovate the two structures was estimated at $6.8 million. An architectural survey revealed that the Depository, despite being at the top of the county's list, was in the worst condition. Nevertheless, the county agreed to pay a monthly option of $2,833 on the Depository.[94]

The Commissioners Court's action was not met by the barrage of negative letters that had typified previous efforts to preserve the building. Only Thomas B.

Rhodes, onetime member of the now defunct Dallas Onward organization, said that he and his associates would try to discourage the county from making the purchase, though his argument notably lacked the conviction present three years earlier. The overall lack of interest in the county's acquisition of the Depository this time around was the result of several factors. Following Mayhew's controversial ownership, Judson Shook had shrewdly downplayed the likelihood of a museum inside the building, though it remained perhaps his strongest personal motivation. Those who did openly contemplate an exhibition were county officials, who saw such a display as part of a functioning county office building, perhaps a small window display of historic artifacts outside a busy conference room. In the months leading up to the bond election, however, even the idea of an actual exhibition was subdued.[95]

By early 1977 Commissioner Orr and Judge Whittington were determined to seek federal funds to maintain the empty sixth floor as a "first-class preserve."[96] Regardless, Dallas residents no doubt perceived any type of county-operated exhibit as less threatening and more satisfying than some type of commercial effort at the site, particularly one developed by a stranger to the area who was not emotionally invested in the sensitive nature of the subject matter. More important from this growing city's perspective, the Depository would be a functional space with offices, conference rooms, a Commissioners Courtroom, and storage space.

On the thirteenth anniversary of the Kennedy assassination in November 1976, Mayor Robert Folsom declared that after more than a decade the city had finally "gotten over the depression" caused by the tragedy.[97] When a mere fourteen people attended the 1975 city-sponsored service at the Kennedy Memorial, Folsom canceled plans for an official ceremony in 1976. Tourists continued to make Dealey Plaza the most popular location in the city, however, and the Depository "one of the world's most photographed structures."[98] The timing was right, it seemed, for the Texas School Book Depository to slip the bonds of its controversial past and become part of an acceptable bureaucratic agenda for Dallas County expansion.

County commissioners initially hoped to hold a proposed $98 million bond election in late 1976. Due to a series of political and tax issues unrelated to the Depository purchase, however, officials postponed the election until the following November, by which point the bond package had grown to $215 million. In the interim the county's original option on the Depository and Purse buildings expired, generating a flood of media speculation that the county's failure to act would result in an embarrassing taxpayer loss of $170,000 for the two structures. In the summer of 1977 commissioners proposed an emergency measure to sell $4 million worth of certificates of indebtedness or general obligation bonds, half of which would provide for the immediate purchase of the Depository and Purse buildings as well as a nearby downtown lot. Although the matter became bogged down in a committee of the Texas Legislature and was never approved, the options were eventually extended until the November election.[99]

The Dallas County bond package of 1977 contained five propositions, one of which provided $20.8 million for capital improvements that included the purchase of the Depository and Purse buildings. The $1.8 million set aside for the Texas School Book Depository would complete the purchase of the building and the first phase of the renovation project, which included structural repairs and remodeling of the building's basement and first two floors to accommodate county offices.[100]

Days prior to the election one local resident wrote a passionate plea urging voters to support the Depository purchase regardless of whether they found the building "infamous or sacred." She implored local residents to help make the structure "a useful part of our community and help remove some of its stigma" rather than let it remain "staring with vacant and accusing eyes."[101]

In the end the long-term social impact of the Depository's purchase at a sum of less than $2 million in a bond package worth $215 million was likely lost on voters concerned with more controversial issues such as the building of a new $50 million courthouse and jail and major state highway, thoroughfare, bridge, and park projects. Most contentious was the revelation in late August that, to cover the purchase of bonds, the county intended to instigate a five-cent tax increase.[102] Nevertheless, county officials noted that all proposed projects "were badly needed." With public support from Sheriff Carl Thomas and long-time Dallas district attorney Henry Wade, the voters agreed.[103]

On November 8, 1977, more than seventy thousand Dallas County residents turned out at the polls; the majority voted in favor of all five propositions in the bond election.[104] Like "children with a new set of toys," the triumphant commissioners met on November 10 to prioritize projects and assign funding. Judson Shook suggested that $5 million of the first bonds be applied toward completing the Depository sale—and other building and land purchases—and planning and designing for the new county facilities. Discussions also began on renaming the Texas School Book Depository building to reflect its new role as the seat of county government. Shook supported the idea, though commissioner Jim Tyson argued that the building would always be known as the Depository, so changing it—although "an 'emotional-type thing to some people'"—remained irrelevant.[105]

The commissioners were undecided, yet their discussion hinted that the renovation of what former mayor Wes Wise once described as "the most unlikely

looking building as a major headquarters of the administration of Dallas County"
would be a long, emotional process. As 1977 drew to a close, however, Judson
Shook was satisfied with his accomplishments. The Depository building was safe
at last. He later reflected: "I always felt that if we couldn't make [the museum]
fly right away, if we could just get the Commissioners Court in there and keep it
in the public interest, then ultimately a new generation would come along and
do it."[106] But it would not take a new generation. The reality of a museum on the
sixth floor of the Texas School Book Depository was only a dozen years away.

Chapter **3**
A SITE OF REFLECTION

The Sixth Floor Museum at Dealey Plaza began in quiet, informal discussions. One of the most significant involved the unlikely trio of a Republican social-ite and community leader, a noted Hollywood film producer, and Judson Shook, the director of public works for Dallas County. Shook's initial tour of the Depository had been a haunting and moving experience, reemphasizing the need, in his mind, to open the sixth floor to visitors. "I wish that the public could experience . . . what I experienced the first time I went into it," Shook reflected in 1992. "Your imagination could easily be carried away to thinking that the place was haunted. . . . And everything was a deep contrast, like a picture taken with ten speed film . . . everything was in . . . deep shadows."[1]

Shook felt that sharing such an eerie, unforgettable experience might moti-vate others to support his efforts. In March 1977, eight months before the bond election, he toured the space with Lindalyn Adams, then chair of the Dallas County Historical Commission, and retired Hollywood executive Martin Jurow, best known for producing films such as *Breakfast at Tiffany's* and *The Pink Panther*. Although Jurow had not practiced law for forty years after earn-ing a degree from Harvard Law School in 1935, he passed the Texas bar exam in 1976 and was immediately hired as a Dallas County assistant district attorney.[2] In this capacity Jurow met with Shook and Adams; ironically, however, it was his Hollywood background that led to his most important contribution to The Sixth Floor project as executive producer of the museum's films a decade later. This initial Depository tour moved Jurow: "As I looked, and as I saw, and as I surveyed . . . the only thing that I [thought was] this must not be demolished. It must not be destroyed. It must be preserved, and the only way of preserving it is to make sure that it [becomes] a museum."[3]

Lindalyn Adams had a similar reaction. "We took the freight elevator up to the sixth floor and . . . walked across that floor to the corner window, and it's a feeling you will never forget," she later recalled.[4] As chair of the Dallas County

Historical Commission, Adams served as the historic preservation liaison for the Commissioners Court and was responsible for recommending local sites for state historical markers with the official goal of preserving and recording Dallas County history. Though this was her first quasi-government appointment, Adams was no stranger to community affairs and leadership positions. During the previous decade, she had served as president of the Dallas County Heritage Society, chair of the prestigious Crystal Charity Ball, chair of women's activities for the American Medical Association annual meeting in Dallas, and in various capacities during the citywide bicentennial celebration in 1976. Yet, as a prominent Republican who was near the Adolphus Hotel in 1960 when vice presidential candidate Lyndon Johnson and his wife were accosted by supporters of conservative congressman Bruce Alger, Adams wondered openly what assistance she could offer such a site.[5]

Although the meeting of Shook, Adams, and Jurow yielded no immediate results, it proved a watershed event in The Sixth Floor Museum's history in introducing Lindalyn Adams to the idea of an exhibition inside the Depository. Prior to that time, she "didn't have a view on the building" but sometimes expressed frustration that visiting friends and associates always wanted to see the site. Soon after touring the sixth floor space, however, Adams's deep and abiding respect for history led her to agree with Jurow and Shook that the sixth floor should become museum space, not office space, if the county did purchase the building. She agreed to help with the project and would remain its driving force for the next decade.[6]

Adams began by talking to friends and colleagues about a Depository exhibition project to gauge public support. As a community leader in historic preservation and a member of the Texas Historical Foundation, Adams had the opportunity to speak to a variety of state and community organizations, including the Dallas Historical Society, the Dallas County Heritage Society, and the state historical commission. Some of her friends were shocked that she had embraced the Depository project, particularly in view of her political leanings.[7] Architect Rodger Burson aptly described Adams as the project's "cheerleader" during these early months.[8]

Judson Shook made the rounds as well, quietly conversing with state and local officials, historians, and staff at Ford's Theater in Washington, D.C., site of the Lincoln assassination. Finding that the theater had been vandalized, gutted, and converted into an office building before being restored to its 1865 configuration a century later, Shook feared that the Depository might suffer the same fate.[9] Having previously visited the "dilapidated Lincoln museum" open at the site prior to 1970, Shook felt he knew the difference between a respectful exhibition and an "amateurish" display.[10] Shook found the Washington staff helpful and encouraging and later sent an exhibition planning committee report to Michael Harman, curator of Ford's Theater, for his review in late 1979.[11]

Not all of the individuals contacted by Shook responded enthusiastically, particularly when he approached local congressmen for assistance in recognizing the building as a historic site. U.S. representative James M. Collins, for example, strongly favored demolishing the Depository and hoped that the shame over the assassination heaped on Dallas by the press would be erased along with it.[12] Collins briefly took his case to the public and advocated a park at the site rather than "a shrine to Oswald."[13]

Frequent local news stories generated even more publicity for the Depository project.[14] So did a February 1978 feature in *Newsweek* magazine. The article reported a meeting the previous month between Shook and National Park Service officials, who, according to Shook's notes from the session, believed that the Depository was "not necessarily a historic site worth preserving."[15]

The immediate result of the publicity about the building was a flood of letters commenting on the county's actions and a myriad of suggestions for using the sixth floor. More thoughtful than many, Norman Redlich, an assistant counsel to the Warren Commission in 1964, suggested a re-creation of the sixth floor as it appeared on November 22, 1963, with a tour guide and an entrance fee to support the site.[16] Redlich followed up with a lengthy letter to the editor at the *Morning News,* expressing confidence that the sixth floor would emerge "tastefully preserved as an historic museum."[17] Other suggestions for the sixth floor included establishing a blood bank or an art display.[18] An Austin sculptor volunteered to fill the area surrounding the infamous corner window with concrete as an artistic statement, because "concrete is a material that will stop bullets."[19] The Dallas County Heritage Society, meanwhile, hoped that some space inside the Depository might house part of their growing collection of local history.[20]

"Someday, This Will Be a National Historic Site"

While Judson Shook fielded comments from individuals from all over the United States, Lindalyn Adams sought the advice of Cindy Sherrell, director of museum services at the Texas Historical Commission. Sherrell, in turn, put Adams in touch with Lonn Taylor, then curator at the Dallas Historical Society. Taylor, whose background included directorship of the Winedale Historical Center in Round Rock, Texas, subsequently toured the empty sixth floor with Adams and Conover Hunt, a museum professional and old friend who had recently moved to Dallas from her native Virginia.[21]

With a BA in art history from Tulane and an MA in early American culture from the University of Delaware, Hunt already had extensive experience in collections, exhibitions, and historic preservation by the time she moved to Dallas in the spring of 1977. In addition to freelance work, she had previously served as curator for the Association for the Preservation and Virginia Antiquities in Richmond and director of the Daughters of the American Revolution Museum in Washington, D.C. Ironically, Hunt also worked with Jacqueline Kennedy Onassis on Hunt's first book project, *Remember the Ladies: Women in America 1750–1815,* which Hunt co-authored with Linda Grant De Pauw.[22]

Visiting the un-air-conditioned space for the first time in intense August heat, Hunt found herself—like so many others—emotionally moved by the Depository's sixth floor. "There are certain spaces that are palpably associative, that put out vibes," she recalled in 1994. "[The sixth floor] came across as one of those." The original plywood floor that Hunt observed that day was dirty; the building itself, unused for nearly a decade and still showing signs of smoke and water damage from the arson attempt, appeared "badly deteriorated." Nevertheless, according to Lindalyn Adams, when Hunt looked out of the sixth floor windows overlooking Dealey Plaza, she said simply, "Someday, this will be a national historic site."[23] Hunt later recalled seeing "a national/international site that would be preserved in perpetuity, that will change as each generation looks at it and reevaluates it and finds new meaning of its own for it."[24]

Although the sixth floor was in a raw state, Hunt immediately recognized its potential educational value. Despite their different backgrounds and personalities, Hunt's experience and intellect impressed Adams, who felt that together they might finally develop a sixth floor exhibition.[25]

After their tour Hunt suggested that the group initially seek a planning grant from the National Endowment for the Humanities and offered to serve as the project's primary research and interpretive coordinator, if the project was funded, while working concurrently for the Dallas Park Department as the curator of the historic DeGolyer Estate.[26] Little did she know that she had embarked upon a journey that not only would occupy much of her life over the next decade but would also significantly change the way in which Dallas and the nation viewed the Kennedy assassination.

While serious work began on the future of the building's sixth floor as it related to the assassination, public works director Judson Shook turned his attention to the Depository's new function as a working Dallas County office building. The county awarded the Dallas architectural firm of Hendricks, Burson, and Walls, which had earlier impressed Shook with its adaptive reuse of the Cumberland

School building, with the contract to work on the first phase of the Texas School Book Depository renovation.[27]

Although the 1977 bond election only provided for phase one of the adaptive reuse of the building—the basement and first two floors—the long-range plan included office space for the county commissioners and a variety of other county officials and departments.[28] The proposed Commissioners Courtroom inside the building seemed symbolic of what Conover Hunt described as the "symbiotic relationship" between the county and the City of Dallas, which first spared the building by blocking all demolition permits in 1972.[29]

Architect James Hendricks understood this connection and how significant the Depository was in the collective memory of Dallas and approached the project with great care. Despite critical comments by some of their colleagues, neither he nor his partner, Rodger Burson, questioned the validity of the project or worried that it might somehow prove detrimental to their professional reputations. As a member of the Historic Landmark Preservation Committee, Hendricks was particularly interested in seeing the Depository put to good use because it was part of the burgeoning West End Historic District. In 1972 the Spaghetti Warehouse restaurant opened in a converted warehouse space in the West End that soon became a popular downtown lunch destination. Retail boutiques, additional restaurants, and office space soon followed, making adaptive use of the districts' various historic structures.[30]

The architects' first task was to assess the Depository's condition, repair any structural damage, and evaluate its exterior. Stress cracks in the wooden arches above the windows posed one early problem and helped push the project over budget. An exterior steel fire escape on the east side of the Depository and a decorative concrete latticework screen over the ground-floor windows, though present on the day of the Kennedy assassination, were not original to the building and were removed.[31]

Judson Shook and the architects remained steadfast that the Depository's exterior should reflect its turn-of-the-century origins rather than its appearance in November 1963; county officials did not oppose this approach.[32] Conover Hunt suggested later, however, that by embracing the earlier period "the architects . . . were following in the traditional Dallas pattern of ignoring the assassination."[33] Aesthetically, the exterior of the Depository was successfully altered to suggest its original 1901 appearance, though Rodger Burson later lamented that the project's tight budget prevented the architects from making all of their desired enhancements. Two badly deteriorated structures to the north and west, which had once been used as a freight loading area and for the nearby railroad, were removed.[34] Hendricks recalled: "The integrity of the shell [of the Depository]

. . . was [of] number one importance. And we wanted to keep . . . the look and the feel and . . . the spirit of the building and . . . of the time period throughout." The Hendricks firm envisioned a dramatic two-story Commissioners Courtroom as the building's dominant feature, though such a plan involved gutting a large central portion of the second floor to accommodate a high ceiling. This posed a challenge for the architects: for example, they had to install a large floor-to-ceiling truss on the third floor and erect new structural columns that ran down to new foundations in the basement. Hendricks, who considered the Dallas County Commissioners Courtroom one of his greatest architectural achievements, ultimately created a state-of-the-art space that respected the Depository's historical integrity with a creative blending of new and old elements, such as original wooden beams punctuating the modern courtroom and restored seventh floor ceiling tiles repurposed for an entry lobby with recessed lighting. With obvious enthusiasm, Hendricks integrated the adaptive reuse of the warehouse space into the new functionality of the courtroom.[35]

During phase one of the renovation, county officials downplayed the building's association with the President's death. County officials told Hendricks: "This is our building. . . . We're putting the Commissioners Court in it, and we don't know what's going to happen on the sixth floor."[36] In private conversations, vague phrases such as "in limbo" or "in reserve" were used when referring to the infamous floor. "Everybody realized how important it was," said Hendricks years later, "but at the same time, nobody had any idea what to do with it."[37] The site's dark history, however, was constantly in evidence. Besides high tourist traffic in Dealey Plaza, television crews used the building on occasion for assassination-related programs. In July 1977, for example, Dallas County permitted a film crew working on the ABC television movie *The Trial of Lee Harvey Oswald* to shoot some scenes inside the Depository building. A reenactment of the assassination in Dealey Plaza involving 300 extras was filmed at the same time, blocking traffic for two days during the July 4 weekend.[38] The following year the building was again utilized when investigators with the House Select Committee on Assassinations staged a four-hour reenactment on August 20, 1978, and fired live ammunition from the alleged "sniper's perch" on the sixth floor into strategically placed sandbags on Elm Street.[39] These occasional distractions did not impede the progress of the renovation project.

While the sixth floor of the Texas School Book Depository may not have been a priority for Dallas County during phase one of the renovation project, a small group of individuals working behind the scenes spent an increasing amount of time contemplating the history and meaning of the space and the ways in which it might be used to educate the people who continued to visit Dealey Plaza. Upon joining the planning team in 1978, Conover Hunt's first task was to conduct an informal study to determine "visible interest" in the building's sixth floor. Hunt immediately learned that no official visitation statistics had ever been gathered about Dealey Plaza as a tourist site despite the obvious public interest in the Kennedy assassination.[40] Dallas tourism in the late 1970s instead promoted sites such as Southfork Ranch, whose exterior was prominently featured on the popular *Dallas* television series, and the city's destination shopping venue Neiman Marcus. Hunt tried to approximate visitor figures by other means—including an inquiry as to whether Dealey Plaza required "more trash pickup than other park areas."[41] An inquiry at the Dallas Convention and Visitors Bureau also was inconclusive, although a veteran employee told Hunt unofficially that individuals asked "frequently" about the site of the Kennedy assassination.[42] Discussions with county employees whose office windows overlooked the plaza yielded similar results and visitor estimates that varied widely, from eight hundred to four thousand people daily. Other Dallas residents admitted that visiting friends and family always wanted to see the spot where President Kennedy had been shot. Hunt's 1978 survey of tourists in Dealey Plaza indicated a 100 percent interest in an exhibition on the sixth floor. Virtually all of those surveyed were visiting the plaza because of the Kennedy assassination. The sample revealed that very few hailed from the Dallas area and only 5 percent were from Texas. All were willing to pay an admission fee to an exhibition if it was not managed by the state or federal government; otherwise, as taxpayers, most expected free admittance.[43] In the final analysis, the survey demonstrated "an extremely high interest in the preservation of the sixth floor and its use for some sort of educational, historical exhibit," though Hunt always remembered the frequently expressed afterthought: "Just don't make it tacky."[44]

Hunt incorporated the survey results into the National Endowment for the Humanities (NEH) planning grant application. She believed that federal involvement of any kind would only help the project, giving it a sort of "seal of approval" that might "help eliminate any media criticisms . . . levied against the community" for trying to develop the Depository's sixth floor commercially.[45] Although Hunt thought that a federal grant was appropriate given the subject, she was unsure whether or not it would be awarded. One NEH employee told her that the idea of restoring the Depository's sixth floor was "offensive," noting that it seemed inconceivable that anyone would want to go inside the building.[46] Despite such reservations, the NEH awarded the Dallas County Historical Commission a planning grant of $8,562 in the fall of 1978. Matching funds from Dallas County increased the amount of planning funds to approximately $11,000.[47]

FIG. 15

A view of the empty sixth floor, captured by restoration architect Eugene George. Note the abandoned Texas School Book Depository signage to the right.

EUGENE GEORGE COLLECTION/THE SIXTH FLOOR MUSEUM AT DEALEY PLAZA

Running against the clock, fearing that some crucial element of the building might be lost or irrevocably changed in the upcoming renovation, Hunt assembled a prestigious planning team tasked with determining the "best use for the sixth floor" and, if approved by Dallas County, establishing an overall plan for the adaptive reuse of the building.[48]

In addition to Hunt, Lindalyn Adams, Judson Shook, and architect Rodger Burson, the planning team included individuals of varied backgrounds and specialties. Local historical agencies—the Dallas Historical Society and the Dallas County Heritage Society—were represented by directors John Crain and Louis F. Gorr, while G. Robert Blakey, then chief counsel and staff director for the House Select Committee on Assassinations, joined as a "historical expert."[49] Others included museum design specialist David Ross of the Texas Historical Commission; security consultant Jack Leo; and Dallas County architect George D. Akins, Jr. Rounding out the committee was respected restoration architect Eugene George. A native Texan and a professor at the University of Texas at Austin, George had previously worked with both Lindalyn Adams in Dallas and Conover Hunt in Virginia.[50] He was fully aware of the controversy and embarrassment over the Depository. But during his initial visit to the sixth floor, he experienced a strong reaction to the space and knew at once that he wanted to be involved in the project.[51]

With this team in place, Conover Hunt prepared for a two-day meeting in Dallas, scheduled for April 1979. By that time public interest in the project demonstrated to everyone involved that their work had a touch of global significance. Wire services carried accounts of the planning meeting throughout the world. The attention surprised Hunt, who characterized such committee work as "pretty much like watching paint dry or grass grow." Keeping discussions private was difficult, and the early planners could not enjoy the electricity of "a creative jam session" for fear of misinterpretation.[52] At the same time, the surprising media attention prompted a greater feeling of responsibility that likely influenced the group's collective thinking. By the end of their day and a half of meetings, Conover Hunt and her planning team had laid "the groundwork for its study" that would eventually lead to an exhibition on the sixth floor of the Texas School Book Depository.[53]

"Things Had Progressed"

The planning committee that met in Dallas in April 1979 recommended that the sixth floor of the Depository house an exhibit rather than a museum. "We did not wish at that time to have it called a museum," Lindalyn Adams later recalled. "We were not displaying artifacts and . . . did not have . . . the requirements that a museum ordinarily would have."[54] Nevertheless, the general public's immediate perception was that some type of sixth floor museum was in active development. The headline on the front page of the *Dallas Times Herald* Metro section on April 13, 1979, typified expectations: "Committee Plans Texas School Book Depository Museum." The accompanying article optimistically said that the sixth floor restoration project—tentatively titled "Tragedy in Dealey Plaza"—could open to the public in as little as one year with the proper funding.[55] Those involved in the planning emphasized the respectful development of the site without sensationalizing the President's death, insisting that it would not be "a cabinet of curiosities."[56]

Meanwhile, the controversy over the use of the Texas School Book Depository was dampened in part by the recently announced findings of the second major investigation into the Kennedy assassination. Three months prior to the Dallas planning meeting, the U.S. House Select Committee on Assassinations wrapped up its hearings, essentially agreeing with the 1964 Warren Commission investigation that three shots were fired by Lee Harvey Oswald from the sixth floor of the Depository. The later investigation also concluded, however, that a second gunman probably fired a fourth shot from the grassy knoll, which missed the presidential limousine. Based upon an acoustical analysis of a recording from a Dallas police motorcycle's radio microphone, this finding immediately came under intense scrutiny and in 1982 was refuted by a follow-up study by the National Academy of Sciences.[57]

In spring 1979 the House Select Committee's chief counsel, G. Robert Blakey, who also served as a historical consultant on the sixth floor project, addressed journalists' questions after the planning conference as frequently as chair Conover Hunt did. When, for example, Hunt indicated that "any exhibits [would] represent only the findings of 'official investigations' into the assassination," Blakey clarified that such displays would include the findings of both the Warren Commission and the House Select Committee on Assassinations investigations, which "embody . . . the consensus of their times."[58]

Initial reactions to the planning committee's work were mixed; at first, Hunt later recalled, the public fell "back on the naïve approach to preservation . . . only a celebration of history, dealing with specific heroes or well-known individuals."[59] One small Texas newspaper called the idea of a "sixth floor shrine a smelly, sick plan."[60] Others also feared that "the Dallas project would create some sort of a memorial to an assassin."[61]

The following week the planning committee recommended to the Dallas County Commissioners Court that an exhibition on the sixth floor of the Texas School Book Depository should historically chronicle the events of November 22, 1963.[62] Though specific details remained vague, the group's philosophy focused on creating an educational exhibition that would deal with the Depository's relationship to history; the planned display would certainly exercise restraint and include photographs, film footage, and diagrams.[63]

At the outset, however, all indications pointed toward an exhibition focused exclusively on the assassination rather than the life and times of John F. Kennedy. The sixth floor of the Depository would not be a shrine to the late President; nor would it celebrate his achievements—interpretive territory already covered by the John F. Kennedy Presidential Library and Museum in Boston, Massachusetts. Rather, it would present the sixth floor as it appeared in 1963, with content drawn from the "raw data" of the official investigative bodies. When the media asked about public access to the sniper's perch corner window, Blakey called the infamous locale "only a small part of the whole." Set low to the floor, the window in question was also a potential safety hazard.[64]

Security was another early consideration. At the planning conference, security consultant Jack Leo recommended that Dallas County seal off the entire sixth floor during the upcoming renovation to prevent vandalism to the floor's most historically important areas.[65] Access to the sniper's perch and the location where authorities found the Mannlicher-Carcano rifle had never been restricted, and some physical damage had occurred. Even after the area was sealed and a chain-link cage was placed around the southeast corner window, souvenir hunters managed to chip off large chunks of bricks. With construction imminent and the two-story Commissioners Courtroom design finalized, the planning committee fought to save as much of the original building as possible.

With the decision to restore the building's exterior to its 1901 appearance, the committee, working under the auspices of the Dallas County Historical Commission, recommended that Dallas County retain 1963-era elements from the building's exterior that had been identified for removal during the upcoming renovation. The restoration architect, Eugene George, recommended the careful removal of the fire escape on the east side of the Depository for storage and the preservation of a sample of the first floor 1963-era concrete screen during its removal.[66] George also requested that the bricklayers match the color of the existing mortar when replacing exterior brick.

The building's freight elevators, scheduled to be removed during phase one of the renovation, were a part of the building's history and germane to the events surrounding November 22, 1963. Oswald used those elevators regularly during his employment, and they were also used by investigators following the assassination. The county architect adopted the committee's recommendation that the freight elevators remain "permanently located at the sixth floor level" when the remainder of the shaft was torn out.[67]

Construction of the two-story courtroom provided space on the second floor earmarked for county commissioner offices. This meant the removal of the building's old second-floor lunchroom, the location where Lee Harvey Oswald was first seen after the shooting. While rushing up the Depository's rear staircase approximately two minutes after the assassination, Dallas police officer Marion Baker saw Oswald through a glass door on the second floor; upon learning that he worked for the Depository, Baker continued upstairs.[68]

This brief encounter was significant to researchers in part because Oswald "didn't seem to be excited or overly afraid" within minutes of the shooting and after having ostensibly run down several flights of stairs, even as officer Baker aimed his pistol at him. This made the lunchroom the most important assassination-related area of the building after the sixth floor.[69] After Hunt's Dealey Plaza survey revealed definite tourist interest in seeing the lunchroom, the committee recommended that the entire room be dismantled for future reassembly, possibly as part of an exhibition on the sixth floor.[70]

In 1978 the lunchroom still included some of the same furnishings present on the day of the assassination, including original doors, booths, and Formica tables.[71] A group of volunteers carefully marked the various parts of the room that they wanted preserved. "We were so serious about it," remembered Lindalyn Adams in 1997. "We labeled every pipe fitting."[72] Their efforts were nearly thwarted by an eager demolition company ironically from the Kennedys' own Hyannis Port, Massachusetts.[73] Adams recalled that her group had barely finished its inventory when "all of a sudden . . . those little wooden steps that led from the first floor up to sixth . . . started disappearing." Fortunately the contents of the lunchroom were saved, though Adams said that the Massachusetts workmen "were tearing [it] down with a vengeance!"[74]

The second-floor lunchroom was not the only assassination-related part of the Texas School Book Depository slated to be removed in the renovation. Architects and engineers also identified the iconic Hertz Rent-a-Car time-and-temperature billboard atop the building as a source of intense structural damage. Measuring approximately twenty-three feet in length, the sign, which ran diagonally across the square roof, acted as a sail and in a strong wind severely racked the building.[75] "The wind load had literally vibrated all the mortar out of between the bricks for the top three floors," Hunt later explained, "and some of [the] large beams, horizontal beams, had been torqued to a 45-degree angle—now, that's powerful wind load."[76] Upon his first inspection, Judson Shook found the roof "so weak that when you jumped up and down, it was like Jell-O on the top."[77]

Dallas County had decided on the removal of the Hertz Rent-a-Car sign as "one of the first steps in the remodeling," long before the planning committee inspected the building in spring 1979.[78] Judson Shook contacted various organizations, including the Smithsonian Institution, hoping to donate the problematic sign.[79] William T. Alderson, director of the American Association for State and Local History, responded that the "curio . . . [with] no genuine historical value" should be destroyed.[80] The Hertz Corporation expressed no interest in its abandoned advertisement, having permanently turned off its electronic time-and-temperature function on December 11, 1973, during the United States energy crisis.[81]

After considerable discussion, which reportedly lasted longer than conversations over whether an exhibit or museum should occupy the sixth floor, the planning committee voted to remove the sign. The large face plate of the billboard was preserved. The exhibition team later considered fabricating a lightweight replica for the roof, though this idea never came to fruition, most likely because it would have interfered with the building's proposed 1901 exterior.[82]

The May 22, 1979, removal of the recognizable Hertz sign—which Dallas politician Louis Toppel once called "a 'tumorous growth' of the past"—forever changed the appearance of the Depository. Regardless of the structural issues involved, it also sent a message to the Dallas community that the adaptive reuse of the building for government business was the priority for Dallas County rather than perpetuating the memory of the Kennedy assassination.[83] Its removal apparently mattered little to the public. In 2009 Lindalyn Adams could not recall anyone ever asking her what had happened to the sign.[84]

Just as the Commissioners Court had initially encouraged the Dallas County Historical Commission to explore ways of utilizing the sixth floor space, it proved quite accommodating to the various recommendations made by the 1979 planning committee, perhaps concerned by predictions that tourist interest in the building could disrupt county business. In fact, according to Conover Hunt, the only recommendation dismissed by Dallas County involved the preservation of the historic paint colors on the building's window frames. The exterior was a terra-cotta color at the time of the assassination while the inside was a dark green. During the renovation, Dallas County opted to paint the exterior of the window edges green as well, including the windows on the sixth floor. If not for the 1979 exhibit planning committee, none of the original Depository windows might have survived the county renovation. County plans called for the replacement of all of the building's windows. But Hunt successfully argued that the windows on the sixth floor, many dating back to at least 1963, should be spared.[85]

Nevertheless, few of the planning committee's recommendations were met with unanimous support from the county commissioners. Hunt later said, "We did everything with a 3–2 vote, three in favor, two opposed . . . [and] it was Mrs. Adams who led the charge and handled everything beautifully, I might add. She said, 'My dear, three votes is enough.'" Opposition to planning committee proposals did not necessarily reflect a lack of support for a sixth floor exhibition but rather the involvement of the federal government, through the National Endowment for the Humanities grant. One county commissioner allegedly told Hunt and Adams: "What's wrong with this thing is a seven letter word. It starts with an 'f' and ends with an 'l.'"[86] The commissioners need not have worried, however: the initial planning grant proved to be the only federal funding ever provided to the Depository project—though federal involvement had been eagerly sought by some early on. For Judson Shook, involving the federal government in the exhibition project had long been a goal, not only for financial assistance but also for credibility.[87]

But as Shook had discovered early on when meeting with representatives of the National Park Service, the federal government was not particularly interested in participating in the management of the site. The Park Service limited its preservation efforts to one historic site per presidency, and the Kennedy family had selected Hyannis Port, Massachusetts. Even "if multiple sites were to be allowed [for] President Kennedy's memory," said one Park Service official, the Depository building would never be a "serious candidate of the family." Disappointed by the reception in Washington, Shook wrote that the county was "now faced with the dilemma of either trying to keep a curious public out of a public building or running the risk of appearing to exploit the depository if we do open it." Ultimately, Shook accepted that Dallas County could carefully proceed on its own so long as it did "not become desensitized to public feelings."[88]

Neither Shook nor Lindalyn Adams seemed particularly concerned that they would have to "go it alone" without the benefit of federal support—financial or otherwise. But both maintained the hope that official recognition for the building would lend respectability to a sixth floor exhibition project and possibly bolster fund-raising efforts.[89] A June 14, 1978, meeting in Washington, D.C., with representatives of the National Register typified the federal attitude toward the Depository at the time.

Two months before Conover Hunt joined the project, Judson Shook, Lindalyn Adams, and architect Rodger Burson traveled to Washington to meet with historians of the Heritage, Conservation, and Recreation Service (HCRS), a short-lived federal entity created in 1977 and absorbed by the National Park Service in 1981. The Dallas trio all had prepared brief presentations in the hopes of adding the Texas School Book Depository to the National Register of Historic Places.[90]

Shook, Adams, and Burson arrived early for their meeting and opted to have lunch at a nearby restaurant. Dr. William Murtagh, one of the HCRS officials with whom the group was scheduled to meet, sat nearby. When Murtagh mentioned his upcoming meeting with the contingent from Dallas, his companions "laughed and made fun of [the idea]."[91] Lindalyn Adams recalled hearing one comment: "Oh, next they'll want to put Watergate on the National Register!" Before Murtagh's group departed, Judson Shook approached their table and introduced himself, saying, "We're going to be in your office about forty-five minutes from now."[92]

The subsequent meeting proved awkward and tense.[93] Rodger Burson and his colleagues felt that they instantly received the "cold shoulder, and [that] they weren't the least bit interested in putting [the Depository] on the National Register."[94] As the trio began discussing the building's troubled past, the upcoming county renovation, and ideas for an educational exhibit on the sixth floor, however, some of the younger members of Dr. Murtagh's staff began to participate in the discussion and vocalized their interest in the project.[95]

Judson Shook's memorandum to the Dallas County Commissioners Court, written one week later, excluded any reference to the restaurant encounter, focusing instead on the positive comments and recommendations on visitor flow, storage of the Hertz sign, and sandblasting the exterior brick of the Depository during the planned renovation that emerged during the formal meeting. Moreover, the "HCRS would continue to advise the Dallas planning committee" and offered the assistance of the Smithsonian Institution in interpreting the sixth floor.[96] Yet the Texas School Book Depository building was never individually recognized by the National Register of Historic Places.[97] Dealey Plaza as a whole—including the Depository—was finally designated a National Historic Landmark District on the thirtieth anniversary of the Kennedy assassination in 1993.[98]

Conover Hunt proposed to the Commissioners Court on November 26, 1979, that a second NEH grant be pursued to cover the costs of exhibition fabrication and all consultant fees, while "county or private sector funding" provided for structural and construction work and staffing.[99] The commissioners, however, were hostile to further federal funding for the project; for a variety of reasons, the grant application was not approved.[100] A few months later they also rejected a request from the Dallas County Historical Commission for $75,000, most of which was intended for a proposed exterior elevator that would take visitors to the sixth floor while avoiding county offices. Disappointed, Adams expressed the view that the project would "not necessarily be scrapped" but admitted that fund-raising would be difficult.[101] With its modest budget and primary mission of recommending historic markers and advising on local historical issues, the commission proved ill equipped to tackle such an ambitious project.[102]

Stymied for the moment in its attempts to raise funds for exhibit design and access, the planning committee turned its attention to the creation of a 501(c)(3) nonprofit foundation charged with creating and operating an exhibition on the sixth floor of the Texas School Book Depository.[103] This effort, too, was delayed, this time by John Hinckley, Jr.'s attempted assassination of President Ronald Reagan in Washington, D.C., on March 30, 1981.

The presidential shooting immediately triggered comparisons or allusions to the Kennedy assassination in the press, amplified by the revelation that Hinckley had grown up in the Dallas area and had purchased the gun used to shoot Reagan at a local pawnshop.[104] Hinckley, authorities soon learned, had even researched the Kennedy assassination and perhaps even admired the accused assassin; photographs of Lee Harvey Oswald and news clippings and articles about the assassination were found among his belongings.[105] With fund-raising for the sixth floor already proving difficult in the Dallas community, Reagan's attempted

FIG. 16

Dallas County public works director Judson Shook stands alongside the Texas Historical Marker recognizing the former Texas School Book Depository building. This ceremony in the newly opened Dallas County Commissioners Court took place on March 29, 1981.
Institutional Archives/The Sixth Floor Museum at Dealey Plaza

assassination pushed "the project underground."[106] Fund-raising would not begin again in earnest until the approach of the twentieth anniversary of the Kennedy assassination in November 1983.

Though the sixth floor project stalled in the early 1980s, the county renovation of the Texas School Book Depository continued unabated. Phase one reached completion by early 1981, and the building wtas formally dedicated. The first two floors were occupied by Dallas County officials and opened to the public for the first time on March 29, 1981. The dedication date was symbolic—one day shy of the 135th anniversary of the founding of Dallas County. A Texas Historical Commission marker was unveiled, recognizing the newly renamed Dallas County Administration Building as "Formerly The Texas School Book Depository Building."[107] The bulk of the plaque, written by Shirley Caldwell, who would shortly succeed Adams as chair of the Dallas County Historical Commission, recognized the site and the building's early history. The final sentence, however, acknowledged its most controversial moment: "On November 22, 1963, the building gained national notoriety when Lee Harvey Oswald allegedly shot and killed President John F. Kennedy from a sixth floor window as the presidential motorcade passed the site."[108]

Judson Shook, who had decided to retire that summer as public works director for Dallas County, sat in the front row during this dedication ceremony. The Texas Historical Commission had recognized Shook's work in 1979 by giving him the John Neely Bryan Award, an annual prize for the individual "who has made the most significant contribution to preservation of Dallas County history."[109] Lindalyn Adams later said: "No one can ever give enough credit to Judson Shook for this whole project, because if it hadn't been for Judson, the county wouldn't have purchased the building. I'm convinced of that."[110] Although Shook remained a supporter of the sixth floor project after his retirement, he never actively involved himself in the planning or fund-raising efforts. His job, he determined, was finished, though he remained pleased at how "things had progressed."[111]

"Plans Are in the Works"

As was their custom, Lindalyn Adams and her husband, Reuben, a Dallas physician, entertained friends at their home on New Year's Eve, 1981. The previous twelve months had witnessed a number of ups and downs for the sixth floor project. Just one day after the dedication of the new Dallas County Administration Building, the attempted assassination of President Ronald Reagan conjured up painful memories and triggered a cessation of fund-raising activities. Before the year drew fully to a close, however, one final piece of sixth floor business remained. Just before midnight John Sissom, who had operated a small John F. Kennedy Museum at 501 Elm Street, across Houston Street from the Texas School Book Depository, visited Adams to sign paperwork donating portions of his museum collection to the Dallas County Historical Commission.[112] While the Adams' guests listened to a recording of Winston Churchill's stirring June 4, 1940, speech in the House of Commons, promising that Great Britain would fight on land, on sea, and in the air, never surrendering, "the only [museum] in Dallas devoted exclusively to Kennedy" closed.[113]

Dallas residents John and Estelle Sissom had established their museum in 1970. In the wake of Kennedy's assassination, the couple had read numerous books and collected memorabilia about the late President, his administration, and his death. By the late 1960s the couple had decided to parlay their interest both as an opportunity for profit and "to set the record straight" about Dallas. "I think it's very ridiculous to blame a city for what one person does," John Sissom later told the *Dallas Times Herald*.[114] In summer 1970, shortly after the dedication of the nearby John F. Kennedy Memorial, construction began on a 10,000-square-foot museum on the first floor of the building across from

FIG. 17

John Sissom's privately owned John F. Kennedy Museum quietly operated across Houston Street from the Depository building for more than a decade.

the Depository. The museum opened without fanfare later that year. Although the Sissoms repeatedly refused to release attendance figures over the years, Conover Hunt estimated in her NEH grant application that "the Museum attract[ed] several hundred paying tourists daily."[115] The year the museum closed, however, the *Dallas Times Herald* called it "one of Dallas' leading tourist attractions."[116]

Throughout Aubrey Mayhew's ownership of the Depository, the battle to save the building from demolition, and the county renovation, John Sissom quietly maintained his private museum next door, garnering little media coverage and suffering more from petty thievery than from controversy over the appropriateness of his displays. Sissom likely escaped the criticism leveled at Mayhew because he operated out of a building not linked directly to the Kennedy assassination.[117]

The centerpiece of the John F. Kennedy Museum was a twenty-two-minute multimedia show in which a series of slides, accompanied by prerecorded narration, walked visitors through the events of November 22, 1963, while a sequence of lights followed the motorcade procession through a scale-model of downtown Dallas and Dealey Plaza. Assorted Kennedy memorabilia, large copies of newspaper headlines, a Kennedy shrine with a portrait done by a local artist,

and a display on Lee Harvey Oswald, complete with a replica of the rifle he allegedly used to assassinate the President, rounded out the presentation.[118] By late
1981 the museum, whose ticket price peaked at $2, had grown tired and stale.
Three empty rifle cartridges once affixed to a wall had been stolen, though "the
hardened yellow glue" remained on display, and a large photograph of Oswald
had peeled off the wall. Assessing the museum on the eighteenth anniversary of
the Kennedy assassination, Jeffry Unger of the *Dallas Times Herald* wrote: "The
bathrooms are dingy, here and there a light is burned out, and several pictures
are missing from displays."[119] Coupled with this lack of attention, however, it was
a major building renovation that eventually drove the John F. Kennedy Museum
out of business.

Arbor Development, which owned the seventy-nine-year-old property at
501 Elm Street, announced a major refurbishment in 1981. Sissom, the only
tenant prior to this renovation, was unable to pay the increased rent.[120] Before
the museum officially closed to the public on January 3, 1982, Sissom opted to
donate his assets—except for the Dealey Plaza model—to the Dallas County
Historical Commission.[121]

Though tourists visiting Dealey Plaza in 1982 no longer had the small
museum across the street to see, they did find the front doors of the former Texas
School Book Depository building unlocked and, as a county building, open to
the public. County employees, however, were constantly turning away sightseers seeking access to the sixth floor, which remained closed to all but occasional
news reporters.[122]

A county commissioner estimated in 1985 that hundreds of tourists visited
the building daily; Shirley Caldwell, after assuming the chair of the Dallas County
Historical Commission in 1983, remembered being offered $100 to show a local
man and his son the famous sniper's perch. In a single month the guest ledger at
the historic John Neely Bryan log cabin, one block from the Depository, regis-
tered visitors from such countries as France, Norway, Israel, Sweden, Germany,
England, Mexico, Belgium, and Taiwan. Like thousands of other tourists, most
had made the pilgrimage to Dealey Plaza to see the site of the Kennedy assassination, not to visit the home of the founder of Dallas.[123] Foreign languages often
could be heard echoing through the plaza.[124]

Behind the scenes, Lindalyn Adams continued to work tirelessly on the
sixth floor exhibit project, briefing Mayor Robert Folsom and other officials,
speaking about it around Dallas, and giving a tour to interested individuals who
might contribute comments or ideas.[125] By late 1980 she had also identified the
exhibition design team who would ultimately create The Sixth Floor exhibit.
Robert Staples and Barbara Charles, heads of a nationally respected interpretive

planning and design firm for museums, had recently completed an exhibition entitled "Puppets: Art & Entertainment" for Puppeteers of America, Inc. After opening at the Corcoran Gallery of Art in Washington, D.C., in summer 1980, the exhibit made its way to Dallas as part of a national tour, hosted at the Hall of State at Fair Park by the Dallas Historical Society. Concurrent with their work on the sixth floor project, Lindalyn Adams was president of the society at the time and Conover Hunt was chief curator.[126] Impressed with the design of the popular show, Adams met with Staples and Charles at the exhibit opening in Dallas and arranged a tour of the Texas School Book Depository.[127]

Bob Staples and Barbara Charles were no strangers to working with historic spaces. The pair had previously contributed to the Gerald R. Ford Presidential Museum in Grand Rapids, Michigan, as well as exhibitions for the Smithsonian Institution and the Chicago Historical Society.[128] During the afternoon tour, Bob Staples observed the Depository's wooden beams and thought that they should be protected and integrated into the exhibition design. "You could see the wheels turning," Adams said; she jokingly suggested on the spot that the pair serve as the exhibit designers for The Sixth Floor.[129] Although initially negative about the project, Staples and Charles found the empty sixth floor to be a powerful space; after returning to Washington, they expressed interest in working on the exhibit and proposed that their firm develop a report, a working budget, and an exhibition model for a fee of $12,500.[130]

Staples later commented that it proved difficult to transition from an exhibit on puppets to one on the death of the President. "You wonder," the designer said. "Should you get involved? Is this the right kind of subject to be part of?" Charles, in contrast, remembered feeling interested from the beginning, though not terribly disappointed when the funding was not immediate. "I think we felt we were the right people to do it," she said after the exhibit opened. "We really felt, they're going to do it, so we'd better get involved."[131] Both Lindalyn Adams and Conover Hunt greeted the Staples and Charles proposal with enthusiasm.[132] Hunt considered their designs "very restrained and very elegant" and called their "their graphic work . . . probably the best in the business."[133]

Over a year passed, however, before the Dallas County Commissioners Court appropriated $66,000 to fund the conceptual design phase of the sixth floor project and to employ Staples and Charles, restoration architect Eugene George, the architectural firm Hendricks, Burson, and Walls, security consultant E. B. Brown, and curator Conover Hunt. An impromptu hallway conversation between Lindalyn Adams and commissioner Roy Orr about persistent tourist interest in the building and the lack of progress on the exhibition got the ball rolling. Adams recalled that Orr immediately flagged down county judge Garry

Weber and said, "Garry, don't you think they need to finish that [sixth floor]?" With Weber in agreement, Orr told Adams: "Well, you have two votes. We just need one more." Fellow commissioner Jim Tyson later lent his support.[134]

With money in hand, Adams, Hunt, and architect Rodger Burson met in spring 1982 and outlined an overall timetable for the sixth floor exhibit: six months for the design phase, six months for fund-raising efforts, and six months for construction contracts and bidding, followed by one year of construction. The trio considered the possibility of opening in time for the 1984 Republican National Convention in Dallas but ultimately opted for a "quiet and dignified" debut a few months later.[135] Despite the sanguine projections, another seven years would pass before the exhibition finally opened.

The schematic design phase moved forward without Rodger Burson, who had left the architectural firm of Burson, Hendricks, and Walls on the same day that the contract from Dallas County arrived. Burson recalled in 2002: "I was very disappointed. . . . I felt like this was my baby, and it hurt a lot."[136] Hendricks, the principal designer of the Commissioners Courtroom during the Depository's initial renovation, now became actively involved in designing a feasible method of transporting visitors by elevator directly to the sixth floor. He would also design what became The Sixth Floor's Visitors Center, a combination orientation and ticketing area.[137] Restoration architect Eugene George, meanwhile, ensured the historical integrity of the sixth floor space and worked closely with Bob Staples and Barbara Charles as their exhibition design plans developed.

The 1982–83 formal conceptual development of the sixth floor exhibit laid the basic groundwork for what ultimately opened at the site in 1989. Critical elements such as the exterior elevator tower, the Visitors Center, and the idea of floating exhibition panels between the floor's original wooden beams emerged through the efforts of a diverse planning team of powerful personalities, each of whom brought unique experience and vision to the project. Fully understanding the nature of The Sixth Floor exhibit that eventually developed requires a brief examination of the contributions of each key participant.

The successful adaptive reuse of the first two floors of the Depository helped familiarize architect James Hendricks with the dynamics of the sixth floor. Early on he realized that direct access to the space, as well as separate restroom facilities, must be provided to avoid interfering with county operations in the building.[138] Thus tourists needed to enter a separate Visitors Center adjacent to the Depository, which connected directly to the sixth floor via an exterior elevator. The 100-by-100-foot Depository structure, Hendricks assessed, had a modular configuration with columns set at approximately fourteen-foot intervals. He extended the same module of columns outward from the building to create an elevator shaft that would serve the sixth floor.[139] Initially the elevator was to be located in the northeast corner of the building, but it later was moved to a center point on the building's north face—the side opposite Dealey Plaza.[140] Hendricks strongly felt that extending the elevator from the building would not disturb the "integrity of its façade."[141]

The architect recognized that entering the Visitors Center and then riding in a closed elevator to the sixth floor might confuse visitors unfamiliar with the site. Thus an important component of his design was a series of skylights in the Visitors Center to serve as a visual explanation to tourists of what was happening, and where they were going, from the time that they entered the building to the moment when the elevator doors opened at the sixth floor. Hendricks believed that tourists should always move forward from ticketing to the exhibition area. Therefore the exterior elevator opened on both sides. Upon arriving at the sixth floor, visitors continued to walk forward into "a transparent connection between the shaft and the building."[142] Similar in concept to a sky bridge, this hyphen, as it was later called, permitted visitor access to the floor through a space that had once been a window on the north side of the building.

The brick exterior of the Visitors Center, connected to the original building by a hallway, closely resembled that of the Depository, almost as if it were an extension of the structure. Hendricks also wanted the interior of the Visitors Center to reflect the spirit of the 1901 renovation of the Depository, with dark wood accents similar to a turn-of-the-century law office.[143] The intended effect was to provide a seamless transition to the sixth floor of the Depository, where Hendricks's responsibilities ended and restoration architect Eugene George took over.

George had served on the 1979 planning committee and, like Hendricks, was already familiar with the building from walkthroughs and intensive structural examinations. Overall, the sixth floor was in good physical condition; George determined that the "heavy timber construction, which was [originally] designed for agricultural equipment, was more than adequate to support human loads" associated with museum traffic. Likewise, he found no structural cracks or deterioration in any of the 14-by-14-foot bays and was particularly impressed by the graded, long-leaf pine wooden beams, though he noted that the builders had used the best pieces on the lower floors in constructing the building.[144]

Like Hendricks, Eugene George found himself fascinated by the classical symmetry of the sixth floor, especially the way in which the sturdy wooden columns separated the space into a series of 14-foot-square bays with 10-foot-high walls, which achieved "a good harmonic design just like they did in ancient books and manuscripts." George particularly felt that the individual structural bays were ideal for positioning exhibits and maintaining control of visiting school groups, with the sniper's perch naturally situated as the floor's "dominant element."[145] Exhibit designer Barbara Charles also recognized the importance of the sniper's perch as a key part of the narrative but did not want to sensationalize the floor's most important area by presenting it in dramatic isolation for "instant tourist gratification." Everyone, in fact, agreed that the sniper's perch required contextual placement within the assassination story.[146]

For Staples and Charles, early planning centered on the logistics of the sixth floor. With visitor access via elevator from the rear of the floor, the designers found themselves geographically limited in their storytelling and had to develop an "elaborate labyrinth" to bring visitors into the narrative chronologically for an appropriate arrival at the window at the proper moment in the assassination story before moving on to the government investigations. The designers agreed with George regarding the organizational use of the original wooden columns and maintaining the original look and feel of the space as much as possible. These columns, as clearly defined markers for all text panels, guided every design of the sixth floor exhibition.[147]

The 1982 exhibition layout developed by Staples and Charles differed substantially from their final design, yet the narrative components established at the outset remained consistent throughout the project. The few topics that were initially excluded demonstrated, perhaps more than the layout itself, how The Sixth Floor exhibition took shape over the years. In the 1982 design visitors exited the elevator and encountered a large image of the sixth floor from the time of the assassination in the form of a black-and-white Dallas Police Department crime scene photograph. Following a panel on the building's history, visitors walking down a corridor along the east side of the floor encountered a single panel about the Kennedy administration's foreign and domestic policies, before immediately arriving at the 1963 trip to Dallas.[148]

An audio component from a November 22, 1963, radio broadcast enhanced a series of motorcade photographs, strategically located to block visitors' view of the sixth floor windows overlooking Dealey Plaza. The sniper's perch and a large surrounding area protected behind a glass wall brought visitors up to a single set of windows to provide a view of Dealey Plaza. In this initial concept, only three of seven window bays—the enclosed sniper's perch, an opening providing a view to Elm Street, and another providing a perspective of the grassy knoll area—were exposed on the south side of the Depository overlooking the plaza, the rest being blocked by exhibition panels. The immediate aftermath of the Kennedy assassination, contained in a large square-shaped central portion of the sixth floor, was dominated by a smaller square alcove labeled "Four Days—In-Depth History,"

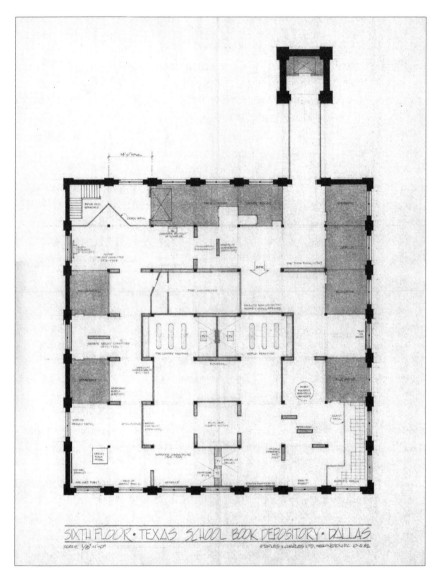

FIG. 18

The Sixth Floor exhibit, conceptual design (October 1982).

Institutional Archives/The Sixth Floor Museum at Dealey Plaza

surrounded by open space and a television monitor near the window playing a loop of news broadcasts. On one side of this central area, a panel describing Kennedy's funeral separated two back-to-back enclosed theaters, playing films on the national and global response to the assassination.[149]

Exiting the central exhibition area, visitors read about the establishment of the Warren Commission investigation—with sections on the evidence, the Abraham Zapruder home movie of the assassination that appeared on an adjacent television monitor, background on Lee Harvey Oswald and Jack Ruby, and a window bay providing a viewpoint of the grassy knoll. Following the Warren Commission's conclusion that Lee Harvey Oswald acted alone, additional panels lined a corridor up the opposite side of the sixth floor and mirrored the path that the visitors followed upon their arrival at the sniper's perch. These touched on Jim Garrison's New Orleans investigation and the second federal investigation, which featured a section on the controversial acoustical evidence. Two additional evidentiary areas behind glass concluded this 1982 concept of the sixth floor: the location in the northwest corner where investigators discovered the Mannlicher-Carcano rifle and the original second-floor lunchroom, relocated to the sixth floor. The lunchroom included a white mannequin in the approximate position of Lee Harvey Oswald when encountered by officer Marion Baker. At this point visitors could read concluding interpretation and pick up a complimentary computer printout bibliography encouraging further reading on the Kennedy assassination, thus completing a clockwise tour through the entire space for a return trip by elevator to the Visitors Center.[150]

Apart from a single panel summarizing key programs of the Kennedy administration, interpretation of the life, times, and legacy of the fallen President was noticeably absent in this original layout. Likewise, though the official investigations dominated the latter portion of the exhibit, no panel detailed the more popular conspiracy theories except those put forth by Jim Garrison's largely discredited investigation. As envisioned in 1982, The Sixth Floor took a low key and straightforward approach, its content primarily influenced by the recent findings of the House Select Committee on Assassinations.[151]

From this conceptual plan came a model designed by Staples and Charles, which was presented to the Dallas County Commissioners Court on April 19, 1983, with an announcement that the exhibition as proposed would cost between $2.5 and 3 million. Lindalyn Adams presented the plans, which called for the bulk of the cost to come from donations, though Dallas County was expected to cover utilities and any structural renovations.[152] To save both time and money, Adams recommended that construction of the exhibition support systems coincide with the next phase of county renovations of the building.[153] County judge Frank Crowley and the commissioners approved of the plans but hoped that the county's investment would be minimal.[154] A few days later Dallas County Historical Commission chair Shirley Caldwell wrote architect James Hendricks: while the commissioners "did not stand up and cheer," they showed enough interest and satisfaction for the project to move forward.[155]

"Plans are in the works to give the 100,000 tourists who gawk at the red-brick Texas School Book Depository each year something to do besides stand in the middle of Elm Street," wrote Laura Miller of the *Dallas Morning News* the day after the meeting.[156] Ironically, an adjacent story detailed Senator Edward M. Kennedy's refusal to speak at the upcoming United Auto Workers convention in Dallas because he still carried "traumatic memories" of his brother's death.[157] Other news outlets carried both stories side by side, some less than enthusiastically. In a lengthy profile on Dallas mayor-elect A. Starke Taylor, Jr., the *New York Times* said that twenty years after the Kennedy assassination Dallas "seem[ed] determined to purge itself of whatever residue of civic shame that might remain" by opening an exhibit in the Depository building.[158] Their description of the proposed exhibition emphasized the life-sized mannequin in the relocated lunchroom and a touristy gift shop filled with Kennedy collectibles—in actuality, only approved books about Kennedy's life and presidency, not his death, had been discussed by the planners as revenue possibilities.[159]

Within days of the *Times* article a twenty-two-year-old New Jersey college student wrote mayor-elect Taylor, imploring him to review the plans for "the apparent garish side-show" intended for the sixth floor, noting that the description of the lunchroom was "akin to placing a Hitler mannequin at Auschwitz."[160] A California resident, responding to a story in the *San Francisco Chronicle,* concluded that "nothing . . . would be in poorer taste" than to construct what she saw as "an attempt to capitalize on one of our national tragedies for commercial purposes." Hinting at the continued national hostility toward the community two decades after the assassination, the letter concluded with the question: "Is Dallas proud that John F. Kennedy was killed there?"[161]

Though still highly controversial, the plans as presented in the spring of 1983 met with the approval in concept of the necessary state and local organizations. Joe Oppermann, deputy preservation officer with the Texas Historical Commission, wrote that the proposed exterior elevator shaft accomplished its goal of providing direct access to the exhibition "without disrupting the views of the major, historically significant facades"; the department of planning and development for the City of Dallas, in coordination with the West End Task Force, provided an "approved 'concept' certificate of appropriateness" for the proposed addition to the building, so long as the elevator tower meshed "with the character of the West End Historic District."[162]

Funding at a national level, however, remained out of reach. The National Endowment for the Humanities rejected a $15,000 planning proposal for additional exhibition research in June 1983, contending that "reviewers were not entirely convinced that there [was] a need for an exhibition concerning the Kennedy assassination out of the context of a broader examination of Kennedy's life and career." It recommended a more focused interpretation, preferably by a historian of the period, though paradoxically the events in question were not yet removed enough for a definitive scholarly perspective.[163] Designer Barbara Charles was told privately that some panel members felt that only the John F. Kennedy Presidential Library and Museum should tackle an interpretation of the assassination. "The word was perfectly clear," said Conover Hunt in 1994. "You all are going to benefit from it, you pay for it." Thus initial fund-raising for the project focused primarily on the local community.[164]

By June 1983 Staples and Charles had prepared a new layout that more closely matched what eventually opened in 1989, with a few significant departures. Revised from their initial 1982 layout, the entire bank of windows overlooking Dealey Plaza remained exposed, providing an eerie and poignant sense of place throughout the bulk of the exhibition. The protected enclosures for the sniper's perch and northwest corner rifle location and stairwell areas were smaller, though the second-floor lunchroom remained as originally designed. Two back-to-back theaters remained, supplemented by four television monitors placed throughout the exhibit to provide brief documentary presentations on specific topics. Most striking were subtle changes in the exhibition narrative, which now included a section on the early 1960s and a concluding panel on the changes in laws and regulations that occurred as a result of the Kennedy assassination, including the Twenty-Fifth Amendment to the U.S. Constitution regarding presidential succession and changes to federal jurisdiction and Secret Service protocol.[165]

Text for a promotional and fund-raising packet, prepared around the same time, provided a walk-through of the space as envisioned in 1983—today offering insight into some of these design changes. An introductory mural of the sixth floor would provide visitors with a visual framework for the space as it appeared in 1963 and set the mood for the entire exhibit. Replacing the originally proposed panel on the Kennedy administration, a new section on the early 1960s would document cultural and political events of the day, including the excitement generated by the "youthful and vigorous approach" of the young chief executive following one of the country's closest presidential elections in

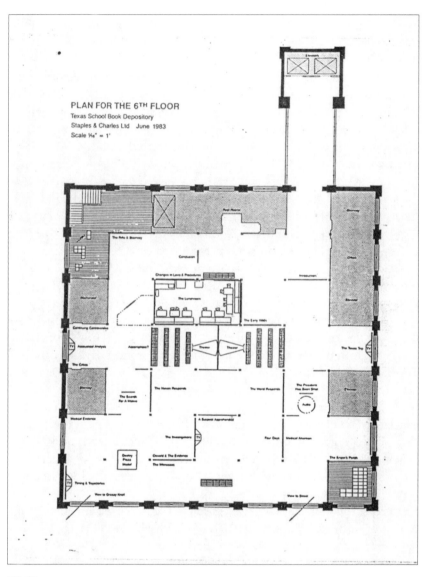

FIG. 19

The Sixth Floor exhibit, conceptual design (June 1983).

history. Within the context of this section, the grief and soul-searching follow-ing the assassination could be more fully understood; likewise, assorted conspir-acy theories could be grasped better with background on the "political milieu" of the Kennedy years.[166]

The central portion of the exhibit would chronicle the events of the assas-sination weekend, with the two theaters each offering fifteen-minute videos detailing the national and global response to the assassination, respectively—designed in part to contextualize the global fascination with the investiga-tions that followed. The designers hoped that seeing various reactions to the President's death would "be an illuminating experience for anyone college-age or younger" as well as "an opportunity to reflect" for those who remembered the assassination firsthand.[167]

While the 1982 concept individually explored the official investigations into Kennedy's death, the revised June 1983 layout summarized the findings of the two main government inquiries in a single in-depth panel with individual sec-tions on four areas of evidence: "the timing of the shots and their angles of tra-jectory," the medical evidence, evidence connecting Lee Harvey Oswald to the assassination, and eyewitness accounts. Nearby stood a scale model of Dealey Plaza. After the section on evidence and investigation, visitors would enter "an area of conjecture and theory." Here the controversial acoustical evidence sug-gesting a second gunman would be featured along with some of the more popu-lar conspiracy theories, including those disproved by science and others "not so easily dispelled."[168]

The caption of a parting photograph of Kennedy's funeral procession noted that while the 1964 conclusions of the Warren Commission might seem "over-simplified," new information and recent scientific analysis supported the find-ing that Lee Harvey Oswald assassinated the president from the sixth floor of the Depository. His motivation, however, and whether or not others were involved, "remains a mystery." Also ambiguous, the 1983 promotional text concluded with the statement that the exhibition could not present any final solution to the "long, unfinished saga" of the Kennedy assassination.[169]

Going into the summer of 1983, the working title of the exhibition, accord-ing to the promotional material, was "The 6th Floor: An Exhibition at the Former Texas School Book Depository." After much discussion, it remained in place, eventually becoming simply "The Sixth Floor." Conover Hunt recalled that the difficulty in naming the exhibition was "conditioned by Dallas' own denial and hesitance to use the 'a' word—the 'assassination' word." Likewise, those involved had avoided including the name "Kennedy" in the title. During its long devel-opment, the exhibit was saddled with a series of vague and innocuous working titles from "A Tragedy in Dallas" to "One November Day," so subtle as to suggest that nothing of remote significance occurred on November 22, 1963. By emphasizing the sixth floor of the Depository, the exhibition connected with its historic site, naturally accented by the proposed design, which maintained the general feel of the infamous warehouse with the bank of windows overlooking the assassination site on Elm Street. Hunt later credited designer Bob Staples with the idea of simply calling the exhibition by its working title because that was its location.[170]

With a working title, a model, a slideshow, and related promotional material for the project, Lindalyn Adams and Conover Hunt in the summer of 1983 embarked on a series of community briefings. Both were optimistic that the exhibition would open in 1985, though a number of challenges and setbacks awaited in the months and years ahead.

Chapter 4

A SITE OF CONFLICT

Dressed in high heels and designer suits and armed with a model of the proposed sixth floor exhibit, Conover Hunt and Lindalyn Adams "briefed over a hundred people in 102-degree heat" during the summer of 1983.[1] Those consulted represented the business, banking, and political elite as well as academic institutions and community organizations in Dallas.[2] Both major Dallas newspapers responded enthusiastically. The publisher of the *Dallas Times Herald* volunteered to run a multipage supplement about The Sixth Floor, while one *Dallas Morning News* executive even suggested that the sixth floor might not be large enough and inquired about additional Depository floors.[3]

Hunt and Adams recalled a handful of these presentations as poignant and indicative of the establishment's response to The Sixth Floor exhibition, particularly in light of the personal experiences of these community leaders during the traumatic assassination weekend. One such briefing took place with Stanley Marcus, the former president and chair of the board of luxury retailer Neiman Marcus. Though retired by 1983, Marcus remained chair emeritus and, as Hunt once put it, the "Dallas establishment's token liberal."[4]

One month before the Kennedy assassination, Marcus, a member of the influential Citizens Council, served as host to U.N. ambassador Adlai Stevenson and was with him when Stevenson was accosted by vocal protesters. Shortly thereafter Marcus warned Vice President Johnson that Kennedy's upcoming visit to Dallas was "a great mistake," because the president would "be subjected to the type of harassment and ridicule that Stevenson" had experienced. According to Marcus, Johnson replied, "It doesn't make a goddamn difference what you think or I think—the president is coming."[5]

On November 22, 1963, Stanley Marcus was in New York City on business and recalled "walking around New York aimlessly" after the assassination occurred; he then attended the president's funeral in Washington, D.C. A frequent international traveler, Marcus endured persistent questioning in the months that followed about how people could live in Dallas after such a traumatic event.[6]

Marcus wrote a brief editorial entitled "What's Right with Dallas" that ran as part of a Neiman Marcus advertisement in national newspapers on January 1, 1964. Marcus praised the community's "dynamic growth" and encouraged national and international understanding during the mourning period after the assassination; he also encouraged the City of Dallas to "take an honest look at its inventory and be willing to consider its faults as well as its assets."[7] Marcus's subsequent thoughts on—and support for—an exhibition inside the Texas School Book Depository would be significant.

During the briefing, Marcus viewed a slideshow on The Sixth Floor projected on a large parchment tacked to an expensive tapestry adorning his office wall.[8] Conover Hunt remembered that Marcus jokingly suggested that the designers should position a mannequin with a gun in the sniper's perch. In retrospect she thought it was the businessman's way of testing the determination of the pair: Adams and Hunt would undoubtedly encounter a myriad of ideas, some of them less than tasteful.[9] In the end Marcus concluded that the Depository should not be punished "for something that a human being made infamous" and lent his support.[10]

Later Adams and Hunt visited the offices of longtime community leader and prominent local developer John Stemmons. The Stemmons Freeway, named for his father, carried the mortally wounded John F. Kennedy to Parkland Hospital. The younger Stemmons, who had helped arrange the presidential luncheon aborted by the assassination, cared deeply for his home city and was so depressed by the shooting that some of his friends feared that he might take his own life.[11] Justifying these concerns, the businessman later admitted feeling "a sense of personal responsibility [because] it had happened in my town."[12]

Before she delivered the briefing, Conover Hunt had no idea that Kennedy's death had created such a deep personal impact on Stemmons.[13] At the conclusion of the presentation, the longtime business leader sat silently then, after an agonizing pause, simply said, "Well, it has to be done."[14] Although Hunt and Adams's presentation had been convincing, Stemmons still had serious concerns that The Sixth Floor exhibition "would be a circus." There is no record that John Stemmons ever visited the exhibit prior to his death in 2001, yet he, too, was willing to lend his influential support to the project, primarily because of his respect for Lindalyn Adams.[15]

Conover Hunt has long credited Adams for whatever community support the project garnered. If this controversial project had the seal of approval from one of the city's best-known volunteer, charity, and historic preservation champions, there was ultimately no need for concern. "She could not have been physically, visually, or in temperament anymore in contrast with the event that she was dealing with," said Hunt. "And it worked. The community trusted her implicitly."[16]

In addition to consulting with community leaders, Lindalyn Adams also proved herself a thoughtful and skilled organizer of issues of governance in shaping, with Hunt, an independent, nonprofit foundation for the management of The Sixth Floor—concurrent with their briefings in the summer of 1983.

When the Dallas County Historical Commission, which had been overseeing the project from the start, could not successfully tackle the required fund-raising and management of The Sixth Floor, planners first explored the possibility that one of city's leading historical agencies might undertake this mission. Ultimately, however, the Dallas County Commissioners Court and its historical commission determined that a new nonprofit organization should be established with a new board and its own bylaws, with a separate Dallas County management contract.[17]

On December 20, 1982, the Texas secretary of state accepted the articles of incorporation for the creation of a tax-exempt entity to be known as the Dallas County Historical Foundation.[18] The purpose of the foundation, as stated in the articles of incorporation, was "to establish, support, maintain, manage, and operate a museum on the sixth floor of the Dallas County Administration building."[19] That document categorized The Sixth Floor as a "museum," though the safer and at the time more palatable term "exhibition" would remain in place for the institution's first five years of operation.[20]

One month after the Dallas County Historical Commission filed the articles of incorporation, the Texas secretary of state granted the new nonprofit corporation its charter. The new body consisted of eleven board members, each serving two-year appointments; five board members were appointed by the Dallas County Commissioners Court, while the rest were selected by local historical organizations.[21]

During the Commissioners Court meeting on April 19, 1983, when the preliminary designs by Staples and Charles were formally unveiled, Lindalyn Adams told the commissioners that the group was ready to move forward with fund-raising.[22] The private conferences and community briefings later that summer raised awareness for the planned exhibit and laid the groundwork for the fund-raising drive that followed. Likewise, it presented the scope of the exhibition honestly to a very wary audience, firmly establishing that any exhibition inside the Depository would be tasteful and not, as many had feared since Aubrey Mayhew's brief ownership, some type of shrine to the alleged assassin.[23]

Those 1983 briefings also aided Lindalyn Adams in her search for community leaders to serve on the foundation's board of directors.[24] Adams intentionally avoided asking the city's leaders who were in power in 1963 to serve on the board because of "the depth of the pain associated with that memory" of the shooting.[25] The primary exception was Joe M. Dealey, president of the *Dallas Morning News* at the time of the Kennedy assassination, who joined the founding board as a Commissioners Court appointee in September 1983. Dealey, too, had a personal connection to the President's death: the tragedy had occurred in a public park named for his grandfather, George Bannerman Dealey, the civic leader who had donated the property on which Dealey Plaza was established. As noted, Joe Dealey's father, E. M. "Ted" Dealey, publisher of the *Dallas Morning News* during the Kennedy administration, famously questioned the President's leadership abilities during a White House luncheon with other Texas newspaper executives in October 1961.[26]

On the morning of the Kennedy assassination, Dealey's newspaper carried a full-page, black-bordered advertisement whose headline "Welcome Mr. Kennedy to Dallas" belied its contents: a vehement indictment of the President's foreign policies and accusations that he was "soft on Communists."[27] Although the newspaper's advertising manager "deemed that there wasn't anything untrue" in the controversial advertisement—paid for by a group of local conservative businessmen—Joe Dealey reportedly reproached his father for allowing the advertisement to be printed.[28] The legacy of that advertisement haunted the *Dallas Morning News* and the Dealey family in the aftermath of the assassination, making Joe Dealey's acceptance of a position on the Dallas County Historical Foundation board of directors all the more significant.

The first board members were appointed on September 6, 1983. In addition to Joe Dealey, the other county commissioner appointees included Boone Powell, Sr., president of the Baylor University Medical Center Foundation; William Cooper, an executive at the Dallas Market Hall complex; Jess Hay, chief executive officer of Lomas Financial Corporation and local Democratic leader; and Becky Power, whose husband, Robert Power (the former mayor of Irving), was instrumental in building Texas Stadium, longtime home of the Dallas Cowboys.[29]

Representing the Dallas Historical Society were attorney William E. Collins, then president of the society, and former Dallas city councilman Samuel Moreno. Lindalyn Adams and Shirley Caldwell were appointed on behalf of the Dallas County Historical Commission. Rounding out the board, representing the Dallas County Heritage Society, were its president, Harriet Weber, and major general (retired) Hugh G. Robinson, then involved in the planning of a major Dallas building project known as City Place Center for the Southland

Corporation.[30] Serving in an ex-officio capacity were Thomas H. Smith, director of Old City Park; and John Crain, director of the Dallas Historical Society, who authored the board's bylaws.[31]

Painstaking and meticulous in her board recruitment, Lindalyn Adams was pleased with the results, proudly stating that the initial members "not only gave great credibility, they worked, and they were loyal, and they stayed with it . . . for years."[32] Conover Hunt added that the first board was "bipartisan . . . culturally inclusive [and] gender inclusive. . . . It had an attorney. It had a finance man. It had strong leadership from a variety of different areas of the community, and it had a series of very cool heads."[33]

"Let's Get On with It"

With a diverse and prestigious board in place, fund-raising efforts began almost immediately. One of the first organizations approached was the Hoblitzelle Foundation in Dallas, a distinguished institution that funded a variety of educational and cultural activities in Texas.[34] Adams requested funds for "an historical, educational display"—the term "museum" was never used—that would objectively chronicle the Kennedy assassination and its aftermath. She extolled the uniqueness of The Sixth Floor project and emphasized the taste with which it would be carried out.[35] Her fund-raising letter included a list of board members, plans and model photographs of the exhibit, the project budget (still estimated at $3 million total), and a list of the community leaders approached by Adams and Hunt earlier in the summer. The proposed budget allotted nearly $2 million for architecture, $800,000 for exhibitions, and lesser amounts for the Visitors Center, security, marketing, and operations.[36]

The Hoblitzelle Foundation generously agreed to provide a challenge grant of $100,000 to be matched by February 1986, providing the Dallas County Historical Foundation with seed money to pursue longer-range goals. The challenge grant was met, thanks to active board efforts, with grants from the *Dallas Morning News*–WFAA Foundation and the Southland Corporation.[37] Despite inroads made with some of the community leaders, however, fierce resistance to the idea of an exhibition on the sixth floor of the Texas School Book Depository continued. Joe Dealey said that the board "had a hell of a time raising that money."[38] A New York company that conducted nationwide inquiries on behalf of the project met with little success.[39]

November 22, 1983, marked the twentieth anniversary of the Kennedy assassination. Although the sixth floor of the Depository remained empty, the project team now had an exhibit layout, model, and background material to share with members of the news media. Beginning in July, representatives of the Dallas County Historical Foundation gave interviews to a host of news outlets, including *Life, Newsweek, Good Morning, America,* and the Tokyo Broadcasting System, in addition to virtually every Dallas newspaper and television station.[40] Most journalists found touring the empty sixth floor "an emotional experience."[41] It was accurately predicted that the assassination would be an item of discussion in the press during the Republican National Convention the following August.[42]

If most of 1983 was filled with optimism and enthusiasm, the following year brought pessimism and controversy. Conover Hunt left the project to return to her native Virginia for family and personal reasons in February.[43] At that moment Adams knew that the project would slow down, though the Dallas County Historical Foundation board continued to meet regularly. Adams read Hunt's letter of resignation at the February 15 meeting, indicating that she would continue to consult on the exhibition.[44]

Despite the loss of Conover Hunt, the board geared up for the Republican National Convention coming in August to the Dallas Convention Center, a few blocks from Dealey Plaza. It was probably not a coincidence that foundation board member Sam Moreno was also a member of the bipartisan Dallas Welcoming Committee for the convention. Prior to leaving Dallas, Hunt had served on the convention's cultural committee.[45]

Aware that the recently renovated Depository and the upcoming exhibit would draw media attention, the Dallas Welcoming Committee, in conjunction with the Republican Host Committee, went to great lengths to present the Dallas story of the Kennedy assassination accurately, including a special JFK bus tour for convention delegates and members of the press as one of the local activities.[46] Though popular with conventioneers, the Kennedy tour was outsold five to one by a tour of Southfork Ranch, where exterior scenes for the television series *Dallas* were filmed.[47]

By all accounts, the Republican National Convention went very well, despite occasional awkward moments, including a live interview with Dallas businesswoman Mary Kay Ash, founder of Mary Kay Cosmetics, Inc., on the *CBS Morning News.* Ash expressed the view that the Texas School Book Depository should have been torn down and the site made into a parking lot.[48] Conover Hunt returned to Dallas during the convention to help give tours of the sixth floor, though visits to the non-air-conditioned space in the intense summer heat were limited to fifteen minutes. Access to the floor by a rickety stairwell made the situation doubly difficult.[49]

On the last day of the convention, Lindalyn Adams received a startling telephone call at 4:00 A.M. Once more the Texas School Book Depository had suffered an arson attempt; the timing, with members of the national news media nearby and eager for a story, could not have been worse. Two reserve officers from the Dallas County Sheriff's Department reported the fire at 2:52 A.M., having smelled and seen smoke in the lobby. According to the official report, the fire began in two locations in the Depository's basement. From the basement, the fire spread up a corridor wall to the first and second floors. Some of the upper floors suffered slight smoke damage; the sixth floor escaped unscathed.[50] Having quickly escalated to five alarms, the fire was extinguished just before 5:00 A.M. after approximately one hundred fire fighters from twenty-three different companies showed up to battle the blaze.[51]

Although stored in the basement, the original building elements removed during the county renovation, the faceplate panels of the Hertz sign, and some materials from the old John F. Kennedy Museum were undamaged. "The Hertz sign was the only thing I was concerned about," Adams told the *Dallas Morning News* after touring the basement. Of greater import, Adams also noted that the fire, which caused approximately $250,000 worth of damage, might delay plans for opening a sixth floor exhibition until 1985 or 1986.[52]

Whereas the *New York Times* and the *Chicago Tribune* reported the fire matter-of-factly, the *Washington Post*'s story struck a more sensational tone.[53] The author of the story, headlined "Landmark Fire Kindles City's Grimmest Memory," concluded that "it was as if fate, or something, conspired in the end to keep Dallas from escaping its long association with Kennedy's murder."[54]

No one was charged with the alleged arson attempt, though Dallas Police Department officials had arrested approximately one hundred political protesters the afternoon before the fire was reported for activities such as spray painting downtown sidewalks, burning a U.S. flag, and causing $12,000 worth of damage to a sculpture.[55]

Lindalyn Adams downplayed any negative publicity generated by the fire, and the Dallas County Historical Foundation acted quickly to ensure that the project was not derailed.[56] In a public statement released a few days after the fire, Adams reaffirmed the board's intent to open The Sixth Floor. In fact, she believed, the response from the news media to the arson attempt only emphasized "the vital importance and need for an historical interpretation of this site."[57]

Ironically, the Depository fire stimulated lagging fund-raising efforts for The Sixth Floor project. Board member Joe Dealey spoke for many when he pleaded: "What are we waiting for? Why are we indecisive? Are we frightened and overly sensitive, so insecure that we shrink before a history that will never fade? Completion of this work is simply something Dallas must and should do. Let's get on with it."[58]

"Three Wars Were Fought"

Repair work to the first two floors of the Depository became the priority for Dallas County in the aftermath of the August 1984 arson attempt. Within a week commissioners authorized an emergency allocation of $92,000, while a team of eighty workers cleaned up the damage. The fire displaced at least one Commissioners Court meeting, temporarily moved to the nearby Dallas County Services Building.[59] Despite Lindalyn Adams's assurances at that meeting that The Sixth Floor would move forward and Joe Dealey's passionate call to action to the community to contribute monetarily, the project languished. Even the commemoration of November 22, 1984, appeared subdued compared with previous years. The Dallas County Democratic Party, which typically sponsored plaza memorial services, opted in 1984 to celebrate President Kennedy's birthday on May 29 instead. Former party chair Bob Greenberg explained that the plan had been to cease holding an annual memorial service after the twentieth anniversary in 1983, noting that Washington and Lincoln's birthdays were celebrated, not their deaths.[60]

While city officials distanced themselves from the Kennedy assassination, Lindalyn Adams continued fund-raising for The Sixth Floor.[61] A typical solicitation letter included a case statement titled "Why Interpret the Kennedy Assassination?" Quoting Abraham Lincoln's admonition: "We cannot escape history . . . we will be remembered in spite of ourselves," the document stressed that visitors flocked to Dealey Plaza more than two decades after the assassination even though no exhibition chronicled the tragedy. Dallas, the paper argued, had a responsibility to meet that need rather than "ignore the phenomenon." The foundation estimated that The Sixth Floor might welcome as many as half a million people in its first year, more than enough visitors at $2 a head for adults to offset an estimated annual operating cost of $300,000.[62]

Charging an admission fee to enter a public building had actually been illegal when Adams had taken her case to the Texas Legislature in the early 1980s. Dallas representative Chris Semos subsequently authored legislation that authorized an admission fee for entrance to a cultural and historical exhibition in a county-owned building.[63] The bill passed with little opposition.[64]

In May 1985 Dallas County moved forward with phase two of the Depository renovation, authorizing $3.9 million as part of a $236.5 million bond package approved in April to complete the third, fourth, and fifth floors and to buy land adjacent to the building for additional county parking.[65] Once again James Hendricks—now of the firm Hendricks and Callaway—served as architect. The upper floors eventually housed departments such as public works and the civil division of the Dallas District Attorney's office.[66]

Efforts to create a sixth floor exhibition stalled. Having successfully matched the Hoblitzelle Foundation's challenge grant by the end of 1984, the board did not actively solicit funds during the following year.[67] On November 22, 1985, Laura Miller of the *Dallas Morning News* criticized the lack of an anniversary ceremony or historical exhibition, blaming what she perceived as "a slow-moving board and lackluster donor interest."[68] A later editorial thought that negative remarks by entrepreneur H. Ross Perot and other influential Dallas citizens were at least partly to blame for lagging funding.[69] Perot commented in a television interview that he "wouldn't put a penny into creating a museum to Oswald" and called the Depository an odd locale for a museum about the assassination.[70] Adams promptly wrote to Perot, offering to brief him personally on the project.[71]

One new fund-raising tool at Adams's disposal was *One November Day,* a short film produced with some of the foundation's seed money in 1985. Combining still images, music, and statements of support from community leaders such as John Stemmons, the presentation made a case for the educational aspects of The Sixth Floor.[72] The narrator intoned that it was "not a memorial or a museum, but an historical exhibit designed to educate."[73] Still, apathy reigned, prompting many board members openly to express their frustration to the news media. In 1985 Adams, who divided her time during the 1980s among twelve different civic appointments, blamed herself for not pushing the project harder.[74] She nevertheless kept the board focused and continued to guide prominent individuals through the sixth floor in an effort to generate national interest.[75]

In 1986 economic hard times delayed the major fund-raising campaign planned by the Dallas County Historical Foundation. Falling oil prices and the Tax Reform Act of 1986 ended the Dallas real estate boom and helped bring about the savings and loan financial crisis. By November news of the stalled exhibition had become an annual anniversary story. Adams lamented that the foundation had not "asked for a cent in two years."[76] A few meager donations, typically $25 or less, nevertheless had come in, most of them after the Depository fire.[77]

The November 1986 cable television broadcast of *On Trial: Lee Harvey Oswald* briefly shined the spotlight on the Texas School Book Depository. The Showtime Network hosted a press conference at the site to promote the show, which took the form of an unscripted courtroom trial featuring authentic assassination witnesses, a Texas judge, and a jury of Dallas County residents. London Weekend Television in Great Britain recorded this forerunner of reality programming, which featured Vincent Bugliosi, the former Los Angeles County assistant district attorney best known for his successful prosecution of Charles Manson, and flamboyant defense attorney Gerry Spence, representing Lee Harvey Oswald. To promote the U.S. broadcast, the two attorneys appeared at the Depository in an event coordinated by Lindalyn Adams on behalf of Dallas County.[78]

Although the press conference brought brief attention to the building, and although the Texas jury convicted Oswald, such theatrics did little to attract attention to The Sixth Floor project. More positive progress was made at the January 2, 1987, swearing-in ceremony of the new Dallas County judge, Lee F. Jackson, who pledged his personal support, saying that "he would do everything he could to make the assassination exhibit a reality."[79] Following the ceremony, Jackson, a Republican, took onlookers on an impromptu tour of the sixth floor.[80] Jackson's announcement surprised and delighted Lindalyn Adams, who had never met the new judge. As it turned out, Jackson's 1987 declaration would be one of the project's defining moments.[81]

Lee Jackson had realized the need for a Depository exhibition as early as 1986. On frequent visits to Commissioners Court meetings, he noticed how earnestly tourists sought access to the sixth floor and was amazed at the blasé attitude of county officials toward the "constant stream" of tour buses and visitors to Dealey Plaza.[82]

Although Jackson never mentioned the Depository during his campaign, shortly after his election victory on November 4, 1986, he began quietly inquiring about the stalled Sixth Floor project. He discovered that the primary problem was a $3 million shortfall in the funds needed to build the Visitors Center and install the elevator.[83] One of the youngest judges in Dallas County history, Jackson was not burdened by painful memories of the Kennedy assassination. As an eighth grader in 1963 Jackson's only awareness of the criticism leveled at Dallas occurred when his Boy Scout troop was warned to anticipate verbal abuse for wearing Dallas badges on their uniforms during a 1964 visit to Pennsylvania.[84]

This new and vocal supporter of The Sixth Floor project, combined with a very positive meeting and tour she had with a National Park Service representative who expressed interest in the site, served as a fresh call to action for Lindalyn Adams, who planned a reunion of all exhibition consultants for March 1987.[85] New board members of the Dallas County Historical Foundation that year included Lillian Bradshaw, appointed by Judge Lee Jackson, and Nancy Cheney among others.

As director of the Dallas Public Library system at the time of the Kennedy assassination, Bradshaw had accepted the cards and notes left in Dealey Plaza in memory of the fallen President after they were gathered by the park department. Later she provided the FBI with Lee Harvey Oswald's library card and related records. A stalwart community leader after her retirement from the library in

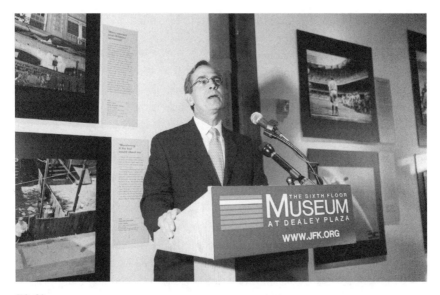

FIG. 20

Dallas County judge Lee F. Jackson, seen here in 2002, played a key role in making The Sixth Floor exhibit a reality.

INSTITUTIONAL ARCHIVES/THE SIXTH FLOOR MUSEUM AT DEALEY PLAZA

1984, Bradshaw soon agreed to spearhead the exhibition's renewed fund-raising campaign.[86]

An appointee of the Dallas County Heritage Society, Nancy Cheney served a vital role as the foundation's direct conduit and liaison to the Kennedy family. Cheney first met John F. Kennedy when the young senator visited Dallas on the 1960 campaign trail; she and her daughter, Allison, also watched the presidential motorcade pass on the day of the assassination. Allison was responsible for introducing her mother to the Kennedy family after meeting Senator Edward Kennedy at the University of Oklahoma in 1979. The Cheney family helped open Kennedy's Dallas campaign office, and Allison worked on Kennedy's staff during his unsuccessful bid for the Democratic presidential nomination in 1980. At the Democratic Convention in New York City that year, the senator invited the family to visit his campaign suite at the Waldorf Astoria.[87]

After learning of Nancy Cheney's connection to the Kennedy family, Lindalyn Adams briefed her on The Sixth Floor project and asked if she would consider passing along information about the Dallas endeavor to Senator Kennedy.[88] Cheney was initially hesitant to approach the late President's brother about the exhibit. But out of respect for Adams, she agreed to tour the space and learn more about it. The experience changed her mind, and she immediately agreed to speak with Senator Kennedy in his Washington office. The day before Cheney left for the East Coast, Adams called with an invitation to join the Dallas County Historical Foundation board of directors.[89]

As Cheney nervously broached the subject of The Sixth Floor exhibit with Ted Kennedy in his private office, the senator's face "turned the color of a [white] sheet." She explained that hundreds of thousands of individuals visited Dealey Plaza every year in memory of the late President with flowers and prayers, wondering "why Dallas hasn't done something at this place to honor the president." When she finished her presentation, Kennedy replied, "Nancy, I have all the confidence in the world in you, and if you say it's going to be all right, I know that it will be."[90]

After that meeting Cheney regularly briefed Melody Miller, the senator's senior aide, who compiled a file for Kennedy's perusal. Before returning to Dallas, Cheney also briefed Senator Kennedy's brother-in-law, Stephen Smith, who volunteered to share this news with Jacqueline Kennedy Onassis. When Cheney returned home, she accepted a position on the foundation's board; feeling a sense of great personal responsibility because of the faith that the Kennedys had placed in her, she decided "to take a very active role in the planning of the exhibit."[91]

At the project's reunion meeting on March 23, 1987, Adams, Conover Hunt, Barbara Charles and Bob Staples, architects Eugene George and James Hendricks, and security consultant E. B. Brown met with Judge Jackson, county officials, and three representatives of the National Park Service. Richard Sellars, chief of the Southwest Cultural Resources Center at the National Park Service's Santa Fe, New Mexico, office, had given Adams great hope about completing the project when he toured the sixth floor in December 1986. In his opinion, the Depository was indeed a historic site in need of recognition.[92] Through Sellars, the Park Service provided valuable counsel and support in the months ahead when the planners battled a myriad of outside forces.

With a newfound sense of energy and optimism, the original exhibition team from 1983 devised a strategy to open The Sixth Floor by the twenty-fifth anniversary of the assassination on November 22, 1988. When Hunt discovered that the construction workers who were renovating the third, fourth, and fifth floors were "using the sniper's nest window as a dump shoot and the corner staircase . . . for the storage of supplies," she successfully lobbied Dallas County to give James Hendricks more direct supervision of the project. The renovation included concrete flooring and a Walkderduct wiring system for both the sixth and seventh floors, literally laying the groundwork for the forthcoming exhibition. Although the two evidentiary areas remained unaltered, a chain link fence now protected the sniper's perch.[93]

Less than ninety days after the March meeting, Conover Hunt returned to Dallas under a two-year contract to work on The Sixth Floor project. On her first day in the office, Richard Sellars of the National Park Service authored an article in the *Dallas Morning News*, succinctly chronicling the efforts to preserve the Depository and convert the sixth floor into an educational exhibition. Comparing Dealey Plaza to the sites of the Lincoln, King, and Robert F. Kennedy assassinations, Sellars provocatively queried: "Do we dare preserve what still hurts?" He concluded in the affirmative, noting that sites such as the Texas School Book Depository allow visitors to confront tragedy in a direct and poignant manner and acknowledge "its lasting historical importance to this nation."[94]

Though public acceptance of The Sixth Floor was key, Conover Hunt faced more concrete challenges upon resuming her duties in Dallas. "In the summer of 1987," she later explained, "three wars were fought."[95] Each threatened to derail, delay, or detrimentally alter The Sixth Floor project. The first was a proposed seven-story parking garage that would wrap around the north and west sides of the Depository, intruding upon space reserved for the proposed Visitors Center and elevator shaft.[96]

Arbor Development Corporation, whose renovation of 501 Elm Street forced out the privately owned John F. Kennedy Museum in 1982, continued to develop the West End Historic District. By the fall of 1985 renovations were underway on a trio of brick buildings across Houston Street from the Depository. The company also transformed a four-story building located at Houston and Pacific Avenue into a multilevel parking garage.[97] Construction of another garage in close proximity to the Depository had been proposed the previous year. Following a series of confrontational meetings with the developer and representatives of the Missouri Pacific Railroad, which owned the property, Lindalyn Adams shored up enough support among the county commissioners to halt the plan. Commissioners instead approved plans for a county-owned underground garage adjacent to the Depository in 1987 but abandoned the idea the following year. No parking garage, either above or below ground, was built next to the Texas School Book Depository.[98]

A second "war" waged by friends of The Sixth Floor during the summer of 1987 centered on the plans of Dallas Area Rapid Transit (DART) to construct a subway system that threatened to have a permanent impact on the historical integrity of Dealey Plaza. Organized in 1983 as the city's mass transit system, DART planned a subway portal—"an open ditch through which the trains [would] rise up to grade from the subway"—near the infamous grassy knoll in Dealey Plaza.[99] As proposed, subway trains would emerge from this hundred-foot-long opening every two minutes.[100] The portal's right-of-way also intruded slightly upon the footprint of the Visitors Center and exterior elevator shaft. This second point was the easier of the two battles with DART; once the organization agreed to provide room for the Visitors Center, however, the problematic portal became a separate issue.[101]

Hunt observed that the subway would emerge "in the most controversial piece of real estate in the world."[102] Many researchers believed that a second gunman fired one or more shots at the presidential limousine in 1963 from the grassy knoll only seventy feet from the projected DART portal.[103] The tracks also threatened a railroad switching tower in the parking lot where a significant assassination eyewitness had been located.

In her typically direct style, Hunt summarized the foundation's opposition to the portal:

1. Passes directly through a major witness area of the assassination.
2. Passes too closely to location of supposed second gunman, who was standing in the parking lot of the rail yards behind the picket fence.
3. Creates a large open ditch into which half a million visitors a year to the sixth floor exhibit will look down. Ditch is over 100 feet long, 34 feet wide, and 22 feet deep nearest the Depository. Trains will rise and go into this tunnel every two minutes.
4. Curve of portal is sharp and will cause squealing.
5. Trains will be noisy.
6. DART drawings showing view from sixth floor are inaccurate, since they are based on photos taken with a wide angle lens. This has the effect of making the portal look farther away than it is.
7. Attractive fencing and trees around portal will not mitigate the view from the sixth floor, which looks directly into the ditch.[104]

Although the foundation did not have the staff, resources, or time to confront DART, its board and the exhibition planners stood firm, for the first time claiming authority for the preservation of the site. They would fight the subway portal.[105] Charles Anderson, executive director of DART, acknowledged that the portal would likely cause "some impact" at the historic site but promised to work with the foundation as "good neighbors."[106] To that end DART had explored a number of alignment possibilities, including two more expensive options that required tunneling underneath Dealey Plaza.[107]

Conover Hunt turned to G. Robert Blakey, the former chief counsel and staff director of the House Select Committee investigations and a member of the exhibit's 1979 planning team, for support in the battle against DART. At Hunt's request, Blakey reviewed the four most popular alignment possibilities. In a letter to Charles Anderson of DART widely distributed by the historical foundation to support their efforts, he advocated tunneling under the plaza without visible disruption.[108] Blakey reminded Anderson that DART was "not just building a railroad" but rather "working with 'consecrated' ground." Treating Dealey Plaza with insensitivity for the sake of progress, Blakey continued, could "mark Dallas poorly once again in the popular imagination."[109]

Also at Hunt's request, assassination researcher Gary Mack, then employed at a local television station, compiled a short video of news footage demonstrating the significance of the grassy knoll, which he screened for the DART board that summer. Mack warned that some in the assassination research community might read DART's plans as part of some conspiracy theory.[110]

At the heart of the subway conflict was a disagreement over whether track should be laid underneath Pacific Avenue or Elm Street—a difference of approximately two hundred feet. The Elm alignment, which called for tunneling under Dealey Plaza, won the support of the Dallas County Historical Foundation, downtown retailers, and some members of the DART board. Although more costly, this route had the potential of revitalizing the city's Main Street shopping district. A majority of DART staff members and some city officials, however, preferred the less expensive Pacific Avenue route, which included the portal on the west side of the Depository in at least two of its proposed alignments.[111] No conclusions were reached by the end of the year.[112]

A decisive DART board meeting occurred in January 1988. Richard Sellars of the National Park Service warned that the Dealey Plaza portal would expose DART to litigation if it disturbed the historical integrity of the Kennedy assassination site.[113] He also advised DART to undertake an impact study under the National Historic Preservation Act of 1966 before finalizing its plans. At the same meeting Adams introduced Charles A. Briggs, recently retired executive director of the Central Intelligence Agency, who was assisting with exhibition research in Washington, D.C. Although Briggs never said a word during the proceedings, his electrifying presence produced a stir among the attendees and further reinforced the national significance of Dealey Plaza.[114]

The DART board scheduled a public hearing in February to resolve the matter. In the interim the *Dallas Morning News* urged the carrier to consider the plaza's historical significance and the financial consequences of a legal showdown over the Dealey Plaza portal, which might also threaten federal funding from the U.S. Transportation Department.[115]

DART agreed in February to consider alternative routes and by May the crisis had been averted, thanks in part to new concerns that the route might damage printing press operations at the *Dallas Times Herald*.[116] In a vote of twenty to two, the DART board approved a $200 million Pacific Avenue subway route that would not endanger Dealey Plaza or the *Times Herald* printing presses.[117]

Ironically, DART never constructed its proposed subway system, opting instead to run a less expensive, above-ground light rail system along Pacific Avenue after voters defeated a $1 billion bond package for the original transit project in June.[118] Eventually the light rail's downtown path ran north and west of the Depository and grassy knoll areas, farther away than the proposed subway. The original railroad switching tower was saved and subsequently restored. Apart from the noise associated with the mass transit system, the light rail does not detrimentally impact the site's historical integrity. A convenient DART light rail station serves the West End Historic District as well as the Dealey Plaza National Historic Landmark District.

The last of the three battles that the foundation fought during the summer of 1987 involved the proposed exterior elevator shaft that would carry visitors directly to The Sixth Floor exhibition. Although the tower design by James Hendricks had received conceptual approval from the Texas Historical Commission and the City of Dallas Landmark Commission in 1983, these same organizations, along with the West End Task Force, now opposed it, largely for aesthetic reasons but also for emotional ones.[119]

Critics balked at the tower's large scale and visual impact on the Depository and the West End Historic District, where it was clearly visible. "At another [level]," wrote *Dallas Morning News* architecture critic David Dillon, the debate was "psychological and philosophical, rooted in Dallas' lingering guilt over the Kennedy assassination."[120] The elevator shaft represented the first physical sign that The Sixth Floor was a reality and generated an emotional reaction among individuals still uncertain about the appropriateness of the project. A member of the Landmark Commission called the entire project "blood and gore and distasteful," noting that many in Dallas were "very upset about the whole thing."[121]

In the years since conceptual approval, however, Dallas County had concluded its renovation of the first five floors of the Depository, precluding the possibility of internal elevator access directly to the sixth floor without considerable financial and logistical consequences. Days after an upsetting meeting in Austin between Adams and the state's new preservation officer, Judge Lee Jackson and all four county commissioners protested the Texas Historical Commission's flip-flop on the issue, to no avail.[122] Adams walked away from a July site visit in tears when historical commission architects repeatedly criticized Hendricks's design.[123]

The argument dragged on for three months as the opposing parties considered alternatives to an external shaft. Craig Melde, an architect on the West End

Task Force, quickly offered an alternative plan with a low-capacity single internal elevator funneling visitors from an abbreviated basement lobby; but it was rejected because it required serious building modifications and ignored the estimated traffic flow of up to half a million visitors annually to the exhibit.[124]

Finally the Texas Historical Commission honored its 1983 concept approval. In August, despite continued opposition from city planning staff and members of the West End Task Force, the City of Dallas Landmark Commission voted ten to one to accept an external elevator shaft. On October 13, 1987, the final design for the elevator shaft won approval from the Dallas body.[125]

In the intervening months James Hendricks made a series of changes to accommodate some of the landmark commission's concerns. He shortened and narrowed the shaft and reshaped the Visitors Center from a square that closely matched the design of the Depository into a rectangle with an enclosed courtyard space. Conover Hunt concluded in December that the elevator shaft controversy had cost the foundation an estimated $40,000 and delayed The Sixth Floor project by five months.[126]

Although serious challenges to the historical and architectural integrity of The Sixth Floor project had been overcome during the summer of 1987, its supporters were constantly reminded of the negative emotions that the exhibition engendered. Some people "just hated that this thing was going to happen," Hunt recalled years later, "and that got mixed up in the process."[127] The *Fort Worth Star-Telegram* spoke for many who saw the elevator shaft and the controversial exhibition "as unwanted reminders of Nov. 22, 1963."[128]

Despite the summer distractions, design and research on the exhibition's content and layout continued apace both in Dallas and in the Washington, D.C., offices of Staples and Charles. As the Dallas County Historical Foundation renewed its formal fund-raising campaign, Judge Lee Jackson told the *New York Times* that he was ready to "unlock the door, let the world look out those windows, see a first-class historic exhibit, and let people draw their own judgments."[129]

"The Last Remaining Demons from 1963"

Fund-raising difficulties had long hampered The Sixth Floor project, preventing its completion in 1985 according to the timetable that Adams and Hunt devised during conceptual planning. When county judge Lee Jackson pledged his support for the project in January 1987, he followed up with direct action. By the summer, at Jackson's urging, Dallas County had agreed to issue over $2 million in revenue bonds to cover construction costs for the exterior elevator and

Visitors Center. The money would be repaid to the county out of the exhibit's ticket revenues.[130]

Earlier in the year, following a ringing endorsement of the project by Richard Sellars of the National Park Service, Congressman John Bryant of the Fifth Congressional District of Texas moved to secure a $3 million appropriation for The Sixth Floor from the Park Service's technical assistance program.[131] If successful in obtaining such funds, Bryant promised to introduce legislation to make the sixth floor of the Depository an affiliate of the National Park Service. When federal funding again failed to materialize, Dallas County stepped in to complete The Sixth Floor by the assassination's twenty-fifth anniversary in 1988.[132]

The county agreed to issue enough revenue bonds to underwrite nearly 60 percent of the project's $3.8 million price tag (the construction of the Visitors Center and exterior elevator), leaving approximately $1.5 million as the responsibility of the Dallas County Historical Foundation for the exhibit design and installation.[133] Ticket revenue for The Sixth Floor would be used to repay the bonds. Critics of this plan worried, however, that the county might be stuck with the bill for an unpopular exhibition. Having observed the tourist presence in Dealey Plaza firsthand, Jackson remained steadfast, and the Dallas County Commissioners Court agreed.[134]

Just over one year away from the exhibit's intended opening, the Dallas County Historical Foundation required between $1.3 and $1.5 million in private contributions to complete The Sixth Floor. The $250,000 that had been raised between 1983 and 1985 was gone, the bulk of it for architectural and design fees, the fund-raising film One November Day, and various studies by national fund-raising organizations. Although the Hoblitzelle Foundation's $100,000 challenge grant in 1984 had to be returned when construction was delayed, the foundation contributed $150,000 to the 1987–88 campaign, the largest individual donation made to The Sixth Floor project.[135]

The final push began on October 7, 1987, with former Dallas County judge David G. Fox, a Republican, and Dallas County Historical Foundation board member Jess Hay, a Democrat, as campaign co-chairs. Judge Lee Jackson and Mayor Annette Strauss served as honorary chairs, with board member Lillian Bradshaw as fund coordinator.[136] Reaching out to foundations, corporations, and the general public, the campaign collected $200,000 in just two weeks. Yet the pace of giving soon slowed considerably. After a year only about two-thirds of the $1.5 million goal had been raised; eventually a private promissory note was issued to open the exhibition on time.[137]

Lillian Bradshaw sought donations from corporations and organizations all over the United States but "didn't get a dime."[138] The planners recognized the irony: although The Sixth Floor's primary audience resided outside the Dallas city limits—in many cases, outside Texas—its funding depended entirely upon the local community.[139] Some local residents contributed without ever intending to visit the exhibition, satisfied, as Conover Hunt put it, in "knowing that the tourists had a place to go because all their houseguests . . . wanted to go to Dealey Plaza."[140] Fund-raisers for The Sixth Floor emphasized this theme time and again while touting the twenty-fifth anniversary as the optimum moment for Dallas to open and interpret the site. "The world is watching what we do here," read one of the solicitation letters. "Your help is needed now."[141]

One issue Bradshaw faced was that the exhibit's deeply serious and emotional subject matter forced her to break one of her cardinal rules by not combining "fun and sociability" in the fund-raising effort.[142] Instead a local agency produced subtle and tasteful campaign brochures. Morton's of Chicago, an upscale restaurant across Houston Street from the Depository, donated lunches for various low-key fund-raising events designed to explain The Sixth Floor project to potential donors.[143] One cocktail reception at Morton's yielded $7,000 in contributions. Attendees could examine the exhibit model, original newspapers, and FBI photographs.[144]

Prominent contributors to the creation of The Sixth Floor included the A. H. Belo Corporation, the Cecil and Ida Green Foundation, and the Eugene McDermott Foundation. A bronze plaque in the Visitors Center would eventually carry the names of fifty major benefactors, patrons, sponsors, donors, and friends.[145]

With funding for The Sixth Floor now in place and with the battles over DART and the elevator design behind her, Conover Hunt faced one final challenge before construction could begin on the Visitors Center. The Antiquities Code of Texas required that an archaeological dig be undertaken before any new building could be constructed on county property.[146] Hunt feared that "the Pompeii of Dallas" might be unearthed or at the very least an Indian burial ground or dinosaur bones. The area in question had been part of Dallas founder John Neely Bryan's original land grant and one of the first blocks to be settled. Archaeological concerns reportedly had negated the county's plans to construct an underground parking garage at the site.[147]

In December 1987 Dallas County authorized up to $75,000 for the dig conducted by the Archaeology Research Program at the Institute for the Study of Earth and Man at Southern Methodist University (SMU). The work ultimately cost the county approximately $50,000 (in part because the county provided its own excavation equipment and operators), paid out of the bond money allocated for the construction of the Visitors Center and elevator shaft.[148] With the exhibition's opening date rapidly approaching, Judge Jackson struck a deal with the state and archaeological team to expedite the process over a thirty-day period between January and February 1988.[149] The dig garnered local publicity as "the first major urban excavation in North Texas."[150]

During the construction of railroad spurs in the late nineteenth century, this area had been filled, preserving cultural deposits from 1850 through 1880. That was a significant period in which industrialization hit the area, turning the largely agrarian village into a prosperous city.[151] The team from SMU excavated a 3,500-square-foot area to a depth of six to nine feet, representing the surface of about 1850.[152]

The team's findings revealed an integrated neighborhood of affluent whites and freed African American laborers. The discovery of nineteenth-century settlers' tools and prehistoric Native American artifacts offered insights into living conditions and lifestyles during the period. Notably, archaeologists unearthed Dallas's earliest water wells, a trench marking the city's first property division and possibly John Neely Bryan's first cornfield, and remnants from the cellar of the five-story warehouse that had once stood on the site.[153]

Within days of the completion of the archaeological dig the Dallas County Commissioners Court voted 3–2 to award a $2.3 million contract to the Thomas J. Hayman Construction Company for The Sixth Floor's Visitor Center and elevator tower, $329,530 above the amount originally proposed. Commissioner John Wiley Price, who supported the contract, told the news media that Dallas County would recoup its investment over a ten-year period "before the foundation [received] a dime."[154]

Construction on the Visitors Center began on March 8, 1988, but was delayed for almost a month by a shipment of bricks that did not match those of the Depository as specified in the contract.[155] When the president of the St. Joe Brick Works in Slidell, Louisiana, who had come to Dallas to resolve the issue, suggested that the color was close enough, Conover Hunt exploded. "I want to make sure to get your name . . . and your phone number," she demanded, "so that when the *New York Times* asks me why the tower is the color of orange sherbet, I can explain to them that only you think it's the same color as the rest of the brick on the School Book Depository."[156] Within two days the material was returned to Louisiana.[157]

Bad weather during the summer of 1988 also delayed construction, as did a rare fall ice storm that hit Dallas before windows were installed in the Visitors Center, with a gaping hole on the north side of the Depository where the elevator sky bridge would connect. Only one week before previews of The Sixth Floor began, the opening on the sixth floor was covered only by a plastic sheet.[158]

FIG. 21

The Visitors Center and elevator shaft under construction in 1988.

INSTITUTIONAL ARCHIVES/THE SIXTH FLOOR MUSEUM AT DEALEY PLAZA

The Visitors Center's bulky security equipment, including a metal detector and x-ray machine, arrived several months earlier than anticipated and had to be stored at an off-site location. Despite these and more minor setbacks, the Visitors Center opened to the public in February 1989.[159]

The previous March, Lindalyn Adams had announced that the exhibition was not likely to open on the twenty-fifth anniversary in November, deeming the solemn date "inappropriate" for a celebratory unveiling.[160] Realistically, the planners recognized that the project could not be finished in time, though it was not until October that the foundation officially designated President's Day, February 20, 1989, as The Sixth Floor's opening day.[161]

Even as contractors and workers swarmed over the building site, controversy continued to dog the project. In late May 1988 Charles Daly, director of the John F. Kennedy Presidential Library in Boston, Massachusetts, and a former aide to the late President, declared The Sixth Floor to be "morbid or disgusting or both."[162] What prompted Daly's unexpected outburst remains a mystery, though it came shortly after the producers of The Sixth Floor's exhibit films made a cordial research visit to Boston. Library staff cooperated in every way, subsequently providing the exhibit team with photographs and other information.[163]

Although the Kennedy family declined to comment on Daly's statement, Senator Kennedy's senior aide, Melody Miller, said that Daly's remarks did not reflect the viewpoint of the family or the Kennedy Library.[164] An anonymous Kennedy family friend revealed to the *Patriot Ledger* in Quincy, Massachusetts, that the family was "dismayed" by the proposed Dallas exhibit. Senator Edward Kennedy told the Associated Press the following day that the Kennedy family would not try to block the exhibit's opening, although he was "disturbed" by the notion of a display inside the Depository.[165]

Charles Daly declined Lindalyn Adams's offer to fly him to Dallas to visit the project, indicating that he had already received The Sixth Floor's briefing material. He strongly felt that the exhibition would dwell unnecessarily on Kennedy's death in Dealey Plaza and not enough on 1960s American history.[166] Nancy Cheney later met Daly at a party held at Hickory Hill, the McLean, Virginia, home of Robert F. Kennedy's widow, Ethel. There the library director graciously promised not to say anything further about The Sixth Floor but stated that his personal opinion about the exhibit's inappropriateness would never change.[167]

In Dallas the response to the tempest was swift. The foundation publicly acknowledged that Senator Kennedy had received a courtesy briefing, though no involvement or support had ever been sought from the Kennedy family.[168] Both Dallas newspapers ran defensive editorials, one stating that Daly's comments reflected "a serious misunderstanding about the project's goals."[169] As a major exhibit contributor, the *Dallas Morning News* worried that Daly's statement might compromise the fund-raising effort.[170] Carl Henry, a volunteer researcher with the foundation, in a letter published by the *Morning News* asked Mr. Daly "to realize that life and history are composed of the unutterably beautiful and the hideously ugly."[171]

A second controversy arose in August 1988 over the proposed admission prices to The Sixth Floor exhibit. When the Dallas County Historical Foundation announced that adult admission would cost $4, with lower price points for children and group tours, naysayers thought the fees were too high compared to other historical museums, some of which did not charge admission at all. A county commissioner feared that the exhibit might "price [itself] out of business." These arguments proved futile, however, as the county readily approved the $4 admission charge in order to recoup its $2.3 million investment in the exhibition's Visitor Center and elevator tower.[172]

The elevator tower was three-fourths complete and the exhibition half-finished when Dallas marked the twenty-fifth anniversary of the Kennedy assassination on November 22, 1988. Greater media fanfare attended the event than Dallas had seen five years earlier at the twentieth observance. The Sixth Floor remained a key component of the news coverage, including a press preview tour of the unfinished space.[173]

With the aid of Tracy-Locke Public Relations (consultants retained through the exhibition's opening the following February) the foundation approached the anniversary with the positive message that The Sixth Floor was "simply a recognition that something important happened here that people still want[ed] to know more about" and that it would satisfy this public desire for interpretation with a tasteful and educational display.[174]

While the city's lingering guilt and shame remained persistent media themes, the exhibition planners developed a "philosophy that [they] were not going to apologize for Dallas." A quarter-century after the shooting, however, some journalists still held grudges against the city, as Hunt experienced firsthand. One out-of-state newspaper reporter interviewing Hunt about the project that fall casually remarked that "Dallas killed [Kennedy]."[175]

The way in which the assassination impacted individuals in Dallas served as the basis for a series of studies by Dr. James Pennebaker, then a social psychologist at SMU, undertaken in 1988 in cooperation with the Dallas County Historical Foundation.[176] Shortly after accepting a position at SMU in 1983, Pennebaker explored the legacy of the assassination in Dallas and found "no schools, streets, or buildings named after Kennedy"; he was rebuffed when attempting to gain access to the Depository's sixth floor.[177] Likewise, the "cold, white box" of Philip Johnson's memorial cenotaph suggested to him that the community wanted to keep its dark secret locked away. In Dealey Plaza, Pennebaker noted, was an "invisible sign . . . that said 'Nothing happened here. Go to South Fork where the TV show *Dallas* [was] shot.'"[178]

In early 1988 Pennebaker attended a meeting at SMU with Lindalyn Adams and Conover Hunt to discuss the impact that The Sixth Floor might have on the Dallas community. It was a fortuitous meeting: Pennebaker's early work as a social psychologist focused on how keeping a secret impacts a person's health and what results when an individual discloses it. Recognizing the assassination as the city's ultimate "secret," he eagerly agreed to investigate the psychological impact of President Kennedy's death.

Working with Hunt and the foundation, Pennebaker randomly harvested tourists in Dealey Plaza for a visit to the sixth floor, where he measured their heart rate and level of perspiration on the hand via a battery-powered apparatus connected to their fingers. During a five- to ten-minute visit, a monitor directed each individual to look out a single window on each side of the building before describing the experience and answering a series of questions. Many wept during the tour, while others expressed anger.[179] "The thing that struck me the most though was how looking out that window validated everybody's world view," said Pennebaker.[180] Viewing Dealey Plaza from the sniper's perch window in the southeast corner either confirmed visitors' beliefs in Lee Harvey Oswald as the lone gunman or convinced them that he must have had accomplices.

After this initial experiment, Pennebaker next conducted a random telephone survey in June and July 1988 with two hundred individuals in Dallas and fifty each in Fort Worth and Houston; Columbus, Ohio; and Memphis, Tennessee, site of the King assassination in 1968. Pennebaker selected Columbus because it approximated the size of Dallas, yet "nothing interesting or important ever happened there."[181] Pennebaker queried respondents in the communities about how often they thought about the Kennedy assassination and whether or not Dallas was to blame. Nearly 20 percent of those surveyed felt that Dallas bore responsibility; interestingly, Dallas natives blamed the city as much as residents in the other communities did. A vast majority of Dallasites also felt that outsiders continued to blame the city. Local residents over age thirty indicated having thoughts about the Kennedy assassination more than sixteen times during the previous year, double the assassination-related thoughts of all others surveyed. All who participated were given the option of calling an answering service to leave personal comments about the assassination, and a number did so.[182] Most spoke of "the humiliation, the embarrassment, [and] the shame" that they felt in the aftermath, and one said: "I drive into downtown Dallas every day and I go by the School Book Depository, and I feel sick every day."[183] Among Dallas residents, 45 percent of the 200 surveyed disapproved of The Sixth Floor and indicated that they would not visit the exhibition.[184]

Pennebaker also studied archival records, finding that deaths from heart disease, murder, and suicide temporarily increased in Dallas in the period after the assassination. A comparative study of Memphis yielded similar results in the aftermath of the King shooting. This comparison drew the most public attention near the time of the twenty-fifth anniversary of the assassination. The *Dallas Morning News* carried the story with the headline "JFK's Death Still Haunts Dallasites."[185] Sociologist Paul Geisel of the University of Texas at Arlington, however, discounted Pennebaker's findings as "ludicrous and . . . hysterical," arguing that suicide rates were so low in the early 1960s "that two or three suicides would completely skew the whole thing."[186]

The Pennebaker study mirrored the local media's emphasis on community reflection during the fall of 1988. Both Dallas newspapers printed special supplements on the assassination anniversary, while the *Morning News* ran more than ten related stories between November 20 and 23 bearing headlines such as "Shadows: Dallas' Dark Journey," "Dallas on Trial: Accusations and Self-Doubts Torment the City," and "JFK Assassination Prompted Soul-Searching in City."[187]

Articles chronicled the extremists who blackened the city's national reputation before President Kennedy's arrival, recounted the anger directed at the "city of hate" in the aftermath, and considered the city's lengthy effort to redeem itself amid racial strife and other issues. Emerging from these oft-told stories around the twenty-fifth anniversary, however, was an overall sense of optimism and recovery. "Dallas survived all that, and even prospered," wrote Ed Timms of the *Dallas Morning News.* "Twenty-five years after the assassination, it is clear that the trauma of Kennedy's death perhaps altered the course of community progress, but could not stop the momentum."[188] Columnist Henry Tatum concurred that "Dallas managed to change its image from the 'City of Hate' to the 'City That Works.'"[189] The Sixth Floor exhibit also was often cited as a concrete example showing that, at long last, Dallas was coming to terms with the assassination. The *Herald* reported, for instance, that the attitudes of prominent Dallasites who initially opposed the exhibition were changing as the project neared completion.[190] Even Tom Landry, legendary coach of the Dallas Cowboys, now lent his support, after publicly criticizing the exhibit in past years.[191]

Not all Dallas journalists agreed with the prominent coverage given to the Kennedy assassination anniversary. One week earlier William Murchison, conservative columnist of the *Morning News,* wrote that Dallas needed to break itself of its awful habit of "wallow[ing] in the past" every November. He considered the upcoming exhibition, nine television documentaries, and three dozen new books the unhealthy symptoms of a morbid public obsession.[192] Ironically, by urging Dallasites to overcome their emotional attachment to the assassination, Murchison agreed with the majority of his colleagues that the twenty-fifth anniversary was the city's designated moment to come to terms with the President's death. Still, the *New York Times* pondered whether "the exhibit and the passage of time could exorcise the last remaining demons from 1963." The results of a national poll taken that November were hopeful. Only 11 percent of respondents cited the Kennedy assassination as their first or second association with Dallas, down from 23 percent at the twentieth anniversary.[193]

Acknowledging the historical significance of the tragedy at this juncture did little to silence the powerful memories of those old enough to recall the events firsthand. Few anniversary articles failed to include some personal perspective. One *Orlando Sentinel* reporter admitted that while Lindalyn Adams talked excitedly about plans for the exhibition during a tour of the sixth floor, his "thoughts were elsewhere" as he touched the wooden window frame in the sniper's perch and thought back to where he was in 1963.[194] Blackie Sherrod, a veteran sportswriter at the *Dallas Morning News*, best captured the feelings of those in Dallas in a reflective essay published on November 20, 1988:

> To Dallas old-timers, the tragedy has become like a birthmark on your child's face. The blemish is there but you have become accustomed to it so that it is no longer a constant heartache. Not until a stranger remarks about it, that is, not until you drive past the old School Book Depository and see tourists staring at the sixth-floor window and unstrapping their Kodaks. And you still feel, however faintly, that stir of resentment and you realize again that the day and its shadow will never be forever erased from memory.[195]

Approximately three thousand individuals gathered in Dealey Plaza to mark the last anniversary of the Kennedy assassination before the opening of The Sixth Floor exhibit. With no official ceremony, a crowd of strangers joined hands along Elm Street at 12:30 P.M., with "their eyes turned toward the same thing: a window on the sixth floor" of the Depository.[196] The *Dallas Morning News* noted that, although many local residents came to the plaza, such faraway places as China, India, and Australia were also represented. For those involved in the exhibition, the anniversary represented an opportunity to document not only the observance but also the attitudes of those involved. Allen and Cynthia Mondell, the documentarians contracted for The Sixth Floor's films, for example, took a video camera to the plaza to capture memories of President Kennedy from individuals around the world for use in the exhibition's film on the Kennedy legacy. Lindalyn Adams hosted a press conference that day to showcase plans for the exhibit.[197]

Four days earlier the Dallas County Historical Commission had presented those involved with The Sixth Floor with a series of well-deserved awards. Lindalyn Adams received the Texas Award for Historic Preservation, Conover Hunt the Professional Award for Historic Preservation, and the Dallas County Commissioners Court a certificate of commendation for helping fund the project.[198] This recognition and the generally positive press coverage that followed during the twenty-fifth anniversary further inspired those working on the exhibit in preparation for its opening on February 20, 1989, a mere three months away. They still had much to do.

PLATE 1

Enthusiastic crowds greet President Kennedy at Dallas Love Field on November 22, 1963.

PLATE 2

The assassination of President Kennedy in Dealey Plaza as captured in frame 230 of the horrifying home movie of Dallas dress manufacturer Abraham Zapruder.

Zapruder Film © 1967 (Renewed 1995) The Sixth Floor Museum at Dealey Plaza

IN PRAYERFUL MEMORY OF
OUR BELOVED PRESIDENT
JOHN FITZGERALD KENNEDY

MEN OF ST BERNARD'S CHURCH

PLATE 3
Mourners transform Dealey Plaza into a shrine in the aftermath of the assassination.

PLATE 4

Dealey Plaza as it appeared in the decade following the Kennedy assassination. The Hertz billboard remained atop the building until May 1979.

George Reid Collection/The Sixth Floor Museum at Dealey Plaza

PLATE 5

The exhibit planners at work in May 1988. *From left to right:* architect James Hendricks, exhibit designer Bob Staples (obscured), Conover Hunt, exhibit designer Barbara Charles, and restoration architect Eugene George.

PLATE 6

Documentary filmmakers Allen and Cynthia Mondell share ideas at a February 1988 meeting.

PLATE 7

A close-up view inside the model of The Sixth Floor exhibit.

PLATE 8
Architect James Hendricks's sketch of the exterior elevator shaft and Visitors Center.
INSTITUTIONAL ARCHIVES/THE SIXTH FLOOR MUSEUM AT DEALEY PLAZA

Chapter 5
A SITE OF HISTORY

The bulk of the work for The Sixth Floor occurred in its final eighteen months of development. The exhibit that opened on President's Day 1989, ultimately shaped by some twenty-seven individuals, was similar and yet strikingly different from the conceptual designs by Staples and Charles in 1983. Remarkably, while Conover Hunt, serving as chief curator and project director, faced outside forces and unrelenting media scrutiny from mid-1987 to early 1989, she remained committed to researching exhibit content, meeting with consultants, writing text, selecting photographs and artifacts, finalizing design issues with Staples and Charles, considering preservation issues with Eugene George, and working with both the documentarians and producers of the audio tour of the exhibit. Hunt later admitted that as she and her team went into "the home stretch," they were "exhausted . . . and also [under] incredible pressure."[1]

Gary Mack, one of Hunt's many research consultants and later The Sixth Floor Museum curator, reflected that Hunt "had the exact vision that was necessary" at the time.[2] Martin Jurow, the executive producer of the exhibit's films, agreed, describing Hunt as "very smart, shrewd, [and] sagacious with a power and kind of an ego which I think she had to have" to get a project like The Sixth Floor completed.[3]

When the team reassembled in 1987, Hunt divided responsibility for content development between her office in Dallas and the Washington, D.C., offices of Staples and Charles. Barbara Charles, in particular, focused on the content, which was unusual for the principal in a design firm but efficient given her close proximity to research material at the National Archives and the Library of Congress.[4] Charles read many assassination-related books during the conceptual design phase; when she returned to the project in 1987, she looked for the broad themes in the larger story rather than the minutiae of the event.[5] Other researchers working on the project in the D.C. office included Abigail Porter, too young to remember the assassination, and Charles A. Briggs, the recently retired executive director of the Central Intelligence Agency, who remembered November 22, 1963, all too well.

Briggs left the agency in 1986 and was working on a genealogy project when he was approached to do research for the upcoming Depository exhibition in Dallas. He jumped at the opportunity and worked on The Sixth Floor for one year.[6] Having joined the agency in 1952, Briggs was unusually well qualified for the position he was offered on the research team. Although Barbara Charles had initially expressed reservations about employing a former CIA official, Hunt remained nonplussed, figuring that the agency wanted to keep tabs on the exhibit.[7]

Although aware of the suspicion that accompanied his joining the research team and personally concerned about how the agency would be portrayed, Briggs quickly developed a close and cordial working relationship with the exhibition designers. His past association with the spy agency was occasionally the subject of office humor.[8] Exhibit interpreters, for example, jokingly threatened to develop the "CIA conspiracy theory totally separate from the FBI conspiracy theory."[9]

Briggs always downplayed his contribution to the project, saying that he primarily tracked down 1963 magazines and reviewed panel text. He only felt compelled to speak up when he noticed outrageous or ridiculous material, such as a period cartoon that showed a CIA agent with a standard-issue assassination kit.[10] In truth, Briggs and researcher Abigail Porter developed the section of the exhibit on the early 1960s, exploring the history and culture of the period and gathering artifacts reflecting the era's popular books, films, television programs, and stage productions. Designer Bob Staples, a collector of ephemera, helped the pair track down 1960s artifacts.[11]

While the exhibition research team in Washington, D.C., placed the assassination in a national and global context, the local story came together in Dallas. Conover Hunt, who had researched the Kennedy assassination over a period of years, sought other experts from the Dallas historical and academic communities. Historian Jackie McElhaney, who saw the Kennedy motorcade, worked on photographic research and content, as did a panel of scholars from Southern Methodist University, including Dr. James Pennebaker. Sociologist Paul Geisel from the University of Texas at Arlington also consulted with Hunt and conducted an evaluation of the exhibition's first visitors.[12]

The Dallas County Historical Foundation hired Adah Leah Wolf as part-time assistant project director in March 1987, and she became the foundation's first salaried employee shortly thereafter. Paid and volunteer assassination researchers included G. Robert Blakey, former chief counsel and staff director of the House

Select Committee on Assassinations; volunteers Jim Moore, Farris Rookstool, and Carl Henry; and veteran assassination researcher Mary Ferrell.[13] Hunt utilized the knowledge and skills of these individuals to counterbalance the more outspoken conspiracy theorists on the team. With films and photographs as key elements of the assassination story, Hunt brought in consultants such as Gary Mack and Robert Groden, who had access to the highest-quality visuals.[14]

Mack, a researcher since 1975 known for his familiarity with visual media associated with the assassination, worked at local television station KXAS-TV when Hunt contacted him in the summer of 1987. He volunteered to assist and introduced Hunt to others in the field, who were for the most part "quite eager to help," although a few expressed reservations about becoming involved in any official project with perceived governmental ties.[15] These researchers responded to questions primarily by telephone, though Hunt brought them all together for a dinner party in which the consultants "ate little, drank a lot and behaved beautifully."[16]

Conspiracy theories had always been a part of the Kennedy assassination story. Even before leaving Parkland Memorial Hospital to take the oath of office, the new President, Lyndon Johnson, voiced his concerns about a larger plot. "Had a great mind for history, Lyndon Johnson did," recalled assistant White House press secretary Malcolm Kilduff. "You can see going through his mind . . . [John Wilkes] Booth . . . and the Mary Surratt conspiracy."[17] With the first published suggestion of an assassination conspiracy emerging in December 1963, it was inevitable that the death of President Kennedy would remain an intriguing and mysterious subject of interest for many in the years that followed. Although most were initially satisfied by the findings of the Warren Commission investigation, which concluded that Oswald acted alone, a barrage of conspiracy literature throughout the 1960s and 1970s—fueled in part by frustration and skepticism over the Watergate scandal, Vietnam War, and lingering doubt in the "lone gunman" deaths of Martin Luther King, Jr., and Robert Kennedy—convinced a majority of Americans that more than one individual was involved in the President's murder in 1963. Collectively, the assassination research community, many members of which invested their lives and personal fortunes in their efforts, uncovered and publicized a great deal of information and raised legitimate questions that continue to be debated today.[18] Author John McAdams concluded that the collective Kennedy assassination conspiracy theory—by now a subject of almost "mystical significance"—is "[t]he greatest and grandest of all conspiracy theories."[19]

Conover Hunt understood that she was involving individuals in a historical exhibition that had a "high level of passion" for the subject matter. She was confident that the group ultimately understood the need for objectivity and that the goal of the exhibit was "history, rather than commenting on the validity of their work or opinions."[20] Nevertheless, some conspiracy researchers, including Gary Mack, were disappointed that the finished product did not delve more deeply into the inconsistencies and unanswered questions in the case. "I don't know what we were expecting," remembered Mack, although he and the other consultants were informed at the outset that the exhibit "would not be devoted to personal theories."[21]

In certain instances, disagreements arose over the use of particular words. Consultants argued, for example, about identifying the controversial Warren Commission Exhibit 399 as the "magic bullet" or "pristine bullet," as it is popularly called. "I thought labeling it . . . as we did in the films and on the wall was somewhat misleading," remembered Jim Moore in 2011. "[Volunteer] Carl Henry and I . . . fought over that—just words obviously—but we were from differing points of view there."[22]

For Hunt, the research community was particularly helpful in determining the exhibit's visuals. Robert Groden, an outspoken conspiracy theorist, possessed enhanced versions of some of the eight-millimeter home movies of the motorcade and shooting, including the Abraham Zapruder film, which he provided to the foundation for a fee. Compiling visual imagery for The Sixth Floor provided a unique challenge: unlike traditional exhibitions where designers sought original negatives, investigators in the case of the Kennedy assassination had spoiled some evidence, forcing researchers to rely on early prints and copies provided by owners vocal in their personal beliefs and emotionally tied to the subject matter.[23]

Nevertheless, by consulting with individuals who had devoted such time and energy to exploring all aspects of the assassination, Hunt successfully navigated an interpretive minefield of content issues given the convoluted, intense, and controversial nature of the subject. She said, "It was problematic to [develop] the exhibit when the actual primary research material contradicts itself to the extent that it does—the Warren Commission exhibits and report in particular." It was essential, therefore, to bring "both sides to the table—the conspiracy theorists and the government authorities who had done the investigations."[24]

Hunt examined about 2,500 photographs before choosing approximately 400 for the exhibition. Fortunately for the budget-conscious project, most of the photographers and agencies waived their usual licensing fees—with one significant exception. *Life* magazine declined to deviate from its standard rates, so very few of its images were included in the exhibit. By contrast, both Dallas newspapers provided free access to their substantial photographic archives.[25] On one occasion the editor of the *Dallas Times Herald* handed Hunt a manila envelope "with 35mm strip negatives coming out like spaghetti." The paper donated its collection of original negatives from the Kennedy assassination weekend and the 1964 Jack Ruby trial. These images marked the beginning of The Sixth Floor Museum's photographic archives.[26]

Hunt's pursuit of visual media focused on the work of Dallas photographers. Among the images she opted to include was one by Squire Haskins photographer Mel McIntire that showed the presidential limousine seconds after the assassination. The Depository building provided the backdrop—with the minute of the shooting, 12:30 P.M., clearly visible on the Hertz sign. Such rarely published photographs clearly demonstrated the significant role that the city's journalists and photographers played in covering this historic event.[27]

The board of the Dallas County Historical Foundation placed few restrictions on Hunt during the content development phase of exhibit design, though it prohibited violent or macabre material of any kind. Graphic imagery of the President's body was not considered, and the board even rejected artistic renderings of his wounds that were created for the House Select Committee on Assassinations investigation. Additionally, they wanted to downplay artifacts and imagery associated with the two alleged perpetrators of violence, Lee Harvey Oswald and Jack Ruby. Conover Hunt recalled several board discussions centered on violence as seen on television, particularly "in an urban center like Dallas."[28]

The chair that Oswald occupied at the Texas Theatre in Oak Cliff at the time of his arrest, once offered to the foundation for display, was rejected for this reason.[29] Apart from its direct connection to the accused assassin, the red chair had been spray-painted black so that it would stand out in its theater row. Hunt and her team also turned down offers to display "a sofa that Jack Ruby sat on" and infant clothing allegedly worn by Oswald's daughters.[30] Nor was a Mannlicher-Carcano rifle similar to the one found on the sixth floor deemed appropriate for the exhibition. The Dallas County Historical Foundation had the rifle once displayed in John Sissom's John F. Kennedy Museum, but Hunt felt that, with such a limited display of artifacts, the presence of any weapon on the sixth floor would stand out in a negative way. She was satisfied with the inclusion of the infamous backyard photograph that showed Oswald holding the Carcano rifle.[31]

The only original artifact requested from the National Archives was the 1964 model of Dealey Plaza built by the FBI and used by both the Warren Commission and the House Select Committee on Assassinations. In a letter to archivist Don Wilson in early 1988, Lindalyn Adams pointed out the model's educational value for an anticipated 500,000 visitors to the site.[32] At first the archives declined, because of excessive exhibit light levels; but some years later they loaned the model, which remains a significant part of the exhibition as of 2013.[33]

The most graphic portions of the Abraham Zapruder film of the assassination were excluded from the audiovisual component of the exhibit, much to the frustration of some of the consultants.[34] Hunt told Gary Mack, who argued that the film should be included in its entirety, that the home movie was too graphic and that the foundation could not conscionably "subject parents and their children to that violence."[35] In addition to its position as one of the most significant home movies in history, the Zapruder film remains the Rosetta Stone of the tragedy for many assassination researchers. As the only visual record of the entire shooting, its contents continue to be debated by researchers.[36] Most notably, some conspiracy theorists feel that the film shows President Kennedy reacting to a shot fired from the front—the grassy knoll area—rather than from the sixth floor of the Depository. Many, however, take an opposing viewpoint, arguing that it instead proves a shot from the rear. By excluding the most significant and graphic section of the film showing the impact of a shot to the President's head—which explodes in a cloud of blood and brain matter—the exhibit team opened itself up to accusations that it was suppressing or withholding important assassination evidence. It was ultimately this decision that "brought us the most criticism," Hunt later observed.[37] As curator of The Sixth Floor Museum at Dealey Plaza, Gary Mack now agrees with the founding board's decision, admitting that "there's no need to see the man die to understand that he did die."[38] The entire Abraham Zapruder film was not shown at The Sixth Floor Museum until 2007, when it was included—prefaced by a discretionary message and accessible only by push button in an enclosed alcove—as part of a special exhibition on home-movie images of President Kennedy.

Only a small number of artifacts were selected for The Sixth Floor exhibit. In 1994 Hunt attributed this situation primarily to the historic building's inadequate environmental controls, yet she acknowledged that careful consideration was given to the types of artifacts put on display.[39] The larger an artifact's scale within the relatively tight space of the exhibit, the more likely it would be rejected. Designer Barbara Charles considered each potential artifact's "intellectual worth" in relation to its size and found the Texas Theatre chair, for example, too large for the small section devoted to the arrest of Lee Harvey Oswald. Hunt and exhibit designers also avoided original material, particularly artifacts associated with the alleged assassin that might be misconstrued as glorifying or enshrining Oswald. No one wanted The Sixth Floor to invite comparisons to Ripley's Believe It or Not or other sensational attractions.[40]

The Sixth Floor opened with the bulk of its artifacts in the introductory section on the early 1960s, including period books, publicity photographs from television shows, and lobby cards from popular films and theatrical productions. Artifacts directly connected to the assassination were primarily limited to newspapers and magazines and a few pieces of ephemera, such as an invitation to the Trade Mart luncheon in Dallas and a United Press International bulletin with word of the assassination. An original Associated Press teletype machine, which Staples and Charles initially opposed because of its bulk, was also included. Hunt argued persuasively that the teletype machine represented how the media disseminated the breaking news in the immediate aftermath of the assassination. The planning team, however, considered the sixth floor of the Texas School Book Depository to be the exhibition's most significant historical feature and "wanted to use the architecture as the primary artifact."[41] The subtle design of Staples and Charles, including their use of natural light from the windows overlooking Dealey Plaza, greatly enhanced the experience.[42]

Though the Dallas County Historical Foundation remained active, board member Glenn Linden recalled that its members did not take a hands-on role in exhibition development.[43] Some board members, however, made specific contributions to The Sixth Floor. Ex-officio member Thomas H. Smith, for example, insisted on a section that acknowledged the country's previous three presidential assassinations.[44] Nancy Cheney, also an active board member, played a key role in the exhibition's bookstore, initially managed by Eastern National Park and Monument. Cheney and fellow board member Lillian Bradshaw reviewed all potential books to ensure their appropriateness. After the exhibition's first year in operation, Cheney recommended that the foundation assume management of the bookstore, which it soon did. During the reorganization, Cheney helped train the staff and develop the inventory.[45]

One of the most important challenges before the foundation board in considering the exhibition's final layout was the portrayal of the life and legacy of President John F. Kennedy. Though early concepts briefly touched on the Kennedy presidency, the exhibit proposed in 1983, Conover Hunt recalled, "was very scientific, had very little humanity, and did not deal with John Kennedy's life at all." The remarks by Charles Daly on the preeminent role of the John F. Kennedy Presidential Library in chronicling the life and achievements of the thirty-fifth President enhanced discussions of this sensitive issue. The board recognized that Dallas's "sole claim of authority was in the matter of [Kennedy's] death" yet also understood that those who made pilgrimages to Dealey Plaza did so because of President Kennedy's life and what he represented to them. For many visitors, the plaza served as a physical link to the unfulfilled promise of JFK, and Hunt recognized that the exhibition required a sense of closure to reflect the site's transformation from a site of international tragedy to a site of commemoration. She compared Dealey Plaza to the Alamo and Pearl Harbor, both sites of death and devastation ultimately remolded into symbolic sites of sacrifice and patriotism. Despite this justification, the board debated an acknowledgment of President Kennedy's life and legacy for years before electing to address these issues.[46]

The 1983 conceptual design included the Depository's relocated lunch-room at the conclusion of the exhibit experience, but by 1987 its position on the sixth floor was in question. The lunchroom mannequin representing Lee Harvey Oswald came under early criticism by the *New York Times*. During the community briefing tour in the summer of 1983, the small wax figure of Oswald in the model of the exhibit melted in the heat—interpreted by the planning team as an omen that it should be nixed. Four years later the planning team eliminated the lunchroom from the exhibit layout altogether.[47] Although Hunt's early outline had justified its inclusion to "reinforce . . . the Oswald connection with the assas-sination," in the final stage of development the planners symbolically shifted their focus from the alleged assassin back to the late President.[48]

In place of the lunchroom, a theater was added in that location for a documentary on the Kennedy legacy. As Conover Hunt explained, with the film and surrounding text panels on Kennedy memorials and tributes around the world, the exhibition team had to find a way to end the traumatic story of the death of a U.S. President on a note of optimism.[49] This *Legacy* video proved to be the filmmakers' greatest challenge. Eventually two panels were also added near the beginning of the exhibit to provide brief information on President Kennedy's life and family. Despite the emphasis on Kennedy in the exhibit's closing seg-ments, the geography of the corner stairwell and rifle location in the floor's northwest corner, which was reconstructed and preserved behind glass, dic-tated its conclusion.[50]

A further departure from the initial approach occurred during develop-ment of the exhibition text when Hunt injected a much needed element of humanity. The highly scientific findings of the House Select Committee on Assassinations heavily influenced previous drafts, though by 1987 and 1988 Hunt elected to emphasize personal stories and the assassination's place in American social history.[51]

The designers configured the exhibition's text panels as a series of large newspaper pages with headlines and subheadings.[52] Utilizing the floor's wooden columns proportionally arranged at fourteen-foot intervals, Staples and Charles created "a newspaper-type grid similar to the column inch."[53] After determin-ing a particular panel's size—based upon the available space between the col-umns—the team used a computer grid to lay out the panel's text, captions, and photographs to resemble newspaper composition.[54] Washington, D.C., graphic designer Kevin Osborne developed this unique system and designed the subtle contemporary logo of The Sixth Floor. The font chosen for the panels resembled that of 1960s newspapers.[55] The result was a "seamless comfort zone in which to move [because] people are accustomed to reading newspapers."[56] Hunt later attributed this design to museum-goers' patience in reading interpretive text, even when lengthy.[57]

While the notion of suspending the exhibit panels between the Depository's wooden columns dated back to the project's earliest concepts, Bob Staples eventually proposed that the individual panels float above the ground rather than extend all the way to the floor, allowing natural light to drift in from the bank of windows on the south side of the floor overlooking Dealey Plaza. The idea helped address the floor's most difficult lighting problem—finding a subtle way to give visitors a hint that they are approaching the windows overlooking the assassination site. From the beginning the designers wanted to maintain the look and feel of a warehouse. They believed that visitors should always have a sense of place as they toured the sixth floor. Staples opted to "leave the funky paint and the bricks exposed . . . [to] set the tone of the coloration of the place."[58] The building's original freight elevator, permanently located on the sixth floor after the remainder of the shaft had been removed, loomed in partial darkness at the exhibition's entrance—representing the 1963 mode of transportation to the floor when it was an active warehouse and immediately establishing the eerie ambiance of the space. In the exhibit itself, the designers used color sparingly, opting for "a black and white journalistic approach" in the narrative before, during, and immediately after the shooting in Dealey Plaza.[59] In certain cases, such as the Abraham Zapruder film, frames were initially presented in black-and-white—when representing the actual assassination—and seen in full color later in the exhibit after the narrative shifted to the government investigations.

"So Robust and Thorough"

The Sixth Floor's final layout reflected years of effort, discussions, community introspection, and compromise. Although thematically consistent with concepts that planners discussed in the early 1980s, the exhibit content and arrangement evolved rapidly during the last year and a half of development. A number of risks were taken with the exhibit's design, making Barbara Charles nervous about the outcome until she toured the space during installation, approximately one month before opening day.[60]

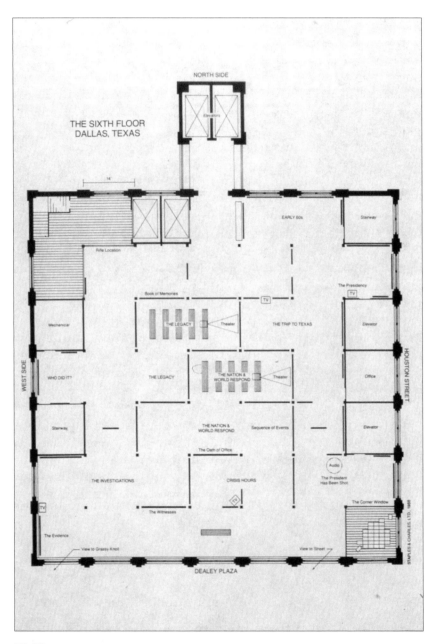

FIG. 22

The Sixth Floor Exhibit, as opened in 1989.

Visitors arrived at the sixth floor via the exterior elevator tower in the center of the north wall of the Depository. An oversized Dallas Police Department photograph of the sixth floor oriented visitors to the crime scene and helped create the historical mood surrounding the assassination.[61] "The Early Sixties," an area larger and more detailed than in previous layouts, introduced the decade with sections on the 1960 presidential election, a biography of John F. Kennedy and his family, the uniqueness of the Kennedy White House, the President's programs, and the major foreign and domestic political issues of the day.[62] Hunt believed that the grief and catharsis associated with the assassination needed "to be understood in terms of the times."[63] For individuals without firsthand knowledge of the assassination, the unique character of John F. Kennedy had to be introduced at the start of the exhibition for younger visitors to invest themselves in the journey and appreciate both the importance of his life and the magnitude of his death.

The President's 1963 trip to Texas was next introduced with background on the atmosphere in Dallas, the political reasons for the visit, and the enthusiastic welcome that the Kennedys received at Love Field on November 22, 1963. Consistent with previous layouts, visitors made their way along a corridor on the east side of the floor, experiencing the motorcade through a series of large black-and-white photographs. At the moment of the assassination, the color of the walls briefly changed from white to dark gray. At this point two large photographs strategically blocked the visitor's view of the sniper's perch and window. A small series of black-and-white frames from the Zapruder film—mirrored on the opposite wall by amateur photographs and frames from home movies taken across Elm Street from Zapruder—evoked a strip of eight-millimeter film and gave the impression of looking at the assassination through the viewfinder of a camera. These views, combined with light from the Depository windows seeping under the dark gray panels and an early radio announcement gravely detailing the shooting, were designed to produce an intense visitor experience and foreshadow the sniper's perch.[64]

Having thus far walked the length of the floor along a very deliberate path, visitors arrived at the reconstructed sniper's perch, protected behind glass, in the southeast corner of the sixth floor—the exhibit's primary physical link to the Kennedy assassination. While visitors could not step up to the famous corner window and see the alleged assassin's viewpoint, the entire bank of windows on the north side remained exposed, with no interpretation, allowing visitors to contemplate Dealey Plaza on their own from a variety of viewpoints and remain in sight of the distinctive sixth floor windows throughout the remainder of the tour. Augmented somewhat from the 1983 design, the exhibit provided a clear

FIG. 23

Looking toward the "Assassination" section of The Sixth Floor exhibit as visitors approach the re-created sniper's perch in the southeast corner.

INSTITUTIONAL ARCHIVES/THE SIXTH FLOOR MUSEUM AT DEALEY PLAZA

and accessible perimeter around the sixth floor for the casual visitor most interested in seeing only the reconstructed sniper's perch, with a large central area available for those interested in exploring the aftermath of the assassination, Lee Harvey Oswald and his shooting, the Kennedy funeral and global response to the assassination, and the establishment of the Warren Commission.[65]

Regardless of whether the visitors were "readers" who examined every label or "runners" who moved quickly through the exhibit, once confronted by the sniper's perch—and the point of the assassination—they had to decide where to go next. At the moment of the shooting in Dealey Plaza, exhibit designers confronted visitors with multiple paths, conflicting information, and no clear direction, deliberately mirroring the confusion immediately following the shooting.[66] Unfortunately, this subtle and creative utilization of the space was almost entirely lost upon visitors, who found this particular juncture frustrating.[67]

From the sniper's perch, visitors could follow three possible routes. They could explore a central area that detailed the shooting of Dallas police officer J. D. Tippit, the arrest of Lee Harvey Oswald, and the shooting of Oswald by Jack Ruby—the only exhibition area prominently featuring Kennedy's alleged assassin. Alternatively they could proceed immediately to eyewitness accounts from Dealey Plaza and the assassination investigations, where they were confronted with forensic, ballistic, photographic, and acoustic evidence, all of which led to the conclusion that Oswald shot President Kennedy, reached by both the Warren Commission and the House Select Committee. The final path from the sniper's perch took visitors along a detailed timeline of the assassination weekend from Friday to Monday—one half detailing the Dallas experience, the other half examining events in Washington, D.C., and elsewhere. A panel near the timeline featured the swearing-in ceremony of President Lyndon B. Johnson aboard Air Force One. The floor's first seated theater nearby showed an eleven-minute black-and-white video of memorial services and tributes to the late President from around the world and Kennedy's funeral on Monday, November 25. These three paths overlapped, and visitors were left on their own to explore all three in any order. This ability to construct their narrative journey through The Sixth Floor also allowed individuals who did not want to see or hear about Lee Harvey Oswald to bypass most references to him.[68]

All three paths ended on the west side of the sixth floor, where a fixed path then guided visitors through the remainder of the exhibit. Moving away from the windows overlooking Dealey Plaza, visitors encountered a freestanding panel labeled "Who Did It?" It carefully acknowledged lingering questions about the assassination and the popular belief that a conspiracy took place. Having established that Oswald was the only individual directly connected with the Kennedy assassination through evidence, a section labeled "Conspiracy?" briefly summarized several major theories. Five years after opening The Sixth Floor, Conover Hunt told staff that this "relatively subdued section" was deliberately designed for later expansion: in the late 1980s no historian had yet undertaken a scholarly examination of assassination conspiracy theories.[69] Adjacent to the conspiracy area was a small panel acknowledging the assassinations of Presidents Abraham Lincoln, James A. Garfield, and William McKinley.

A "Legacy" area, instead of re-creating the Depository's second-floor lunchroom, concluded the visitor's journey with an examination of President Kennedy's accomplishments while in office and a summary of the major issues tackled by the Kennedy administration in the 1960s, including space exploration, the Peace Corps, the Vietnam War, and the civil rights movement. Tributes and memorials to the late President were also represented, including the John F. Kennedy Presidential Library and Museum in Massachusetts. Articulating the Kennedy legacy in a small space proved difficult: though the President exuded confidence and style, public doubt and speculation about his death, the shadow of Vietnam, and other issues proved problematic.[70] Conover Hunt directly linked the assassination and its impact to the challenge of embracing the Kennedy legacy in her introduction to this area:

> The assassination of John F. Kennedy had a profound effect on millions of people at home and abroad. Historians have found it difficult to assess Kennedy's Presidency because it was cut short. Some of them assert that he accomplished little; others believe that he will ultimately rank among America's most significant leaders. Most concur that he deserves credit for "what might have been."[71]

At the conclusion of the exhibition, visitors were encouraged to register their thoughts and memories on the pages of one of the Memory Books provided for this purpose. According to label copy accompanying the books, visitor responses would "assist future historians to interpret the meaning of this part of history to our nation and to the world."[72] Barbara Charles, who saw similar books at a history exhibition in Munich, specifically requested unlined paper for The Sixth Floor to encourage thoughts and reflections rather than names and addresses. The Memory Books were an instant hit: The Sixth Floor ran out of paper during the exhibit's first preview. By 2012 well over half a million pages had been collected, either onsite or via the online Memory Book, available since 2003 on The Sixth Floor Museum's website.[73]

Conover Hunt incorporated her thoughts for each section of the exhibition in a twenty-eight-page outline composed prior to the elimination of the second-floor lunchroom. She demonstrated a keen awareness of the exhibit's diverse audience and justified the structure and path of the exhibit at every turn. She also recognized the space limitations imposed by the architecture of the sixth floor and the additional problems in presenting such a broad and convoluted story.[74] The computer grid used in layout assisted her in streamlining the exhibition narrative and "influenced the text considerably." Strictly following the "newspaper" format, Hunt limited the text of each of the main didactic panels to thirty-one lines or less, with "smaller substatements" fixed at seven lines or less. All captions were restricted to two lines of text.[75]

Twenty years after the opening of the exhibit, Nicola Longford, executive director of The Sixth Floor Museum at Dealey Plaza, called Hunt's work "so robust and thorough that it has remained untouchable." Curator Gary Mack remarked, "We can sit here twenty years later and argue about minor details about the exhibit itself, but the fact that it's essentially not outdated says everything."[76] With the exception of a few minor updates, the original text compiled and largely written by Hunt between 1987 and 1988 remains on view to museum visitors as of 2013. Remarkably, despite the density of text and the overlap of information between the exhibit panels and the six video presentations, many visitors spend a great deal of their visit reading interpretive label copy. In the spring of 1989 an employee of the Smithsonian Institution stopped Hunt during an American Association of Museums annual meeting and exclaimed: "There's a hundred pages of text [on the sixth floor], and that's not allowed! [But] I was there, and every person read every word. It works."[77]

"Today We Stand Whole Again"

One of the last projects to fall into place during the final phase of development of The Sixth Floor between 1987 and 1988 was the exhibition's six video presentations. In addition to the partially enclosed theaters for longer subjects on the Kennedy legacy and the global response to the assassination, four standing kiosks scattered throughout the space provided six-minute videos covering the Kennedy presidency, the November 1963 trip to Texas, the aftermath of the assassination through the shooting of Lee Harvey Oswald, and an overview of the government investigations. The videos repeated about one-third of the information contained in the exhibit's text panels in an effort to connect with The Sixth Floor's diverse audience of "readers" and "runners" and their different methods of learning. The kiosk screens were also a reminder of the growing importance of television in the early 1960s, especially during the weekend of the Kennedy assassination.[78]

Although Staples and Charles intended personally to supervise production of the exhibit videos, their ongoing work on the exhibition *Imperial Life in the Qing Dynasty* for the Empress Place in Singapore forced Conover Hunt to look elsewhere for filmmakers.[79] Hunt and the designers critiqued submissions from at least ten documentarians, covering subjects from butterflies to real estate development. A little over one year before the opening of The Sixth Floor, Allen and Cynthia Mondell of the Dallas-based Media Projects, Inc., were selected as the project's documentarians.[80]

Although neither was native to Texas, the Mondells felt aptly suited to produce documentaries on the presidency, death, and legacy of John F. Kennedy. Stimulated by Kennedy's call to service, Allen Mondell had joined the Peace Corps in June 1963 immediately after his college graduation. He had been teaching English literature and world history in Sierra Leone in West Africa for two months when the assassination took place. His future wife, then a student at the University of Maryland, spent the weekend watching television, like millions across the country. The couple married in 1969 and moved to Texas in

1973 when Allen Mondell (a writer and director at a Baltimore television station) accepted a position at the Dallas Public Broadcasting System (PBS) station. Cynthia Mondell pursued her own film projects in Dallas. After her first documentary aired on public television in 1977, the Mondells formed their own nonprofit company.[81]

Hunt prepared an outline detailing what each video needed to cover and accomplish, though the Mondells recalled that they were never shown artwork, blueprints, or text prior to joining the exhibition team.[82] The Mondells proposed films conveying two distinct stories, one covering the life and death of President Kennedy and the other about the Kennedy "charisma that was able to re-kindle the American spirit and captivate the imagination of the entire world." They hoped that their films would help young people to understand the life, death, and legacy of John F. Kennedy; rememberers to reflect on their personal experiences from the period; and Dallasites to stop viewing the assassination "through a haze of guilt, anger or defensiveness."[83]

Allen and Cynthia Mondell spent one year compiling the six exhibition videos, collectively titled *Films from The Sixth Floor,* for their 1989 home video release. Avoiding a journalistic approach, the Mondells opted for imagery with emotional appeal. The young documentarians had never worked on a museum exhibition, so the Dallas County Historical Foundation also hired former Hollywood producer Martin Jurow, who first toured the empty sixth floor alongside Lindalyn Adams in 1977, to oversee the production and work closely with both the Mondells and Conover Hunt.[84]

Credited as executive producer for *Films from The Sixth Floor,* Jurow brought "knowledge and experience" to the media project, reviewing the Mondells' raw footage, offering commentary, and supervising the editing of the videos.[85] Despite occasional friction, the Mondells enjoyed the opportunity to work with such an experienced filmmaker.[86] Allen Mondell remembered that Jurow, "a philosopher poet," always framed his suggestions with eloquence.[87]

The finished products emphasized the life and legacy of John F. Kennedy rather than the lingering questions about the assassination. Conover Hunt sat in on several of the editing sessions with Jurow, the Mondells, and film editor Bart Weiss. During the editing of the exhibition's funeral video, Jurow directed the placement and length of archival footage to the second. He edited out a woman in a crowd scene, for example, because she was "interfering" with Jacqueline Kennedy, the focal point of the funeral sequence.[88] Hunt concluded that Jurow's work represented "the genius of film—what film can do that nothing else can do."[89]

Most of the institutions and organizations approached by the Mondells were pleased to open their film archives, including the John F. Kennedy Presidential

Library. The Dallas ABC affiliate, WFAA-TV, owned by the Belo Corporation (prominent supporters of The Sixth Floor) offered a great deal of footage at no charge. The Mondells also sought footage from NBC and CBS News as well as cinema verité pioneer Robert Drew, who had produced three landmark documentaries on John F. Kennedy between 1960 and 1963. Consultant Gary Mack identified some privately held film and video material from the weekend of the assassination. As the exhibit took shape, the Mondells frequently worked with Staples and Charles. Mirroring the designers' limited use of color, the Mondells used only black-and-white footage through the Kennedy funeral, permitting color only after the narrative shifted to the government investigations.[90]

In the *Crisis Hours* video, detailing the assassination aftermath through the shooting of Oswald, Cynthia Mondell replicated her personal experience using black-and-white television footage devoid of narration. To heighten the drama, she intercut the TV images with audio from original radio broadcasts, in order to "feel the emotion because radio people [were] so descriptive." Hunt approved the first cut she saw, and Allen Mondell used the same approach in the longer theater-based film exploring the national and world response to the assassination. After a tearful first viewing of the video, designer Barbara Charles worried, however, that without narration visitors might not be able to identify world leaders such as France's President Charles de Gaulle at the Kennedy funeral. "Let the walls provide the information," Allen Mondell told her. "Let this film do exactly what it did to you."[91]

The videos exploring the Kennedy presidency, the 1963 trip to Texas, and the government investigations, by contrast, required narration for clarity. Dallas resident Robert Strauss, former chair of the Democratic National Committee and later U.S. ambassador to the Soviet Union, was asked to secure legendary CBS News anchor Walter Cronkite as the host for *The Legacy* film.[92] Strauss had previously assisted the Mondells by encouraging the heads of all three major television networks to donate the use of proprietary footage for The Sixth Floor exhibition.[93]

For *The Legacy* video, the Mondells initially proposed a series of "scholars, pundits, politicians and plain folks," with linking narration by host Bill Moyers, Garrison Keillor, or Ted Koppel.[94] The foundation board, however, wanted Cronkite, "the most respectable . . . news figure in the country in those years . . . [to] put it in its proper perspective."[95] The network anchor had also received the Kennedy family's unofficial approval to serve as the film's host. Lindalyn Adams and Martin Jurow asked Robert Strauss in July 1988 to approach Cronkite.[96]

Adams provided Strauss with a two-page outline on the exhibition's six documentaries, hoping that Cronkite would provide "thoughts, ideas, and collaboration on the script." The summary described the proposed *Legacy* film as dealing "with the long-term meaning of the assassination." In addition, noted the letter, "Kennedy's legacy of hope and the questions about the real impact of this event on American and international thought will be explored."[97]

A month later Robert Strauss saw Cronkite in Atlanta, Georgia, and received his tentative verbal agreement to host the film. Ecstatic, Adams offered to fly the Mondells to New York City for a meeting with Cronkite, although he still had not formally committed to the project.[98] Cronkite soon volunteered to host the film at no charge to the foundation; but due to time constraints, he could not contribute to the script.

Allen Mondell wrote the host script himself, imagining the rhythm and style of the broadcaster's distinctive voice as he summarized Kennedy's legacy.[99] He aptly tied the assassination and legacy of John F. Kennedy together by quoting journalist James Reston: "What was killed in Dallas was not only the president but the promise. The heart of the Kennedy legend is what might have been."[100] In the fall of 1988 Allen Mondell and editor Bart Weiss flew to New York City to videotape Cronkite in his CBS office. Cronkite went through Mondell's script on camera once and, after a minor one-word change, recorded the final version in a second take.[101]

Apart from the script and Cronkite's narration, the development of *The Legacy* film was slow and difficult. An early outline listed a series of themes needed in the final video, including the notion of "collective memory," changes in specific laws, how President Johnson fulfilled many of Kennedy's programs, and finally "the 'intangibles' (a good or bad president and a public perception that may have accorded him greater glorification by his death than had he lived)."[102] In the final product host Cronkite eloquently summarized these themes, interspersed with footage of the late President and contemporary video recorded in Dealey Plaza on the twenty-fifth anniversary as individuals tearfully shared their thoughts and memories of Kennedy and the assassination. Mondell spoke for an entire generation when he wrote:

> How do we explain this personal affection for John Kennedy? His good looks, his youth, his style, his charisma? Or is it a search for lost innocence and a renewed sense of optimism? Perhaps we associate him with happier times. Whatever the explanation might be, it didn't take long for the nation, tormented by its young president's death, to transform him into a legend.[103]

Properly ending *The Legacy* video proved to be the Mondells' greatest challenge, because the parting image would undoubtedly linger in the minds of

FIG. 24

The "Legacy" section of The Sixth Floor exhibit as seen in 1989. The theater shows the concluding shot of the film *The Legacy,* in which two hands reach out to touch President Kennedy's face.

INSTITUTIONAL ARCHIVES/THE SIXTH FLOOR MUSEUM AT DEALEY PLAZA

visitors as they exited The Sixth Floor. Early in the project's development, the board of the historical foundation, still hesitant to emphasize the late President's life, refused to end the film with an image of John F. Kennedy.[104] The suggested conclusion in May 1988 (a mix of still images and documentary footage showing Kennedy in action from 1956 to 1963) was rejected, as was a montage of the President's gravesite at Arlington National Cemetery.[105] With the opening bearing down and the Mondells desperate for a final determination, Hunt disregarded the board's concerns and told the filmmakers to "put Kennedy in there and maybe [the board members will] forget what they said."[106] They did.

The Mondells ended their film with a rarely seen clip of Kennedy in an unexpected embrace with a bystander. While he is shaking hands in a crowd of people, two hands reach up and gently grasp either side of Kennedy's face in an affectionate manner; Kennedy briefly closes his eyes and reacts with his characteristic smile.[107] Martin Jurow selected the image, wanting "a most compassionate shot of President Kennedy" and imagining the unknown hands "as if every hand in the world—and certainly mine as well—[were] there touching his face."[108]

The audiocassette tour of The Sixth Floor, produced by Antenna Tours, was an afterthought during the exhibit development. After meeting for a year with audio-tour companies and uncertain until the last moment if the budget would allow it, Hunt finally signed a contract with Antenna in November 1988, only three months before the opening of the exhibition.[109]

Hunt rejected the company's first script, which suggested narrative contributions by presidential advisor David Powers and others in "the Kennedy court" frequently interviewed for documentaries, as "passé." She wanted the Dallas story emphasized with the voices of actual participants; Antenna's second script "was right on the money."[110] Antenna began production in late 1988 with former Dallas broadcaster Pierce Allman, one of the first journalists inside the Texas School Book Depository after the assassination, as the narrator of the audio tour written by David Helvarg and Char Woods. New interviews recorded over the Christmas holidays in 1988 included assassination eyewitnesses Bill and Gayle Newman; journalist Ike Pappas; photographer James Altgens; Parkland Hospital nurse Audrey Bell and Dr. M. T. Jenkins; law enforcement officials James Leavelle, Eugene Boone, and Bobby Hargis; Warren Commission counsel David Belin; and author and conspiracy researcher Josiah Thompson.[111] Pierce Allman's narration, recorded on February 2, was mixed, edited, and available for distribution less than two weeks later. The audio tour was remixed several months after The Sixth Floor opened to eliminate noticeable glitches. For over two decades, it guided visitors through their Sixth Floor experience. A new audio tour, also produced by Antenna, premiered in the fall of 2012.[112]

While exhibition, documentary, and audio content was developed, Conover Hunt worked with the restoration architect, Eugene George, and the exhibition design team on restoration issues connected to the Depository's sixth floor. One week before construction began on the Visitors Center, Hunt detailed the exhibition installation schedule to Dallas County judge Lee Jackson. By the end of March 1988, with the final design in place, Hunt hoped to have a team of workers begin restoring the sixth floor. Scheduled for completion by August 15, 1988, in anticipation of exhibition installation and a public opening in late November, the restoration phase soon fell behind and was not completed until February 1989.[113]

As adaptively reused, the sixth floor functioned as both an exhibition venue and a historic site.[114] The task of effectively blending the warehouse's "dark and dreary environment into a subdued setting appropriate for a dual-purpose education and commemorative space" fell upon Eugene George and the exhibit design team of Staples and Charles.[115]

Restoration was minimal. The wooden columns—along with original ceiling components and the sprinkler system—were not washed, only dusted. The distinctive light fixtures, visible in news film and photographs from the day of the assassination, were restored to working order; existing water stains remained untouched. Likewise, newly installed mechanical systems, additional sprinklers, and security cameras were left visible on the ceiling of the sixth floor.[116] George felt a deep respect for the environment, which he once described as "not a good space to design within but . . . a fabulous space."[117] He consulted with structural engineers and historians and interfaced with heating, ventilating, and air conditioning (HVAC) workers, a team of electricians, Visitors Center and elevator tower architect James Hendricks, and the exhibition designers to ensure that the floor reflected its 1963 appearance.[118] Those who worked with George on the project vividly recalled his motto: "We're here to preserve the dirt."[119]

During the restoration phase, accommodations were made for the contemporary displays. Two emergency stairwell exits were added as well as an enclosed mechanical room. Another room was built around the internal county elevator, which opened onto the sixth floor by means of a special key to hide its use from exhibition visitors. Originally identified as a private "crying room . . . for anyone who gets upset" during a tour, this room has been alternatively used over the years as a staff break room, VIP back entrance, and storage, meeting, and office space. Stress cracks in the wooden arches above the Depository windows were not repaired with bracing on the sixth floor as they were throughout the rest of the building. Instead, to maintain the windows' original appearance, steel lintels were installed behind the original brick and wood, invisible to exhibition visitors. The windows on the sixth floor, many of which dated back to 1963, remained in place.[120]

George also ensured that all exhibit components were reversible to avoid causing permanent damage to the Depository if they were later removed. He insisted that the floating text panels between the floor's wooden support columns be attached with minimal damage to the original structure.[121] Assembled on-site by Heritage Display (the firm contracted for exhibition fabrication and restoration work), the exhibit panels were composed of steel frames covered with a laminate and a wooden trim with an expensive finish that Hunt felt demonstrated a "respect for history."[122] Photographic prints, produced by The Color Place of Dallas, were mounted on a thin layer of tin before being coated with plastic and sealed. Proto Productions completed the silk screening of the large text panels in Chicago; but due to time constraints photograph captions and other small blocks of text on the main laminate panels were vertically silk-screened on-site after being installed in position—a difficult, expensive, and lengthy process.[123]

FIG. 25

During exhibit construction, a worker repairs the damage to the southeast corner window caused by vandals and souvenir hunters over the years.

INSTITUTIONAL ARCHIVES/THE SIXTH FLOOR MUSEUM AT DEALEY PLAZA

Before the 14-by-14-foot area known as the "sniper's perch" could be enclosed by glass, it was restored to its appearance in the Dallas Police Department crime scene photographs from November 22, 1963. Workers repaired the badly chipped brick work around the window that had been damaged over the decades by souvenir hunters and removed the plywood flooring laid by Depository employees at the time of the assassination (and completed following the tragedy) to expose the original wooden floor.[124] According to Hunt, removal of the plywood flooring unleashed a shower of debris on the assistant district attorney whose fifth-floor office was directly beneath the sniper's perch. Hunt recalled: "When we pulled up the plywood, about fifty pounds of bird guano and feathers fell down on the . . . office below, which was the head of the civil section of the DA's office—who was bald." When Hunt inspected the office in question, she discovered guano "on the ledges of the pictures of his wife and kids . . . on the top of all the awards he'd won . . . [and] stuck in his sofa."[125] To minimize any further damage, Heritage Display promptly encased the impacted office in plastic to catch remaining debris until the work was finished.[126]

FIG. 26

The reconstructed sniper's perch in The Sixth Floor exhibit, as photographed in 1989.

INSTITUTIONAL ARCHIVES/THE SIXTH FLOOR MUSEUM AT DEALEY PLAZA

An accurate re-creation of the sniper's perch also required carefully arranged cardboard schoolbook boxes. To reproduce these 1963-era boxes, large photocopies were made of some of the originals in the National Archives. A Munsell Color System chart allowed researchers to match the color. The Lane Container Company of Dallas manufactured the replicas, and owner Rick Lane became directly involved with their placement on the sixth floor. He carefully examined existing photographs of the boxes to determine the manufacturers and then set out to obtain original printing dyes from each company to re-create box labels. The box manufacturers were initially incredulous when Lane called to inquire about 1960s-era printing dyes. "They were very cautious," he remembered, "especially after I told them that their boxes had ended up [in the Texas School Book Depository]. . . . Boy, things got quiet." The companies ultimately agreed to loan vintage dyes from their archives for printing the box labels.[127]

According to Hunt, over five hundred reproduction boxes were arranged in the two evidentiary areas. Several exhibit consultants participated in the painstaking placement of the boxes, using all existing crime scene photographs and still frames from black-and-white news footage. Volunteer Jim Moore recalled that, with the 1963-era flooring exposed, specific markings on the wood could be matched to those seen in the Dallas police photographs. Additionally, the week-long effort was a dirty and physical process: the boxes had to be artificially aged, while some were weighted down with loose Depository bricks removed during elevator construction. Based upon the precise arrangement of boxes, Moore left this experience convinced that Oswald had acted alone. He went on to write the best-selling lone gunman book *Conspiracy of One* in 1991.[128]

As opening day approached, the exhibition experienced a variety of glitches, ranging from difficulties with electricians and contractors to the delay of kiosk button mechanisms by Canadian customs to a display of commemorative Kennedy stamps for the "Legacy" section that was trapped for months by an ice storm in International Falls, Minnesota, and did not arrive until after The Sixth Floor opened.[129] Tensions ran high during the final push. Dallas County Historical Foundation president David Fox, a longtime Dallas home builder and a former Dallas County judge, oversaw the project directly and ordered a num-ber of budgetary cutbacks, including the arched glass skylights for the Visitors Center that would have oriented visitors and offered a preview of their jour-ney to the sixth floor via elevator.[130] Hunt and Adams also pushed hard to com-plete the task, working in tandem, in Hunt's words, as "the good cop/bad cop . . . needed to get this thing done."[131]

Previews of The Sixth Floor exhibit, *John F. Kennedy and the Memory of a Nation,* were held between February 11 and 19 prior to opening to the pub-lic on President's Day. The preopening glimpses were scheduled amid count-less last-minute changes and adjustments. With the "hyphen" connecting the exterior elevator to the sixth floor still not finished, the foundation held pre-views for construction workers and their families and Dallas County employ-ees on February 11 and 12.[132] The following two days were set aside for practice school tours, with three and a half hours per day allotted for continued exhibi-tion work. Print journalists toured on February 15, followed by broadcast news media the next day—a point of contention amid charges of preferential treat-ment.[133] Volunteer Carl Henry, who checked press badges at the elevator, was shocked at the number of gate crashers who tried to "rush past [him] or get through on phony credentials."[134]

The final days before opening were marked by preview tours for state and local historical societies, government officials, convention and hotel executives, board members of the Dallas County Historical Foundation, exhibition con-sultants, lenders and donors, and members of the museum community. The response was overwhelmingly positive.[135] Lindalyn Adams, who attended all of the exhibit previews, called riding the elevator to the sixth floor for the first time

FIG. 27

This publicity image of Conover Hunt (*left*, with exhibit plans) and Lindalyn Adams was taken days prior to the exhibit's opening on February 20, 1989.

INSTITUTIONAL ARCHIVES/THE SIXTH FLOOR MUSEUM AT DEALEY PLAZA

"one of [her] greatest thrills."[136] Her fears that they might be too slow or inefficient proved unjustified.

When designer Barbara Charles asked Hunt when the exhibition was scheduled for peer review by the museum community, she replied, "It will not be reviewed . . . for a long time [because] it'll be initially covered as a breaking news story." As Charles worried aloud what might happen if the media did not enjoy the exhibit, Hunt drolly observed: "Barbara, it's very simple. None of us will ever work anywhere again."[137]

Hunt's statement about breaking news coverage proved accurate, particularly among the local media. They covered even minute aspects of the exhibit's development, including the Commissioners Court's approval in December 1988 of a thirty-six month contract with Ticketron for the sale of admission tickets.[138] The *Dallas Morning News* ran nine exhibit-related stories over a five-day period between February 15 and 20, 1989. Likely reflecting the feelings of many

Dallasites—and certainly every member of The Sixth Floor's planning team—
Henry Tatum of the *Morning News* wrote that his "fingers [would] be invol-
untarily crossed Monday when Dallas finds out what 'spin' the national press
intends to place on the opening of the Sixth Floor."[139]

Media reviews of the exhibition were typically though not universally positive. Multiple stories placed great emphasis on the exhibit's controversial history
and development. Echoing the sentiments of the recent twenty-fifth anniversary
coverage, they suggested that Dallas had finally come to terms with the death of
President Kennedy. For many reporters, commentary on the exhibit was heavily
influenced by memories of 1963. Columnist Steve Blow wrote: "My tour became
a personal experience, not a professional one. . . . Tears welled in my eyes at several points, and I chewed on the cap of my pen. It's not professional to cry on
assignment."[140] Former *Times Herald* editor A. C. Greene devoted nearly three
pages of his seven-page exhibit review in *Southwestern Historical Quarterly* to his
own experiences during the Kennedy assassination; he acknowledged that the
sixth floor was "well used" and the information was "accurate, insofar as accu-
racy can be ascribed to clippings, broadcasts, and notes written or published
during the tense hours of the assassination."[141]

Tom Kennedy of the *Houston Post* said that the absence of artifacts, such
as the sixth floor's original book boxes, was acceptable under the circumstances
because this was "an exhibit, not a museum."[142] Ironically, after covering the
controversial exhibit's lengthy development, the *New York Times* did not initially plan to cover its opening. Reportedly, photographer George Tames, whose
iconic image of President Kennedy in the Oval Office was featured in the exhibit,
insisted that the *Times* acknowledge the opening of The Sixth Floor. The newspaper ran two related stories chronicling the exhibit's development but offered no
subjective commentary on its contents.[143] *Time* magazine's article on the opening, written without seeing the exhibition, debuted under the cynical headline
"See Oswald's Lair—$4."[144] The periodical's commentary on The Sixth Floor
inaccurately described the sniper's perch as the exhibit's only feature, warn-
ing that all "gun toters" would be stopped by metal detectors in the lobby.[145]
With much greater sensitivity, the *Chicago Tribune* said that the somber display
"help[ed] Dallas face its past."[146] Accompanied by glowing coverage of the opening, the front-page headline of the *Dallas Times Herald* on February 20 read simply: "Today We Stand Whole Again."[147]

Tracy-Locke Public Relations, which completed a content analysis of early
media coverage of the exhibition, found "a marked increase in positive messages
in both national and local coverage" compared to reporting before September
1, 1988. The firm recorded fifty-six positive national stories and only thirteen

FIG. 28

The completed Visitors Center and elevator shaft adjacent to the former Texas School Book Depository, 1989.

INSTITUTIONAL ARCHIVES/THE SIXTH FLOOR MUSEUM AT DEALEY PLAZA

negative stories between the fall of 1988 and the exhibit's opening, as opposed to fifty positive and thirty-six negative prior to September 1. The results were even more pronounced from February 16, 1989, to the beginning of March, by which time The Sixth Floor had been open for less than two weeks: twenty-five positive national news stories and only four negative stories. No negative stories were written locally about The Sixth Floor between September 1988 and February 16, 1989, and only four appeared in its first month open to the public. The most positive messages were that the public demanded this educational display, Dallas had a responsibility to history, and The Sixth Floor would help the city recover from the Kennedy assassination. Negative messages included identifying The Sixth Floor as controversial, as a commercial effort, and as being in "poor taste/exploitative/morbid."[148]

On Monday, February 20, 1989, individuals lined up two hours early to be among the first public visitors to experience The Sixth Floor. Admission was complimentary on opening day, and over 1,700 people toured the exhibition at a rate of approximately 300 per hour.[149] Prior to its official opening at 10:00 A.M. a dedication ceremony was held in the Commissioners Courtroom on the first floor of the former Texas School Book Depository. Dallas County treasurer Bill

Melton served as the master of ceremonies, with comments by Mayor Annette Strauss, Judge Lee Jackson, and Lindalyn Adams.[150] In his opening remarks, Jackson called the exhibition "a thankless and unpopular effort" and emphasized its intended purpose: "We are here to dedicate an exhibit created in response to a heartfelt need. A need shown by thousands who come here in pilgrimage each year, seeking to understand modern American history. And a need, felt by many in the Dallas community, to answer the challenge of history."[151] The proceedings were marked by performances by the brass quintet of SMU, the Arts Magnet High School Chorus, and the Up with People dance group. J. Jackson Walter, president of the National Trust for Historic Preservation, provided the keynote address.[152] He acknowledged that history was being made with the opening of this exhibition, which continued "a proud tradition of private, stubborn, individual initiative" through its long and painful development.[153]

Judge Jackson may have called The Sixth Floor a "thankless" effort, but both Dallas newspapers extended unflinching public gratitude to the planning team, specifically Conover Hunt and Lindalyn Adams, with editorials noting that "the people of Dallas owe them more than they know."[154] Perhaps more meaningful for those involved in the creation of The Sixth Floor were the comments and thoughts that individuals wrote in the Memory Books during the exhibit previews and the first days of operation. Many reflected on their own memories of the Kennedy assassination, acknowledging that the exhibit brought the era back to life for a few moments. "Today I was 16 again," wrote one visitor. A Dallas transplant who had long refused to bring family and friends to Dealey Plaza penned the following: "This exhibit is necessary. It reminds us of a great tragedy yet it also reminds us of a time when some of us were fresh, hopeful of the future and secure in the thought we could change the world for the better. To that end this exhibit is inspirational. I'll bring others." And one lifelong city resident wrote that after Kennedy was shot, she "was angry and shamed" to live in the community. "Today in '89 on the 6th Floor," she wrote over twenty-five years after the Kennedy assassination, "I'm proud to be a Dallasite."[155]

"As Memory Fades into History"

After the exhibit opened on February 20, 1989, over 32,000 individuals visited The Sixth Floor during the month of March. The *Dallas Morning News* reported in November that approximately 1,000 people per day had visited The Sixth Floor during its first nine months; the exhibit even extended its hours that summer to accommodate increased visitation. Yet, mired in debt, The Sixth Floor was not an immediate financial success.[156]

Conover Hunt continued to work with the staff and board until the summer of 1989, primarily training docents and writing the official guidebook, which was released in August along with a home video version of the Mondells' *Films from The Sixth Floor*.[157] When Hunt's formal relationship with the exhibit ended in summer 1989, she was presented with a Depository brick mounted on a wooden base with a brass plaque.[158]

Hunt remained in Dallas as a freelance consultant for several years, with a third-floor office across the street from the Depository at 501 Elm Street, the former location of the private John F. Kennedy Museum in the 1970s. She returned to The Sixth Floor at various times as a consultant and historian, drafting long-range plans, writing the application to designate Dealey Plaza as a National Historic Landmark District in 1993, and authoring a revised guidebook in 1995 and the museum's publication *JFK for a New Generation* in 1996.[159]

Two executive directors left The Sixth Floor during its first year of operation. Director of operations Bob Hays was interim director by October 1989 and was named executive director by the Dallas County Historical Foundation the following year. A Fort Worth native, Hays had been a writer, poet, and professor of Oriental languages and philosophy in Mexico City before accepting a job as a part-time guard and later as security chief at the Dallas Museum of Art. He joined the staff of The Sixth Floor one month prior to its opening, assuming the duties of executive director nine months later. Though not particularly interested in the Kennedy assassination, Hays remained fascinated by the event's impact, particularly its historical, sociological, and psychological context. He was supportive of the approach that Conover Hunt and her exhibit team had taken with The Sixth Floor's narrative and structure and tried to provide visitors with a fulfilling emotional experience.[160] "The Sixth Floor is helping . . . the nation and this community to come to a measure of emotional resolution on this subject, even though we may not know it all," said Hays in 1993, shortly after stepping down as director.[161]

The Sixth Floor opened with a conservative business plan in place. By foundation mandate, Hays's first task as interim director was to cut the institution's operating budget by one-third following a series of layoffs. Despite an encouraging beginning, the board was uncertain how long-term visitation patterns would play out.[162] Potentially complicating matters was the unanticipated announcement in April 1989 that a for-profit exhibition named the JFK Assassination Information Center would soon open on the third floor of a nearby restaurant and retail space called the West End Marketplace. Co-founder J. Gary Shaw, an architect and assassination conspiracy researcher, got the idea from The Sixth Floor's development.[163] Shaw "felt like the full story would not be told by a government entity" and wanted to provide interested researchers with programs, displays, and information giving them access to the Assassination Archives and Research Center (AARC), an organization founded by political assassinations researchers Bud Fensterwald and James Lesar in Washington, D.C.[164]

After failing to secure a location at 501 Elm Street across Houston Street from the Depository, Shaw and his business partner, Larry Howard, rented a three-room space in the nearby West End Historic District. When critics called the plan "distasteful and offensive," the pair insisted that it would be an educational institution. Unlike The Sixth Floor, however, the JFK Assassination Information Center would show the entire Abraham Zapruder film of the assassination and sell new and out-of-print conspiracy books and souvenirs of questionable taste, such as assassination trading cards and "paperweight replicas of the '[magic] bullet' that struck both Kennedy and former Texas Gov. John Connally." Lindalyn Adams, still serving on the foundation's board, publicly wished the organizers well, hoping that they would create "a tasteful and appropriate display and exhibition."[165]

The 3,000-square-foot center, whose entry fee was one penny less than the $4 admission to The Sixth Floor, opened in August 1989 with a display featuring films, photographs, government documents, and a forty-seat theater and resource area; but it was never a serious competitor to The Sixth Floor exhibition at the Depository. By November center officials reported that only one hundred people visited their exhibit daily, as opposed to approximately one thousand daily visitors at The Sixth Floor. Shaw, who left Larry Howard to run the center on his own in the early 1990s, later acknowledged that the center was "not successful financially at all."[166] Despite compensation from Hollywood director Oliver Stone, who used the center for research during the production of *JFK* and hired Howard as a film consultant, the JFK Assassination Information Center closed after Howard's death in 1994. Although a related for-profit venture, the Conspiracy Museum, opened in the historic Katy Building on Market Street across from the John F. Kennedy Memorial Plaza the following year, it closed in 2006 after losing its lease.[167]

The Sixth Floor welcomed approximately 280,000 visitors during its first year, less than the hopeful estimate of 500,000 but enough for the media to consider the exhibition a success. "The need for such a display was a controversy for many years," wrote *Austin American-Statesman* reporter Robin Doussard. "That need no longer is a question."[168] In November 1990 director Bob Hays estimated an average daily attendance of seven hundred, with as many as fifteen hundred on some weekends throughout the year.[169]

During his three-year tenure, Hays concentrated primarily on day-to-day operations and financial stability, with less thought about long-range plans and collections, programming, and education initiatives. However, he was also an eye-witness and participant in the controversy brought about by Oliver Stone and his 1991 film *JFK*, which had a profound impact on The Sixth Floor's development.[170]

Academy Award–winning director Oliver Stone's magnum opus on the Kennedy assassination focused on the largely discredited investigation by New Orleans district attorney Jim Garrison, portrayed in the film by actor Kevin Costner. Location filming took place in New Orleans and Washington, D.C. As expected, however, a portion of Stone's film was set in Dallas. The filmmaker approached both the Dallas County Commissioners Court and the Dallas County Historical Foundation in early 1991 about using the Texas School Book Depository. News of the Stone film terrified Lindalyn Adams, who recognized the director's earlier work as dark and violent.[171] Like many on the foundation's board, she worried that the movie might be detrimental to The Sixth Floor. Board member Glenn Linden feared that Stone might include something bizarre or offensive, such as putting "Jackie in bed with Oswald."[172] Nevertheless, Stone was creating a major Warner Brothers motion picture with a budget of approximately $40 million. North Texas film commissioner Roger Burke estimated that "$5 million to $8 million of that [would] stay in Dallas."[173]

In an effort to re-create an accurate version of the Dealey Plaza of November 1963, Stone sought to dismantle The Sixth Floor exhibit and relocate it to the empty seventh floor for up to three weeks, in addition to installing a replica Hertz Rent-a-Car billboard atop the Depository, altering some of the building's windows and signage, and placing gravel, faux railroad tracks, and two small buildings in the county parking lot adjacent to the building. While a majority of the county commissioners opposed any attempt to disrupt public access to The Sixth Floor, and county engineers forbade the installation of a replica billboard atop the Depository, a split occurred regarding Stone's other requests. The filmmaker's biggest county advocate, commissioner Chris Semos, touted the value of this film for tourism and the local economy.[174] Semos also felt "very strongly that an artist [had] a right to do [his] thing, as long as it's not immoral or illegal."[175] Judge Lee Jackson countered that any intrusion by Stone would disrupt exhibition traffic and county business. Furthermore, he felt that the Depository interior could easily be constructed on a soundstage. He noted that a number of "great movies . . . have included the Oval Office in them, and . . . not a single one of them has ever been filmed in the Oval Office."[176]

At the heart of the controversy, however, was a much older discussion about potential commercial exploitation at the site of the Kennedy assassination. Dallas County tried to consider the precedent it would set by granting Stone's requests. *Austin American-Statesman* reporter Paul Weingarten thought it ironic that "after years of efforts by some Dallas leaders to raze the depository as an unpleasant reminder of the past, the site has now been embraced by some as sacred and not to be sullied by commercial ventures."[177]

The Dallas County Commissioners Court rejected all three of Stone's proposals for utilizing the sixth floor. One involved relocating the entire exhibit, and the other two called for dismantling portions of the exhibit for access to the sniper's perch. In a split vote on March 5 the county granted Stone access to the seventh floor and roof of the building and permitted temporary alterations to the exterior and parking lot. The following week the county approved a contract that provided a minimum of $52,000 for the right to use the Depository.[178]

Stone, however, refused to give up his pursuit of the sixth floor. The Dallas County Historical Foundation was fiercely opposed to any proposals that required even a partial dismantling of the exhibition.[179] But after Stone personally attended at least one board meeting to explain his vision and express his interest in filming in the sniper's perch some of the foundation board's opinions began to change. In late March 1991, just a few weeks before filming began, the historical foundation voted five to four to permit "limited access to film on the sixth floor," pending the approval of the county commissioners.[180] Adams, who was among those opposed to Stone's use of the floor, explained that by this time several new individuals had joined the board, who "were all very young and not of my generation . . . and they saw nothing wrong with having an Oliver Stone film at The Sixth Floor."[181] Board member Meg Read remembered the Stone situation as "one of the most divisive times I've ever seen on that board."[182]

In another split vote the Dallas County Commissioners Court rejected this proposal, only to change its mind a week later when commissioner John Wiley Price switched positions after meeting with a production official about the minimal use of equipment, lighting, and crew members on the sixth floor. With the county's approval, historical foundation board president David Fox negotiated with Stone's Camelot Productions for use of the space, ultimately allowing limited availability for a two-day period in the morning before the exhibit opened to the public. According to Stone's location manager, Jeff Flach, the production crew specifically wanted to film inside the sniper's perch looking out the windows onto Dealey Plaza and to film from the street below looking up at actors positioned in the infamous corner window.[183] Additional scenes set on the sixth floor were filmed on the seventh floor, dressed to replicate the look of the sixth floor in 1963. Adams marveled at Fox's gift for bargaining, and Stone later described the foundation president as "a tough fellow to negotiate with."[184] The foundation used the compensation received for Stone's access to the sixth floor to settle the private promissory note that had been issued years earlier to help complete The Sixth Floor exhibit.[185]

Dallas shooting for Stone's *JFK* began on April 15, 1991. For two weeks several streets on the west side of downtown Dallas were blocked from 7:00 A.M. to 7:00 P.M., rerouting some 21,000 automobiles per day. His crew transformed Dealey Plaza through vintage signage, period automobiles, and carefully trimmed trees.[186] "The downtown area was 1963 again," said board member Glenn Linden, who watched many of his SMU history students serve as extras.[187]

Conover Hunt, whose office at 501 Elm Street was one floor above the location of one of Stone's various gunmen teams, agreed that the filming was a cathartic if surreal experience for Dallas. She remembered that the actors portraying John and Jackie Kennedy had lunch in costume at the nearby Palm Restaurant after morning filming. Meanwhile, special effects technicians on a crowded city street repeatedly tested the prosthesis used to simulate the explosive head shot that killed the President.[188] Besides Dealey Plaza, filming took place at several other locations in the Dallas area, including the Texas Theatre in Oak Cliff.

The highly controversial film opened on December 20, 1991, eventually grossing over $205 million worldwide and winning two Academy Awards (best film editing and best cinematography) out of a total of eight nominations, including best director and best picture. Neither The Sixth Floor nor the Dallas County Historical Foundation was acknowledged in the film's credits after the board declined recognition of any kind following a pre-release screening. In addition to being one of Stone's most financially successful films, *JFK* introduced a new generation to the Kennedy assassination and its enduring mysteries, though many historians and mainstream journalists argued that it did a great disservice to history by distorting facts.[189] Walter Cronkite called *JFK* "an abomination," adding that "if there is any reason in the world for press censorship, that film would go right to the top of the evidence."[190]

Stone's *JFK* did, however, make the nearly thirty-year-old event relevant to individuals born after 1963. One concrete result of this renewed interest was the passage of the President John F. Kennedy Records Collection Act of 1992, signed into law by President George H. W. Bush, which mandated "the gathering and opening of all records concerned with the death of the President."[191] The five members of the subsequent Assassination Records Review Board were appointed by President Bill Clinton and confirmed by the U.S. Senate in April 1994. The board concluded its work four years later.[192]

The Sixth Floor felt the immediate impact of Stone's film through increased attendance. Visitation was up by 30 percent in January 1992, usually the exhibit's

FIG. 29

Executive director Bob Hays and a TV news crew surprise the exhibit's one millionth visitor in June 1992.

INSTITUTIONAL ARCHIVES/THE SIXTH FLOOR MUSEUM AT DEALEY PLAZA

slowest month.[193] For months one attendance record after another was shattered, peaking at over 41,000 during March. Exhibit visitation for the first three months of 1992 was up a total of 69 percent over figures from the same period the year before, and the exhibit welcomed its one millionth visitor that June.[194] The Sixth Floor ended fiscal year 1992 with a budget surplus, after a total visitation of 404,834 people.[195]

In the years since its release, Oliver Stone's *JFK* has frequently been cited by staff members as the primary catalyst for the discussion to shift from a so-called temporary exhibition to a more permanent position as a museum and collecting institution. Director Jeff West later credited *JFK* with helping build The Sixth Floor's audience at a critical time, noting that it brought the institution "natural success."[196]

In March 1993, shortly after he stepped down as executive director, Bob Hays acknowledged the progress beginning to take place at The Sixth Floor. He explained that "as the years have progressed, we have begun to add one thing at a time . . . to fulfill the original vision . . . of what the board has wanted for this great institution."[197]

It became the responsibility of a new executive director to achieve this "original vision" for The Sixth Floor. The Dallas County Historical Foundation selected Jeff West, then managing director of the Dallas Theater Center, for that position. Although the Alabama native had no previous museum experience, the foundation wanted someone, as board member Glenn Linden explained, who "could reach out more to the community."[198] West did not initially consider the position a good match with his theatrical background, but he concluded that it was a good opportunity, because he had studied political science and considered Kennedy a personal hero.[199] He took over as director in January 1994 and remained at The Sixth Floor more than a decade.

West immediately considered adding the word "museum" to the institution's title. As he later explained, The Sixth Floor was originally "perceived within a bureaucratic mindset as perhaps having a lifespan of maybe four to five years," after which the exhibit might give way to additional Dallas County offices. The founders, West surmised, "were scared of the word 'museum' for a variety of reasons, which meant permanence, and as a result, when I was hired, I did the old 'walks like a duck, quacks like a duck, oh, it must be a duck.'"[200]

Neither Conover Hunt nor assistant project director Adah Leah Wolf understood The Sixth Floor to be a temporary display with a limited lifespan, let alone the future site of county office expansion.[201] West, however, noted during his tenure that the exhibits could "be popped out and be gone in six days" if necessary.[202] To the present day many museum staff and board members believe that The Sixth Floor began as a temporary display and could have closed after the public had satisfied its curiosity if not for Oliver Stone's *JFK*.[203]

In the interim between Hays's departure and West's arrival, Conover Hunt returned to The Sixth Floor to coordinate an application to recognize Dealey Plaza as a National Historic Landmark District.[204] Hunt's diligent work, which involved getting seven property owners to agree to the terms of the designation among other issues, marked the end of a seven-year effort by the Dallas County Historical Foundation that began with Richard Sellars's initial interest in the site on behalf of the National Park Service in December 1986.[205] Board member Meg Read, who had joined the foundation in 1987, championed the designation and raised the issue at virtually every board meeting for over a year and a half. Six months before the thirtieth anniversary of the assassination the board finally established a National Historic Landmark designation committee.[206] With city and county cooperation, Hunt hurriedly wrote the draft nomination, which was finalized by a representative of the National Park Service.[207] Congress bestowed the designation just six weeks before the formal dedication in Dealey Plaza on November 22, 1993.[208]

Hunt felt that even in 1993 "there was still a great need for the community to cleanse itself of this lingering memory, and so [the ceremony] was turned into a major event."[209] Planners closed Dealey Plaza and erected a large platform near the triple underpass, adorned with Texas and U.S. flags. A crowd of 4,000 people gathered for the hour-long ceremony, which included remarks by U.S. senator Kay Bailey Hutchison, assistant secretary of the interior Bob Armstrong, and Judge Lee Jackson, followed by the flyover of a pair of F-14 aircraft. Nellie Connally, widow of former Texas governor John Connally, removed a black cloth covering a replica National Historic Landmark plaque on the speaker's platform, while the actual plaque was unveiled in the grass on Elm Street.[210] The placement of the plaque proved controversial. Some Dallas political leaders wanted it put at the base of a statue of civic leader George Bannerman Dealey, for whom the plaza was named. Hunt, however, successfully argued that this location was tied too closely to local history and that a more appropriate site was along Elm Street "at the foot of the grassy knoll . . . in the approximate area where—for all intents and purposes—Kennedy died." The original plaque, she recalled, arrived with the word "Dealey" misspelled and had to be replaced before the ceremony. The Dallas Park Department installed the plaque that morning; the large hole dug the previous Friday to accommodate it was surrounded by wreaths and flowers left by tourists.[211]

After Jeff West's arrival in January 1994, Hunt remained on to brief the new director and consult with staff about the future of The Sixth Floor. In a meeting that focused on the responsibilities of being a museum, Hunt told the administrative staff that the debt had been repaid and educational programming was underway, so it was time to start thinking and acting like a museum. She explained that when the historical foundation was established in 1983 The Sixth Floor exhibition was expected to evolve into a full-fledged museum, complete with educational and interpretive programs. Long-range planning in the early 1990s confirmed this view.[212]

Over the next few years a number of changes took place at The Sixth Floor, not least of which was the name change to The Sixth Floor Museum in the mid-1990s—later expanded to The Sixth Floor Museum at Dealey Plaza. This identity shift came only after extensive board meetings, introspection, and discussion. The name change, however, did not garner media attention because journalists and tourists alike already referred to the exhibition as a "museum" regardless of its official designation.[213]

The museum hired professional collections and exhibits staff, including its first director of interpretation, Dr. Marian Ann Montgomery; registrar Megan Bryant, later named director of collections and intellectual property;

and Gary Mack as archivist and later curator. Additional artifacts were added to the exhibit, including the long-awaited FBI model of Dealey Plaza and a display of cameras used by motorcade spectators. As time passed, the staff incorporated a few minor updates into Hunt's original exhibit label copy and relocated or removed certain panels, including the section on earlier presidential assassinations, replaced by a display highlighting the museum's growing collections. Despite these changes, the visitor experience on the sixth floor remains largely the same as on its opening day.[214]

The museum's collections have grown exponentially over the years, now totaling approximately forty thousand items, making it "one of the world's largest and most important sources of visual, audio, documentary and artifactual documentation of the assassination and legacy of President John F. Kennedy." Among its holdings is a first-day, first-generation print of the Abraham Zapruder film, donated along with the film's copyright and related materials by the Zapruder family in 1999. In addition to a number of other amateur home movies and photographs of President Kennedy, the museum's collections include nearly 250 hours of news coverage relating to the assassination.[215]

Although always a part of the long-range plan for the institution, the museum's ongoing Oral History Project, which has thus far captured more than one thousand interviews regarding the life, death, and legacy of President Kennedy and the history and culture of Dallas and the 1960s, began informally after the exhibit opened in 1989 when interested individuals volunteered to share stories with staff members. Hunt recalled borrowing "a dictating machine from one of the DAs in the civil section" on the fifth floor to record the earliest oral histories.[216] This handful of impromptu audiocassette interviews became the foundation for a videotaped archival project launched in 1992 that continues to the present day with new interviews and programs recorded in high-definition.

With an expansion of its Visitor Center in 1997, the museum presented free rotating exhibits in the lobby across from the admissions desk. This small, annually changing display addressed "timely and newsworthy topics" more quickly than larger and more involved shows, which often took several years to develop.[217] The museum's exhibit in response to the September 11, 2001, terrorist attacks, for example, was conceived, written, designed, produced, and opened within two months. This well-received exhibit, *Loss and Renewal: Transforming Tragic Sites*, presented five American sites of tragedy—including Dealey Plaza—through text, photographs, and artifacts and explored how each was subsequently memorialized as part of the national healing process. It also addressed early concepts for memorializing the World Trade Center site, encouraging visitors to present their own ideas via an interactive component. Another small-scale temporary exhibit,

Unfinished Business: Kennedy and Cuba, provided historical context for the Elián González affair in 2000. Still another, on the history of Dealey Plaza, was linked to a major restoration effort.

Later lobby exhibits moved away from breaking news stories and instead highlighted examples of the twenty-five thematic categories of the museum's Oral History Project and its rich artifact collections. In 2003 and 2004, for example, the lobby display detailed the history of the John F. Kennedy Center for the Performing Arts in Washington, D.C., following a synergistic partnership between The Sixth Floor Museum and the Dallas Symphony Orchestra. To mark the assassination's fortieth anniversary, the orchestra staged a special performance of Leonard Bernstein's *Mass,* the piece commissioned by Jacqueline Kennedy Onassis for the opening of the Kennedy Center. As part of this collaboration, the museum opened a concurrent display—complete with a second set of artifacts—for the Morton H. Meyerson Symphony Center on the dates when *Mass* was performed. This was not the first time that The Sixth Floor Museum had extended its interpretive reach beyond the Texas School Book Depository. To commemorate the thirtieth anniversary of the John F. Kennedy Memorial, the museum, with city and county support, led a conservation effort to restore the monument "to its original vitality" in the summer of 1999.[218] The memorial's architect, Philip Johnson, was consulted on the restoration process. It was implemented by Phoenix I Restoration and Construction, Ltd., with several local companies donating materials and labor. The museum hosted a rededication ceremony on June 24, 2000.[219]

In the second half of its twenty-year history The Sixth Floor Museum has continued to engage a local audience. A desire to bring Dallasites to the museum and establish itself as a venue for community discussion and interaction was a major catalyst for its largest expansion project to date. On President's Day 2002, the institution's thirteenth anniversary, the seventh floor opened as a changing exhibition gallery with "innovative installations, exhibitions, performances, educational activities, special events, and public discourse."[220] At a time when 85 percent of the approximately 460,000 people who visited The Sixth Floor Museum at Dealey Plaza annually hailed from outside Texas, Jeff West explained that the seventh floor expansion solved the museum's capacity problems and provided "a reason for Dallas, Texas, to visit the museum."[221] West's interest in expanding the museum experience to the seventh floor developed almost immediately after he accepted the position of executive director. He shared expansion plans with news media in November 1995 and during a private program on the empty seventh floor the following year.[222] Without any major fund-raising drives, grants, or endowments, the museum ultimately covered the full $2.5 million in design and construction costs, added 9,000 square feet of exhibit space, and extended the exterior elevator shaft by one floor.[223]

A diverse series of national touring exhibits and in-house productions occupied the seventh floor in its first few years, from a Pulitzer Prize retrospective placing the Kennedy assassination within the context of world history to an exhibition of Andy Warhol's *Jackie* paintings, created in partnership with the Andy Warhol Museum in Pittsburgh. Over the past decade the floor has hosted artwork inspired by September 11, 2001; photographer spotlights showcasing the work of Kennedy family photographer Jacques Lowe, freelance photojournalist Stanley Tretick, and Pulitzer Prize–winning *Dallas Times Herald* photographer Bob Jackson; a series of Collections Spotlights highlighting newly acquired and rarely seen artifacts; and several assassination-specific exhibitions utilizing the museum's Oral History Collection and rich photographic, film, and document collections.

In 2004, in association with the Museum of the Moving Image in New York City, the museum created an exhibit of presidential campaign commercials, 1952–2004. Tied to the upcoming election, the show included a live community screening of the first presidential debate between George W. Bush and John Kerry, followed by a town hall discussion. Emphasizing the breadth of its mission to chronicle the assassination and legacy of President John F. Kennedy, interpret and support the Dealey Plaza National Historic Landmark District and the John F. Kennedy Memorial Plaza, and present contemporary culture within the context of presidential history, the museum has sought programming opportunities beyond the assassination to discuss civic responsibility in the context of current events shaping the global community.[224] This effort, though still in its infancy, helps keep the stories told by The Sixth Floor Museum relevant for younger audiences and, with the frequently changing seventh floor exhibitions, opens up opportunities for return visits, particularly by local residents.

A brief exhibit in 2006, *Call to Action,* was the museum's first dedicated to community interaction. Serving as a backdrop to an inaugural series of free public programs (including lectures, documentary screenings, and panel discussions), this exhibit on social activism inspired by the words and vision of John F. Kennedy drew heavily upon stories and artifacts provided by Dallas residents. The exhibit also prompted a new series of oral history interviews that centered on the local experience during the civil rights and peace movements. Local resources such as the Dallas Peace Center and the Juanita J. Craft Civil Rights House helped pinpoint individuals with unique stories to share.

A second program series focusing on Dallas law enforcement followed the next year, and record audiences attended programs that examined not only the events of the assassination but also issues such as women in the Dallas Police Department. The museum hosted a Crime Scene Investigation (CSI) Family Day on Father's Day 2007 that attracted over one thousand visitors, who learned about fingerprinting, blood spatter analysis, and other CSI techniques. This activity fair—a first in the museum's history—has become an annual event. The Sixth Floor Museum also invited the local community to share family films in 2007 as part of Home Movie Day, for which the museum was named the National Spotlight Venue by the nonprofit Center for Home Movies. As part of this day-long event, the nearby Dallas Holocaust Museum screened home-movie oral histories with Holocaust survivors and the Dallas chapter of the Juvenile Diabetes Research Foundation (JDRF) showed video diaries of diabetic children. Later that year the museum raised over $2,500 during the JDRF "Walk to Cure Diabetes."[225]

Much of this focus on community engagement in the past few years is the result of the vision of Nicola Longford, who became executive director of The Sixth Floor Museum at Dealey Plaza in 2005. A native of Pembry, in Kent, England, Longford brought decades of museum experience to the task, including seven years at the Colonial Williamsburg Foundation. Before relocating to Dallas, she served as vice president for community services at the Missouri Historical Society in St. Louis.[226] After discovering that very little demographic information had been captured over the years, Longford has tried to identify and maximize the museum's present and future audience.[227]

Although Longford feels that the museum today does not yet have the resources for sustained community engagement, it remains one of her primary goals and fuels her ambitious plans for the future. She hopes to create a "campus look" in Dealey Plaza that includes the John F. Kennedy Memorial Plaza.[228] In September 2009 the museum launched a cell-phone walking tour of Dealey Plaza, narrated by curator Gary Mack, to extend interpretation outside the Depository building to an area where a variety of street vendors share personal theories, provide impromptu tours, and sell souvenir magazines and videos. The somewhat carnival-like atmosphere of the plaza compared to the integrity and decorum of The Sixth Floor Museum led Judge Lee Jackson to declare: "What we do upstairs is the Smithsonian, [while] what happens out there is Graceland."[229] Beyond the walking tour, the museum continues to expand, moving its administrative offices across Houston Street to 501 Elm Street in 2008 and opening a series of new facilities in summer 2010. Located on the ground floor of 501 Elm, ironically in the same location that once housed John Sissom's private John F. Kennedy Museum, the award-winning Museum Café + Store "welcomes Museum guests and local residents with an ever-changing mix of unique offerings in a contemporary yet historic setting."[230] The Museum's Reading Room on the ground floor of the Depository building provides a reflective environment for students, teachers, researchers, and historians to access books, magazines, oral history interviews, and artifacts from the museum's collections. The nearby Media Room provides a dedicated space for media interviews, distance learning educational programs connecting to schools and other venues around the globe, and high-definition oral history video recordings. With these new resources and other ongoing initiatives, Director Longford feels that The Sixth Floor Museum will alter the imprint of the surrounding area and eventually reshape how the community views Dealey Plaza well beyond the fiftieth anniversary of the Kennedy assassination in 2013.[231]

The twenty-plus-year-old exhibition provides another interpretive challenge: as the museum's audience changes, two-thirds of its visitors possess no firsthand knowledge of the 1960s. Although the content developed by Conover Hunt and her team remains a solid foundation, future plans call for "a multilayered interpretation" that will emphasize the diverse narratives being gathered by the museum. Fully realizing a new iteration of the sixth floor experience will take years of careful assessment, focus groups, and community involvement. Many still feel that the exhibition produced in 1989 is fine.[232]

Nicola Longford and her staff recognize that the museum has a long and difficult road ahead as it explores and interprets the Kennedy assassination "as memory fades into history."[233] They are challenged with interpreting the story in new and creative ways, reaching larger audiences, and remaining relevant while maintaining integrity. Few can dispute that the museum's position in the local community has changed dramatically since individuals argued over the fate of the controversial building. Its recent pursuit of community engagement stands in stark contrast to those troubled days and brings the tragedy and its uneasy relationship with Dallas full circle.[234]

The Sixth Floor's long development and its twenty-plus-year history as an exhibition and museum remain testaments to the dedication of its founders and reflect the changing face of Dallas and its slow embrace of a tragic moment in history, distilled in part by the passage of time. Although a visitor to Dealey Plaza in 2013 finds a remarkably different experience than a visitor in 1973, the international level of interest surrounding the Kennedy assassination has not abated. Modern-day pilgrims to the site still contemplate both the history and the mystery of the events played out there in 1963. Some mourn the loss of the young President or their own innocence. The inquisitive ones try to reconcile the potential bullet trajectories from the grassy knoll and the Depository's sixth floor. Others come to protest war or government policy or perhaps demand a new investigation into the assassination. Every so often—while street vendors peddle their merchandise and theories, school groups eat sack lunches on the grassy knoll, teenagers rush into Elm Street to have their photo taken, and senior citizens appear lost in memory—someone leaves a bouquet or a rose atop the bronze historical plaque by the side of the street as downtown traffic rushes past. Year after year they come to this place of necessary pilgrimage—to mourn, to learn, to ponder.

CONCLUSION

P resident's Day, February 16, 2009: I waited, patient and silent, a few feet away from my camcorder as footsteps echoed down the hallway leading to the south gallery on the seventh floor of the former Texas School Book Depository. On this day The Sixth Floor Museum at Dealey Plaza celebrated its twentieth anniversary with a special luncheon honoring the institution's founders. My responsibility as oral historian was to document the private event for the archives. Already six months into initial work on this manuscript as my master's thesis, I had given the history and development of this museum a significant amount of thought. Days earlier I had poured over notes, correspondence, and preliminary exhibit layouts in the museum's institutional archives. Perhaps more than at any other moment in my nine years of employment, I felt as though I were a part of the museum's history, a small part of the history of the controversial building, and perhaps a minuscule part of the overall narrative of the Kennedy assassination and its aftermath. As the luncheon guests made their way down the corridor, I realized that this would be an extraordinary opportunity to meet the subjects of my study in person—and all in one place.

My position at the entrance to the gallery provided the occasion for me to serve as an unofficial greeter as the guests made their way to their assigned tables. At the front of the line, as expected, was Lindalyn Adams, who warmly shook my hand, alongside former board members Nancy Cheney and Glenn Linden—my mentor as an undergraduate at SMU in Dallas. Architect James Hendricks nodded, remembering me from our extensive oral history sessions the previous fall. I met restoration architect Eugene George for the first time and was struck by his booming baritone and dominating presence, even at the age of eighty-six. I recalled Lindalyn Adam's comment that "every time he spoke, it was like Moses speaking."[1] Exhibition designers Bob Staples and Barbara Charles followed with their friend Charles A. Briggs, once of the CIA. As The Sixth Floor's assistant project director Adah Leah Wolf walked by,

I quickly introduced myself and obtained her business card for a future oral history recording.

Board members past and present, consultants, and county officials soon followed in the procession. Exactly one week before his eighty-fourth birthday, Judson Shook entered the gallery with his wife, introducing himself to me for the first time—though I instinctively felt as though we were old acquaintances. It was a personally remarkable moment to see all of these individuals gathered together on The Sixth Floor's anniversary. Speechless, I was reduced to nodding, smiling, and shaking hands, silently reminded of the conclusion of James Cameron's *Titanic* when those who perished aboard the doomed luxury liner gathered together at the grand staircase in a dream sequence.

One of the last individuals to enter the south gallery was Conover Hunt. As I stepped forward to say hello—noticeably flushed as if in the presence of a rock star or royalty—she rushed passed me, lost in conversation, and disappeared in a crowd of people. We eventually spoke at length later that day and well into the evening. At that moment I dutifully took my place behind my camcorder for the luncheon.

Executive Director Nicola Longford welcomed the founders back to the museum, acknowledging that their work was still clearly visible—indeed, mostly untouched—two decades later, yet The Sixth Floor Museum at Dealey Plaza remained "a balanced and lasting experience that reaches . . . many types of people . . . on deeply personal levels." Over the next hour a series of speakers remarked upon the development, creation, and success of The Sixth Floor Museum, including Paul Coggins, current chair of the board of the Dallas County Historical Foundation; former Dallas County judge Lee Jackson, now chancellor of the University of North Texas System; and Lindalyn Adams, who was introduced by Longford as "the fairy godmother of Dallas historical institutions."[2]

Over the past twenty years Adams has remained active in local preservation efforts, having recently participated in a lengthy restoration of the Old Red Courthouse near Dealey Plaza, which opened as a local history museum in 2007. Adams spoke frankly about the early struggles that she endured with the Depository project, praising many in the audience by name and acknowledging some, such as the late David Fox, Martin Jurow, Chris Semos, and Annette Strauss, who sadly did not live to witness The Sixth Floor's twentieth anniversary. In summing up, the individual who dedicated more than a decade of her life to this project said, "It has been a great adventure, and I am so glad to have been a part of it." Conover Hunt spoke for only a fraction of the time, reading a handful of media quotes—a few negative and wary—from 1979 to 1988 and recounting a few oft-told, characteristically humorous stories from the exhibit's development:

My memory—these are the things I will tell you—is filled with details of the national resistance to the idea, innumerable awkward social events, the attempt to burn the Depository down, the war over the tower . . . preservation wars which ultimately involved the National Park Service, an attempt by DART to move their tracks through the grassy knoll, and statements from historians who swore Kennedy's memory would soon fade into oblivion. The cast of real life characters [included] politicians, community volunteers, original participants in the events of 1963, museum and historic preservation professionals, international media, leaders in government investigations, conspiracy fanatics, Kennedy liberals, anti-Kennedy conservatives, academic historians, sociologists, and a few psychiatrists and psychotics—we all know who we are. Over the years, people have asked me what has been my greatest professional challenge and what has been my greatest accomplishment. The answer is getting The Sixth Floor open.[3]

One of the day's highlights was a presentation by Dallas County judge James Foster, who read a proclamation naming "February 16, 2009, as a day of recognition to the founders of The Sixth Floor Museum, and as a day to celebrate the twentieth anniversary of The Sixth Floor exhibit."[4] Presentations of commemorative Depository bricks were made to Adams, Hunt, and Jackson, followed by an anniversary cake-cutting alongside museum staff and the general public in the Visitors Center. Like a child on Christmas morning, I took full advantage of this unprecedented gathering to secure as many oral history recordings as possible, particularly from those who had traveled to Dallas from out of state—a few visiting for the first time since the opening in 1989.

Late that afternoon, after the luncheon tables had been cleared from the south gallery, I walked back to the seventh floor. In a few hours many of the museum founders would return for an evening reception to mark the opening of our latest seventh floor exhibition, *A Photographer's Story: Bob Jackson and the Kennedy Assassination*. In a brief moment of downtime, I walked over to the southeast corner window overlooking Dealey Plaza—the same location that Oliver Stone once used to replicate the sixth floor during the filming of *JFK*. As always, I saw pockets of individuals milling about below me, reminding me again of the value of the museum's presence and the continuing significance of Dealey Plaza. In light of my research, it also made me think about the human need to contextualize tragic events and renew them into sites of reflection and understanding.

I visited The Sixth Floor with my parents and grandparents during its first week of operation, unaware of the long and painful journey that the exhibition had taken during its development. It had a distinct smell, as I recall, which has stayed with me through the years. I remember being somewhat frightened by the image of Lee Harvey Oswald holding a rifle in the backyard of his Oak Cliff apartment house, snapped by his wife when the Oswalds lived on Neely Street in March 1963. I remember signing the exhibition's Memory Book in a large, child-ish scrawl. Still, more than anything else from that first visit twenty years ago, I vividly recall my mother's reaction to The Sixth Floor. She was in the fifth grade in the Dallas suburb of Mesquite when the assassination took place and went to bed on November 22, 1963, feeling that certain sense of dread or endangerment that young people feel when something unexpected occurs that shakes the foun-dations of their world. Lying in bed, she thought that an assassin or assassins might come and get her in the night. The Sixth Floor transported her back to that childhood, prompting tears and catharsis as she relived that moment of horror and reflected on her life and the country's history since that time. Hers was not an isolated experience. My father told me that his family started locking the front door around 1963. Eyewitness Bill Newman—a family friend who accompanied us on that first visit—admitted to me later that, for the first time in his life, he put a shotgun underneath his bed on the night of the assassination, just in case.

My mother grew up amid the skepticism of the 1960s, compiling a com-prehensive library of assassination-related books, magazines, and documen-taries that I devoured in my youth and that somehow led, through a series of circumstances, to my employment at The Sixth Floor Museum at Dealey Plaza. My daughter Deanna, born in March 2008, has already visited the museum a half-dozen times. In contemplating my mother's reaction as a rememberer and my own as part of that "next generation" that Conover Hunt spoke of during the exhibit development, I wondered for a moment what my daughter would find here in Dealey Plaza. Born more than forty-four years after President Kennedy's death, she will probably view the assassination as ancient history. Yet within the context of my stories and her own historical pursuits between home and school—augmented by documentaries, Oliver Stone's film, and interpretations yet to be devised—perhaps she may find some personal meaning within the con-fines of this site.

I concluded in those quiet moments on the seventh floor that the power of Dealey Plaza is left to individual perception, whether someone visits as a tour-ist, a mourner, a researcher, a historian, or an unwilling member of a school group, tour, or family unit. Like Ford's Theater, Pearl Harbor, the Lorraine Motel in Memphis, the Alfred P. Murrah Federal Building in Oklahoma City, and the footprint of the World Trade Center, Dealey Plaza, "stained by the blood of vio-lence and covered by the ashes of tragedy, force[s] people to face squarely the meaning of an event."[5] For the high school groups that I encounter, personal significance is often found within the context of their collective response to events in their lifetime, whether it be the September 11 terrorist attacks or the inauguration of President Barack Obama.

The site itself, however, maintains a unique aura, connecting instantly with visitors because the plaza is recognizable from books, film, and documentaries—the familiar concrete colonnade and abutment where Abraham Zapruder stood, the graffiti-covered stockade fence on the grassy knoll, the gentle curve downhill toward Stemmons Freeway, the Triple Underpass, and the red brick of the Depository building. Although he was writing about the National Civil Rights Museum in Memphis, Professor Keith Woods's comments about the personal impact of a historic site also apply to Dealey Plaza: "History learned this way is real. It breathes, it bleeds, it cries, it rejoices. It's not easily dismissed, nor easily forgotten, because it's no longer just what you read in a book or saw on a grainy film clip. It embraces you and draws you so close that it becomes more than just a lesson. It becomes you."[6] These were my thoughts in that brief moment of introspection, looking out onto the faces of Dealey Plaza—the gateway to downtown Dallas—and its collection of concrete, grass, and bricks.

EPILOGUE

S o, yeah, why is this all important?" The high school student asked me her question without irony, seated on the front row of an informal question-and-answer session that I was hosting in the south gallery of the museum's seventh floor. A young man seated behind her, briefly intrigued by this charged inquiry, glanced up from his iPhone. For me, it was not a startling question but one that I have been considering, along with the rest of my colleagues at The Sixth Floor Museum at Dealey Plaza, for a very long time.

In the immediate aftermath of the September 11 terrorist attacks, it was easy for me to make understandable comparisons to the emotional impact of the Kennedy assassination. These students seated in front of me, however, though burdened with early childhood memories of 9/11, were likely exhausted from relentless media references to the tragedy over the past decade. And, of course, no one in the audience had firsthand memories of the Oklahoma City bombing or the explosion of the *Challenger*. Without a frame of reference, the exhibition's black-and-white news film—showing eyewitnesses falling to the ground in Dealey Plaza, investigators searching the Texas School Book Depository, mourners overcome by grief outside of Parkland Memorial Hospital—seems so antiquated and inaccessible to young people who are prone to wonder aloud in disbelief why a president would travel into a knowingly hostile environment completely unshielded. The situation remains the same in the museum's school and community outreach programs and its distance learning video connections with classrooms as far away as Alberta, Canada, and Sydney, Australia.

When recording oral history interviews for the museum, I often ask participants if the assassination will matter once the rememberers are gone. John F. Kennedy remains fixed in the popular imagination at the age of forty-six, without any trace of gray hair, while many of the schoolchildren who cheered his arrival in Dallas on November 22, 1963, have started to collect Social Security checks. His charisma and his timeless and easily applicable quotations live on through media, posters, coffee mugs, and T-shirts, yet the individual and the realities of his presidency have slipped largely into myth. The idyllic happiness of "Camelot" diminishes the true cold war danger of the Cuban missile crisis and ongoing civil rights struggles in the South. The grandeur of the Kennedy legacy belies the fact that he was a complex politician whose approval rating had actually fallen during 1963, reaching an administrative low of 56 percent less than two months before the assassination.[1]

The fiftieth anniversary of the President's death in 2013 may be the last significant anniversary witnessed by those participants who played key roles in the Kennedy story. In 2011 alone, sixteen of the museum's Oral History Project participants passed away, including one of the president's pallbearers, the KRLD-TV camera operator who captured the shooting of Lee Harvey Oswald on videotape, and one of Oswald's arresting officers at the Texas Theatre. The few remaining eyewitnesses from Dealey Plaza, constantly in demand for documentaries and public programs, remain the world's last direct links to the tragic moments of the Kennedy assassination.

Executive director Nicola Longford views this crucial anniversary as "the conduit through which we hope to make transformative change for the museum." In addition to enhancing the museum's facilities and developing a series of commemorative programs, Longford and her team see the fiftieth anniversary as a beginning. "It's a renewal," she said, "for new generations of people who will be interested in the subject of the assassination and, more broadly, the context of the assassination."[2]

In addition to supporting a fiftieth anniversary committee established by Mayor Mike Rawlings and working with the City of Dallas on a Dealey Plaza restoration project, the museum finds itself in the unique position of "making positive contributions in numerous ways in [the Dallas/Fort Worth] community." The Sixth Floor Museum at Dealey Plaza has emerged as the primary destination for factual information, audiovisual imagery, and firsthand accounts relating to the Kennedy assassination and its aftermath. As other institutions and organizations contemplate ways of marking or interpreting the fiftieth anniversary, this museum—which many in the community were once so slow to embrace—has started to "reposition itself in the arts and cultural community in a way that it hasn't been."[3] Artists seeking oral histories for inspiration for musical pieces, paintings, or sculptures; students in need of basic information and guidance for school projects; documentary producers in search of both familiar and largely unseen news footage; and dedicated researchers hoping to access original artifacts that might shed light on the mysteries of the assassination now turn to the museum as a valuable historical and cultural resource.

At the heart of this role is a determination to maintain relevancy and ensure that those not alive in 1963 understand the impact that the President's death had on the nation and the world. The museum's series of "Living History" programs, started in 2008, allows school groups and the general public the opportunity to listen in on a live oral history recording and then interact directly with an eyewitness, reporter, or law enforcement official involved in the events of 1963. Public programs on aspects of the Kennedy legacy, such as the Peace Corps or the *Apollo* space program, "make a connection with younger audiences, making this . . . 'ancient history' seem more real."[4] For educators, the museum has offered a number of workshops and institutes that provide teachers with tools necessary to explore the Kennedy years in their classrooms. Most recently, aided by a National Endowment for the Humanities planning grant, the museum's Shared Stories project provides an opportunity to use children's theater as a vehicle for conveying the emotion and drama of the Oral History Project.

Despite this community engagement, many continue to wonder how future generations will view the assassination of President Kennedy. Curator Gary Mack fears that, as time passes, the primary focus will be on conspiracy theories and whodunit conjecture. With the President himself shrouded in the myths and legends of a fictitious Camelot, Mack feels that "the Kennedy legacy will diminish in stature the farther away [we move] from the period. It is the mystery that draws the most people, and in the future, it will be only the mystery."[5] Nicola Longford, in contrast, considers major anniversaries to be opportunities to enhance the story's relevance by bringing "back to the surface opposing points of view, conflicting memories, [and] historical records where things were consciously destroyed or not."[6] Few can dispute that the mystery of the assassination will continue to be a major draw to Dealey Plaza. But once visitors arrive at this National Historic Landmark District perhaps they will find something more, whether it be inspiration from a particular artifact or meaningful oral history account or simply an intangible connection to history through the site itself. Professor Edward Linenthal sees no "'term limits' on emotional engagement," suggesting that even those not alive in 1963 can achieve "a sense of what was lost." Young people make connections to the powerful stories of the Holocaust and the civil rights movement, and even "the emotional engagement with the Civil War is still present."[7]

I began researching this manuscript as my master's thesis at the University of Oklahoma in late 2007 while my wife was pregnant with our first daughter. Now, more than five years later, my precocious Deanna Rose persistently asks questions about the redbrick building where her father works. From the Museum Store, I bought her a plush Kennedy doll that has received a lot of affection over the years as well as a plastic action figure of the late President, who now incongruously lives with Scooby Doo, Spiderman, and Doctor Who in a wooden dollhouse in our living room. Deanna proudly recognizes and identifies John F. Kennedy on an almost daily basis, surprising everyone except close friends and family, who would expect nothing less from my daughter. She sometimes mistakenly believes that I work for President Kennedy or that I have to go to visit him when I leave for work each morning, but she nonetheless understands that he has a connection to that city park downtown. One day very recently I tried to explain to her the basics of the President's death. She stared at me solemnly, finally asking, "He got shot?" I nodded, and she placed her small hand on my shoulder. "I'm sorry, Daddy. It's OK." I suppose that in this tiny personal moment between a father and his daughter I realized in a much larger way that there will always be more to the story of the Kennedy assassination, and more to the story of Dealey Plaza and Dallas, than the question of conspiracy. History, at its best, is full of meaningful drama, tragedy, hubris, and redemption. Whether it is America's struggle for independence, emancipation from the bondage of slavery, the horrors of world war, the aftermath of devastating natural disasters, wondrous achievements in science and medicine, or the triumph of humankind setting foot on the moon, history imprints its mark on the nation's psyche and moves people in profound and often unexpected ways. And if that history is shared and truthfully embraced for all its human moments of loss, frailty, hope, and joy, I believe that we will find meaning in an event such as the Kennedy assassination in 2013, 2063, and beyond.

Back on the museum's seventh floor, I smiled briefly, knowingly, before answering the student's question: "So, yeah, why is this all important?" One possible answer comes from John F. Kennedy, whose words still linger, frozen in time, on a museum exhibit panel a half-century after his death: "History, after all, is the memory of a nation."

NOTES

Introduction

Epigraph: Josiah Thompson, interview by Bob Porter, November 21, 1998, transcription p. 17, Oral History Collection, The Sixth Floor Museum at Dealey Plaza (hereinafter OHC/SFMDP).

1. David Flick, "Grief, suspicion linger on anniversary," *Dallas Morning News*, November 23, 2003.
2. "40th Anniversary Symposium Outline," unpublished internal memorandum, November 2003, Institutional Archives, The Sixth Floor Museum at Dealey Plaza (hereinafter IA/SFMDP). The Sixth Floor Museum at Dealey Plaza; Carlton Stowers, "MASS appeal: Bernstein's Big D story," *Dallas Observer*, November 20, 2003.
3. Glen Gatlin, interview by Stephen Fagin, April 17, 2003, transcription p. 14, OHC/SFMDP.
4. Conover Hunt, interview by Stephen Fagin with Gary Mack, March 26, 2003, transcription p. 9, OHC/SFMDP.
5. Helen B. Callaway, "Plaza area provides stroll through history," *Dallas Morning News*, November 18, 1967.
6. Jack Valenti, interview by Stephen Fagin, February 24, 2004, transcription p. 12, OHC/SFMDP.
7. Memory Books, The Sixth Floor Exhibit, April 1995 and September 2001, IA/SFMDP.
8. KRLD-TV Videotape, November 22, 1963, KRLD-TV/KDFW Collection, The Sixth Floor Museum at Dealey Plaza (hereinafter SFMDP).
9. Bishop and Polk, editors, *And the Angels Wept,* p. 88.
10. "Recent Quotes," *Loss and Renewal: Transforming Tragic Sites* exhibition research, September 24, 2001 (copy in author's files).

Chapter 1. A Site of Tragedy

1. Buell Wesley Frazier, interview by Gary Mack with Stephen Fagin and Dave Perry, June 19, 2002, transcription p. 19, OHC/SFMDP.
2. Ibid., transcription p. 3; *Hearings before the President's Commission on the Assassination of President John F. Kennedy* (hereinafter *Hearings*), vol. 2, p. 212.
3. Posner, *Case Closed,* pp. 199–201.

4. *Hearings,* vol. 3, p. 213.

5. Ibid., pp. 213, 214.

6. *The Warren Commission Report: Report of the President's Commission on the Assassination of President John F. Kennedy,* p. 137.

7. Frazier interview, June 19, 2002, transcription pp. 8–9, 14; Posner, *Case Closed,* p. 202.

8. Posner, *Case Closed,* p. 203.

9. Fagin, "American Biography: Lee Harvey Oswald," p. 72.

10. Ibid., p. 18; *The Warren Commission Report,* pp. 377–78.

11. *Hearings,* vol. 21, pp. 484–95 (quotation on 485).

12. Dorothy M. Bush, interview by Stephen Fagin with Al Maddox, September 11, 2003, transcription p. 5, OHC/SFMDP; *The Warren Commission Report,* pp. 383–84.

13. Fagin, "American Biography: Lee Harvey Oswald," p. 20; *The Warren Commission Report,* pp. 384–86; Posner, *Case Closed,* pp. 27–28 (quotation).

14. Fagin, "American Biography: Lee Harvey Oswald," p. 22 (quotation); *The Warren Commission Report,* p. 687.

15. Fagin, "American Biography: Lee Harvey Oswald," p. 22; *The Warren Commission Report,* pp. 393–94, 691; Posner, *Case Closed,* pp. 51–53, 60–61.

16. Fagin, "American Biography: Lee Harvey Oswald," p. 22; *The Warren Commission Report,* pp. 702–13.

17. Fagin, "American Biography: Lee Harvey Oswald," p. 22; *Hearings,* vol. 1, pp. 10–12; *The Warren Commission Report,* pp. 395, 400–402; Fagin, "American Biography: Lee Harvey Oswald," p. 22.

18. *The Warren Commission Report,* pp. 402–403, 723–24.

19. Ibid.; Fagin, "American Biography: Lee Harvey Oswald," p. 70; *The Warren Commission Report,* pp. 724–28. This theory prompted New Orleans district attorney Jim Garrison's later investigation and subsequently served as the basis for Oliver Stone's 1991 film *JFK.*

20. Fagin, "American Biography: Lee Harvey Oswald," p. 70; *The Warren Commission Report,* pp. 730–36.

21. The commission's controversial findings continue to be debated among researchers and theorists.

22. *The Warren Commission Report,* pp. 111–16.

23. Hunt, *Dealey Plaza National Historic Landmark,* p. 42.

24. Catton, *Four Days,* p. 132.

25. MacNeil, *The Way We Were,* p. 216.

26. David Koenig, interview by Stephen Fagin, August 7, 2007, video recording, OHC/SFMDP; "Theaters, entertainment to observe JFK mourning," *Dallas Morning News,* November 25, 1963; "Parade canceled," *Dallas Morning News,* November 23, 1963; "Most Dallas firms, offices shut doors," *Dallas Morning News,* November 23, 1963.

27. Vivian Castleberry, interview by Stephen Fagin, August 19, 2004, transcription pp. 19–20, OHC/SFMDP.

28. Hunt, *Dealey Plaza National Historic Landmark*, p. 42; Tom Landry, interview by Wes Wise with Bob Porter, April 14, 1996, transcription p. 10, OHC/SFMDP; Gary Cartwright, "Glass not fragile," *Dallas Morning News*, November 24, 1963; Gary Cartwright, "Browns smother Cowboys," *Dallas Morning News*, November 25, 1963.

29. Warren Commission Report, p. 143.

30. Hunt, *JFK for a New Generation*, p. 22; Hunt, *Dealey Plaza National Historic Landmark*, p. 33.

31. Maurice "Nick" McDonald, interview by Stephen Fagin, November 20, 2003, transcription pp. 7–8, OHC/SFMDP. During the arrest, McDonald grabbed Oswald's pistol in such a way that the firing pin caught the flesh of McDonald's hand between his thumb and forefinger so that the gun did not discharge.

32. Ibid., transcription p. 8; *The Warren Commission Report*, p. 200.

33. Fagin, "Dallas Police vs. the World Press: November 1963," p. 38.

34. Hunt, *JFK for a New Generation*, p. 30; Fagin, "Dallas Police vs. the World Press: November 1963," p. 37; *The Warren Commission Report*, p. 200.

35. KRLD-TV Videotape, November 23, 1963, KRLD-TV/KDFW Collection, SFMDP.

36. Robert MacNeil, interview by Stephen Fagin, April 16, 2004, transcription p. 15, OHC/SFMDP.

37. WFAA Radio broadcast, November 22, 1963, WFAA Collection, SFMDP.

38. Darryl Conine, interview by Gary Mack with Stephen Fagin and Arlinda Abbott, January 15, 2002, transcription p. 3, OHC/SFMDP; Organ, "Murder Perch to Museum."

39. Organ, "Murder Perch to Museum"; Conover Hunt, "Lecture 13 of 13," interview by Jeff West with Bob Porter et al., July 29, 1994, transcription p. 12, OHC/SFMDP; "History of 411 Elm Street," IA/SFMDP.

40. Organ, "Murder Perch to Museum"; "History of 411 Elm Street"; Conine interview, January 15, 2002, transcription p. 4.

41. Organ, "Murder Perch to Museum"; Hunt, "Lecture 13 of 13," transcription p. 12; "History of 411 Elm Street"; Frazier interview, June 19, 2002, transcription p. 5.

42. Organ, "Murder Perch to Museum."

43. Luke Mooney, interview by Gary Mack with Stephen Fagin, December 4, 2002, transcription p. 18, OHC/SFMDP.

44. Bert Shipp, interview by Wes Wise with Bob Porter, November 17, 1992, transcription p. 6, OHC/SFMDP.

45. "Spiral of Hate," *New York Times*, November 24, 1963.

46. "The Shame of Dallas, Texas," *Saturday Evening Post*, 237, no. 14 (April 11, 1964): 82.

47. D. V. Harkness, interview by Stephen Fagin, June 29, 2006, video recording, OHC/SFMDP.

48. Charles Elwonger, interview by Stephen Fagin, May 5, 2003, transcription p. 12, OHC/SFMDP.

49. Fagin, "Dallas Police vs. the World Press: November 1963," p. 38.

50. François Pelou, interview by Stephen Fagin, July 22, 2005, video recording, OHC/SFMDP.

51. James Chambers, interview by Wes Wise with Bob Porter, June 10, 1994, transcription p. 14, OHC/SFMDP.

52. Felix McKnight, interview by Bob Porter, March 9, 1995, transcription p. 12, OHC/SFMDP.

53. Erik Jonsson, interview by Wes Wise with Bob Porter, June 30, 1992, transcription p. 17, OHC/SFMDP.

54. Leslie, *Dallas Public and Private,* p. 9.

55. Letters to Mayor Cabell, Earle Cabell papers (Box 11, Folder 1, "Earle Cabell Mayoral Correspondence, Kennedy Assassination, November 24, 1963"), DeGolyer Special Collections Library, Southern Methodist University, Dallas.

56. West, "Wiser Heads Prevailed," p. 61; Chambers interview, June 10, 1994, transcription p. 15.

57. Shelia Irons, interview by Stephen Fagin, March 19, 2009, video recording, OHC/SFMDP.

58. George Jefferies, interview by Stephen Fagin, March 5, 2007, transcription p. 15, OHC/SFMDP.

59. Leslie, *Dallas Public and Private,* pp. 8–9.

60. Blow and Attlesey, "The Tenor of the Times," p. 2.

61. Tom Russell, interview by Stephen Fagin, March 16, 2004, transcription p. 12, OHC/SFMDP.

62. Blow and Attlesey, "The Tenor of the Times," p. 2.

63. Payne, *Big D,* p. 353.

64. Wright, *In The New World,* p. 16.

65. Belli and Carroll, *Dallas Justice,* p. 17.

66. H. D. Quigg, "Flowers wilt where shots once echoed," *Dallas Morning News,* December 1, 1963.

67. Russell interview, March 16, 2004, transcription p. 4.

68. John Birch Society, "About the John Birch Society"; Payne, *Big D,* pp. 351–52; Holloway, ed., *Dallas and the Jack Ruby Trial,* p. 42.

69. Texas State Historical Association, "Walker, Edwin A."

70. Payne, *Big D,* p. 351.

71. Texas State Historical Association, "Walker, Edwin A."

72. Warren Bosworth, interview by Bob Porter, September 24, 1997, video recording, OHC/SFMDP.

73. Marshall Terry, interview by Stephen Fagin, June 18, 2003, transcription p. 14, OHC/SFMDP.

74. Payne, *Big D,* pp. 351–52.

75. Ibid., p. 353; Texas State Historical Association, "First Baptist Church, Dallas."

76. Payne, *Big D,* p. 354; Leslie, *Dallas Public and Private,* p. 87. The National Indignation Convention was alternatively known as Committee or Conference.

77. Payne, *Big D,* pp. 323–24; David Flick, "Sanders' career has embraced history, controversy," *Dallas Morning News,* November 4, 2006.

78. Bruce Alger, Keynote Address at Dallas County Republican Convention, May 14, 1960, Box 8, Folder 19, Bruce Alger Collection, Dallas Public Library.

79. Jess Hay, interview by Bob Porter, February 22, 2001, transcription p. 6, OHC/SFMDP; Payne, *Big D,* p. 324.

80. Terry interview, June 18, 2003, transcription p. 11.

81. Leslie, *Dallas Public and Private,* p. 90.

82. James Chambers, interview by Wes Wise with Bob Porter, June 10, 1994, transcription p. 7, OHC/SFMDP.

83. Ibid.; Payne, *Big D,* p. 351.

84. Payne, *Big D,* p. 353.

85. Segura, *BELO: From Newspapers to New Media,* p. 107.

86. "Change of mounts," *Dallas Morning News,* November 9, 1961.

87. Chambers interview, June 10, 1994, transcription pp. 7–8.

88. James Lehrer and Sue Connally, "LBJ, wife remain calm," *Dallas Morning News,* November 5, 1960; Leslie, *Dallas Public and Private,* pp. 180–81; Belli and Carroll, *Dallas Justice,* pp. 17–18.

89. Leslie, *Dallas Public and Private,* p. 182; Payne, *Big D,* p. 349.

90. Leslie, *Dallas Public and Private,* pp. 182–83; Lehrer and Connally, "LBJ, wife remain calm."

91. Payne, *Big D,* p. 350.

92. Mike Quinn, "Comment continues over demonstration against Johnson," *Dallas Morning News,* November 7, 1960; Leslie, *Dallas Public and Private,* pp. 183–84.

93. "Readers back, rap LBJ demonstration," *Dallas Morning News,* November 7, 1960.

94. Lehrer and Connally, "LBJ, wife remain calm."

95. Allen Duckworth, "LBJ calls pro-Nixon fans at his rally 'discourteous,'" *Dallas Morning News,* November 5, 1960.

96. Richard M. Morehead, "Critics twist Dallas event," *Dallas Morning News,* November 25, 1960; Mike Quinn, "Comment continues over demonstration against Johnson," *Dallas Morning News,* November 7, 1960.

97. Leslie, *Dallas Public and Private,* pp. 184–85; Belli and Carroll, *Dallas Justice,* p. 18.

98. Duckworth, "LBJ calls pro-Nixon fans at his rally 'discourteous.'"

99. Quinn, "Comment continues over demonstration against Johnson"; Donald Janson, "Jeering Texans swarm around Johnson and his wife on way to rally," *New York Times,* November 5, 1960; John J. Lindsay, "Johnson hissed and shoved around by Dallas crowd of Nixon boosters," *Washington Post,* November 5, 1960.

100. Morehead, "Critics twist Dallas event."

101. Leslie, *Dallas Public and Private,* pp. 190–93; Payne, *Big D,* pp. 353–54.

102. Payne, *Big D,* p. 355; Leslie, *Dallas Public and Private,* pp. 194–95.

103. "Banner at U.N. Day rally swaps sides in mid-act," *Dallas Times Herald,* October 25, 1963.

104. Payne, *Big D,* pp. 355–56; Leslie, *Dallas Public and Private,* p. 195.

105. Stanley Marcus, interview by Wes Wise with Bob Porter, July 11, 1995, transcription p. 14, OHC/SFMDP.

106. "Stevenson gets Dallas apology for treatment," *Dallas Times Herald,* October 26, 1963; Payne, *Big D,* p. 356.

107. "Dallas disgrace," *Dallas Times Herald,* October 25, 1963.

108. Ibid.; Leslie, *Dallas Public and Private,* p. 197.

109. Leslie, *Dallas Public and Private,* pp. 197–98; Payne, *Big D,* p. 360.

110. Leslie, *Dallas Public and Private,* pp. 199, 358–59.

111. Helen Holmes, interview by Wes Wise with Bob Porter, May 5, 1993, transcription p. 12, OHC/SFMDP; Leslie, *Dallas Public and Private,* p. 205.

112. Leslie, *Dallas Public and Private,* p. 205; Hunt, *Dealey Plaza National Historic Landmark,* p. 26.

113. Hunt, *Dealey Plaza National Historic Landmark,* p. 26; Payne, *Big D,* p. 361.

114. Payne, *Big D,* p. 361.

115. Wright, *In The New World,* p. 15.

116. Hunt, *Dealey Plaza National Historic Landmark,* p. 26; Evadeane Peters, interview by Stephen Fagin, April 12, 2005, video recording, OHC/SFMDP.

117. Dr. A. Jack Jernigan, interview by Stephen Fagin, August 16, 2007, video recording, OHC/SFMDP.

118. Tom Dillard, interview by Wes Wise with Bob Porter, July 19, 1993, transcription p. 15, OHC/SFMDP.

119. Connally and Herskowitz, *From Love Field,* p. 7.

120. Rev. William A. Holmes, interview by Stephen Fagin, March 2, 2007, transcription pp. 4–5, OHC/SFMDP.

121. Ibid., transcription p. 7; Payne, *Big D,* p. 366.

122. Holmes interview, March 2, 2007, transcription p. 7.

123. Ibid., transcription p. 9.

124. Jonsson, interview, June 30, 1992, transcription p. 17.

125. Kent Biffle, "Reporters question tag of 'trial of century,'" *Dallas Morning News,* February 18, 1964.

126. Holloway, *Dallas and the Jack Ruby Trial,* pp. 55–56, 65; Huffaker, Mercer, Phenix, and Wise, *When the News Went Live: Dallas 1963,* p. 134.

127. Holloway, *Dallas and the Jack Ruby Trial,* p. 66.

128. Ibid., pp. 69–70; Dempsey, *The Jack Ruby Trial Revisited,* p. 9.

129. Holloway, *Dallas and the Jack Ruby Trial,* p. 5; Huffaker et al., *When the News Went Live: Dallas 1963,* p. 135.

130. Belli and Carroll, *Dallas Justice,* p. 153; Holmes interview, May 3, 1993, transcription p. 55.

131. Holmes interview, May 3, 1993, transcription p. 55.

132. KRLD-TV Videotape, March 14, 1964, KRLD-TV/KDFW Collection, SFMDP.

133. Murphy Martin, interview by Bob Porter with Stephen Fagin, June 22, 2001, transcription p. 20, OHC/SFMDP.

134. KRLD-TV Videotape, March 14, 1964.

135. Belli and Carroll, *Dallas Justice*, pp. 1, 3.

136. Tony Zoppi and Larry Grove, "Jack Ruby fires Belli as chief defense counsel," *Dallas Morning News*, March 19, 1964; Associated Press, "Belli plea ignored as court recesses," *Dallas Morning News*, July 30, 1964.

137. Belli and Carroll, *Dallas Justice*, pp. vii (quotation), 4 (quotation)–5, 17, 258, 3 (quotation).

138. Tom Russell interview, March 16, 2004, transcription p. 6; Jonsson interview, June 30, 1992, transcription p. 21.

139. Leslie, *Dallas Public and Private*, pp. 63–65.

140. Gatlin interview, April 17, 2003, transcription p. 6.

141. Bert Holmes, interview by Wes Wise with Bob Porter, August 3, 1993, transcription p. 3, OHC/SFMDP.

142. Leslie, *Dallas Public and Private*, p. 64.

143. Payne, *Big D*, p. 317.

144. Jonsson interview, June 30, 1992, transcription p. 20.

145. Payne, *Big D*, p. 367.

146. Ibid., pp. 367–68; Jonsson interview, June 30, 1992, transcription p. 22.

147. Jonsson interview, August 17, 1992, transcription p. 3.

148. Payne, *Big D*, p. 378.

149. Ibid., p. 379; "Bryghte Godbold Inducted into Alabama Hall of Fame," p. 2.

150. Bryghte Godbold, interview by Stephen Fagin, October 11, 2007, transcription p. 7, OHC/SFMDP.

151. Payne, *Big D*, pp. 372, 379.

152. Steve McGonigle, "Survey: JFK's death still haunts Dallasites," *Dallas Morning News*, November 8, 1988.

153. Gatlin interview, April 17, 2003, transcription p. 14.

154. Dr. Glenn M. Linden, interview by Bob Porter with Ray Langston, August 4, 1997, transcription p. 7, OHC/SFMDP.

155. Lacie Ballinger et al., *The Rededication of the John Fitzgerald Kennedy Memorial: June 24, 2000*, pp. 2, 5–11.

156. Ibid., p. 2.

157. Ibid., pp. 3, 9–15, 18.

158. Ibid., pp. 26–27; "History of the John F. Kennedy Memorial Plaza."

159. Ballinger et al., *The Rededication of the John Fitzgerald Kennedy Memorial*, p. 30.

160. James K. Lambert, dir., *From That Moment On*, IA/SFMDP.

161. Jacquielynn Floyd, "Love JFK Memorial or hate it, at least we're talking," *Dallas Morning News*, March 10, 2006; David Dillon, "Let it be—Don't move it or redesign

it," *Dallas Morning News*, April 10, 2006. Occasional arguments that the memorial should be moved or replaced continue to gain local media attention, most recently in 2006 following a widely publicized negative review by Canadian architect and critic Witold Rybczynski. As of 2013, it remains at the original site, with no current plans for relocation or removal. To help explain Philip Johnson's intent with the cenotaph, The Sixth Floor Museum at Dealey Plaza installed interpretive text panels at the site as part of a renovation project at the memorial's thirtieth anniversary.

162. "Death site memorial sought," *Dallas Morning News*, June 19, 1965; Ballinger et al., *The Rededication of the John Fitzgerald Kennedy Memorial*, p. 9.

163. Carl Harris, "Park Board to get plans for bronze JFK marker," *Dallas Morning News*, March 6, 1966; "Kennedy memorial marker," *Dallas Morning News*, March 8, 1966; "Council asks new study of JFK marker," *Dallas Morning News*, March 22, 1966; "Data approved for JFK marker," *Dallas Morning News*, April 5, 1966; Gene Ormsby, "Kennedy plaque placed," *Dallas Morning News*, November 17, 1966.

164. "Data approved for JFK marker"; Ormsby, "Kennedy plaque placed."

165. Ormsby, "Kennedy plaque placed"; Maryln Schwartz, "Tribute paid to Kennedy," *Dallas Morning News*, November 23, 1966.

166. Carlos Conde, "Grieved turn drab building into Dallas shrine to JFK," *Dallas Morning News*, November 24, 1963.

167. Ike Pappas, interview by Wes Wise with Conover Hunt and Bob Porter, March 1, 1993, transcription p. 19, OHC/SFMDP.

168. Joe Thornton, "Reverent, curious come to pay final respects," *Dallas Morning News*, December 22, 1963; Conde, "Grieved turn drab building into Dallas shrine to JFK."

169. Tom Russell interview, March 16, 2004, transcription p. 9.

170. Ibid., transcription p. 10. Russell's impressive tribute appears in several films and photographs taken that weekend, but he was soon asked to remove it by the Dallas Park Department because the display's accompanying sign included the name of his development corporation and was considered advertising (ibid., pp. 9–10).

171. Pappas interview, March 1, 1993, transcription p. 19.

172. Quigg, "Flowers wilt where shots once echoed."

173. Ibid.; Conde, "Grieved turn drab building into Dallas shrine to JFK."

174. Conde, "Grieved turn drab building into Dallas shrine to JFK."

175. "Depository 'off limits,'" *Dallas Morning News*, January 4, 1964.

176. Bill Holt, interview by Stephen Fagin, June 26, 2008, transcription pp. 3–4, OHC/SFMDP.

177. Hugh Aynesworth, "Visit proves 'invaluable' to 3 probers," *Dallas Morning News*, May 10, 1964; Carlos Conde, "Russell startles sightseers by aiming rifle from window," *Dallas Morning News*, September 7, 1964.

178. "Candidates for Senate seat speak," *Dallas Morning News*, October 31, 1967. The sign's electronic time and temperature were permanently turned off on December 11, 1973, during the United States energy crisis (see Jim Lewis, "Hertz calls 'time out' on roof sign," *Dallas Morning News*, December 12, 1973).

179. Douglas Domeier, "School Book Depository will be sold at auction," *Dallas Morning News,* March 12, 1970.

180. Gary Mack, interview by Stephen Fagin, October 17, 2008.

181. Domeier, "School Book Depository will be sold at auction"; James Overton, "Depository for sale," *Dallas Morning News,* April 11, 1970. An article in the *Dallas Morning News* suggested that Byrd, then age seventy, simply wanted to dump the controversial building along with an estimated $4 million of other Dallas properties that he owned to devote more time to fishing and other recreational activities.

182. Domeier, "School Book Depository will be sold at auction." Prior to the auction, the building was named as a possible location for an extension of the Dallas County Jail in an "emergency situation" (see John Geddie, "Action put off on old jail use," *Dallas Morning News,* March 27, 1970).

183. Overton, "Depository for sale."

184. Ibid.

185. Maryln Schwartz, "The mysterious Mr. Mayhew," *Dallas Morning News,* August 29, 1971.

186. Ibid. By allegedly liquidating a publishing company he owned, Mayhew secured the $168,000 down-payment within the required ten-day time frame.

187. Tom Johnson, "Nashville man bids $650,000 for building," *Dallas Morning News,* April 17, 1970.

188. Terry Kliewer and Bryan Martin, "JFK Museum slated for Depository," *Dallas Morning News,* July 23, 1971.

189. Schwartz, "The mysterious Mr. Mayhew."

190. Ibid.; Gary Mack, e-mail to author, April 13, 2012.

191. Hugh Aynesworth, "Depository controversy lingers," *Dallas Morning News,* November 18, 1971.

192. Kliewer and Martin, "JFK Museum slated for Depository."

193. Maryln Schwartz, "Buyer of Book Depository planning display of items," *Dallas Morning News,* July 27, 1971.

194. James L. Hendricks, interview by Stephen Fagin, September 19, 2008, transcription pp. 4–5, OHC/SFMDP.

195. Schwartz, "Buyer of Book Depository planning display of items."

196. Ibid.

197. "Fund drive planned for center," *Dallas Morning News,* April 11, 1972; Mike Fresques, "Depository hit By arson blaze," *Dallas Morning News,* July 21, 1972.

198. Mack interview, October 17, 2008.

199. Schwartz, "The mysterious Mr. Mayhew."

200. Mack interview, October 17, 2008.

201. Don Mason, "Old Depository in money trouble," *Dallas Morning News,* July 7, 1972.

202. "Cornerstone removed from old Depository," *Dallas Morning News,* July 17, 1972.

203. Mason, "Old Depository in money trouble"; Fresques, "Depository hit by arson blaze."

204. Hendricks interview, September 19, 2008, transcription p. 5.

205. "Cornerstone removed from old Depository."

206. Fresques, "Depository hit by arson blaze." Ironically, the same sprinkler system that saved the building from fire in July had caused severe flooding in January—another headache for Aubrey Mayhew in the twilight of his ownership of the Depository. Pipes on the seventh floor, having thawed after frigid weather, caused water to seep "down through all of the floors to the basement, where it was about six inches deep" ("Water hits Depository building," *Dallas Morning News,* January 6, 1972).

207. Fresques, "Depository hit by arson blaze"; Schwartz, "Buyer of Book Depository planning display of items."

208. Schwartz, "Buyer of Book Depository planning display of items."

209. Ibid.

210. Tony Castro, "Mayhew to file fire suit," *Dallas Morning News,* July 30, 1972; "Missing fee blocks appeal," *Dallas Morning News,* August 12, 1972.

211. "Weather vane," *Dallas Morning News,* July 30, 1972.

212. "Missing fee blocks appeal." At the time Mayhew told the *Morning News* that the bank officials "had been reasonable" with him. Twenty-five years later, however, he blamed the powerful leadership of Dallas and "the people who killed Kennedy" for the foreclosure by ensuring that the bank would not extend additional credit or alter the terms of his loan (Mack interview, October 17, 2008).

213. George Proctor, "Mayhew loses old Depository at auction," *Dallas Morning News,* August 2, 1972. After the sale Mayhew's attorney appealed to the federal court; but according to the *Dallas Morning News* the appeal was summarily rejected because Solon failed to pay the $5 filing fee. Solon countered that, as a full-time mechanic, he could not visit the clerk's office during business hours and was forced to "slip his written motions under the door, no questions asked" ("Missing fee blocks appeal").

214. Pete Oppel, "Promoter faced sentence," *Dallas Morning News,* September 10, 1976.

215. Conover Hunt, "Lecture 2 of 13," interview by Jeff West with Bob Porter et al., February 11, 1994, transcription p. 3, OHC/SFMDP.

216. Holt interview, June 26, 2008, transcription p. 9.

217. C. Judson Shook, interview by Wes Wise with Bob Porter, August 13, 1992, transcription p. 6, OHC/SFMDP.

218. Oppel, "Promoter faced sentence."

219. Castro, "Mayhew to file fire suit."

220. Mack interview, October 17, 2008.

221. Ibid.

222. Bill Hunter, "McKool to propose buying Depository," *Dallas Morning News,* December 14, 1968.

223. L. A. Mote, "Demolish Depository," *Dallas Morning News,* September 10, 1972.

224. R. Miles, "Parthenon for Dallas," *Dallas Morning News,* September 17, 1972.

225. "Council halts alteration of landmark," *Dallas Morning News,* September 6, 1972.

226. Hunt, "Lecture 2 of 13," transcription p. 3.

Chapter 2. A Site of Shame

1. Fred M. Zeder II, "A memorial to what?" *Dallas Times Herald,* September 10, 1972.

2. Ibid.; L. A. Mote, "Demolish Depository," *Dallas Morning News,* Letters from Readers, September 10, 1972.

3. "Book building solutions sought," *Dallas Morning News,* September 11, 1972.

4. Ibid.; Jerry McCarty, "Depository demolition ruled out," *Dallas Times Herald,* September 12, 1972.

5. Marc Bernabo, "Council rejects razing," *Dallas Morning News,* September 12, 1972.

6. "Book building solutions sought," *Dallas Morning News,* September 11, 1972.

7. Bernabo, "Council rejects razing"; Doug Domeier, "Lack of volunteers, funds plague civic organizations," *Dallas Morning News,* June 6, 1976.

8. Bernabo, "Council rejects razing"; "Sedco Board sees changes," *Dallas Morning News,* February 13, 1973.

9. "Book building solutions sought."

10. Wes Wise, interview by Bob Porter, January 25, 1993, transcription p. 34, OHC/SFMDP.

11. Wes Wise, interview by Stephen Fagin, September 22, 2005, transcription p. 25, OHC/SFMDP.

12. Shook interview, August 13, 1992, transcription p. 6, OHC/SFMDP.

13. Ibid., transcription p. 8; Wise interview, September 22, 2005, transcription p. 25.

14. Wise interview, September 22, 2005, transcription p. 25.

15. Shook interview, August 13, 1992, transcription p. 7.

16. Ibid.

17. Ara Haswell, "Grim reminder," *Dallas Morning News,* Letters from Readers, September 20, 1972.

18. Charles J. Steeger, "Reminder enough," *Dallas Morning News,* Letters from Readers, September 30, 1972. The arguments on both sides were remarkably straightforward. For many, the continued existence of the Texas School Book Depository was nothing more than "a sad and disquieting reminder of [the] assassination for which [Dallas] was criticized by many." For others, it was recognized as a historic site or, at the very least, an artifact that might further embarrass the city by its conspicuous absence from Dealey Plaza.

19. "Councilmen studying depository," *Dallas Morning News,* August 31, 1972.

20. Hunt, "Lecture 2 of 13," transcription p. 3, OHC/SFMDP.

21. Zeder, "A memorial to what?"

22. Ibid.; Michael Fresques, "Old Depository is reconsidered," *Dallas Morning News,* January 22, 1973.

23. Bill Hunter, "McKool to propose buying Depository," *Dallas Morning News,* December 14, 1968.

24. Bill Hunter, "Dallas races uncertain," *Dallas Morning News,* November 4, 1968; Dennis Hoover, "Thriller-Diller," *Dallas Morning News,* November 10, 1968.

McKool was elected as part of a Democratic landslide, resulting in twenty-nine Democrats and two Republicans in the Texas State Senate.

25. Hunter, "McKool to propose buying Depository."

26. Mary G. Crawford, "State Sen. McKool must be kidding," *Dallas Morning News,* Letters from Readers, December 21, 1968; W. B. Hallmark, "No economy," *Dallas Morning News,* Letters from Readers, December 23, 1968.

27. Crawford, "State Sen. McKool must be kidding." Contrasting this view, an Ohio resident wrote a letter urging Dallas to "seize this opportunity to make a unique contribution to our national heritage" (James M. Lyons, "McKool's proposal," *Dallas Morning News,* Letters from Readers, January 5, 1969).

28. Hunter, "McKool to propose buying Depository."

29. Ibid.; "McKool suggests panel for museum," *Dallas Morning News,* January 14, 1969.

30. Hunter, "McKool to propose buying Depository."

31. Ballinger et al., *The Rededication of the John Fitzgerald Kennedy Memorial: June 24, 2000,* p. 6.

32. Mary Brinkerhoff, "Chairman launches democratic forces," *Dallas Morning News,* January 10, 1964.

33. Jimmy Banks, "School fund ruling may add to state's taxing problem," *Dallas Morning News,* March 2, 1969.

34. Jimmy Banks, "Kennedy Commission gets approval," *Dallas Morning News,* March 6, 1969; "Kennedy Memorial plan garroted by fund lack," *Dallas Morning News,* September 16, 1970.

35. Ballinger et al., *The Rededication of the John Fitzgerald Kennedy Memorial,* p. 18.

36. Jimmy Banks, "Vote backs bus driver bargaining," *Dallas Morning News,* March 18, 1969.

37. Jimmy Banks, "McKool bill survives fire," *Dallas Morning News,* March 19, 1969.

38. "Woman left out by rule," *Dallas Morning News,* March 26, 1969.

39. Stewart Davis, "Divorce, minimum wage bills win approval of Texas House," *Dallas Morning News,* May 17, 1969.

40. "3 Dallasites to serve on commission," *Dallas Morning News,* July 14, 1970; "Smith's appointments confirmed by Senate," *Dallas Morning News,* May 23, 1971.

41. "Kennedy Memorial plan garroted," *Dallas Morning News,* September 16, 1970.

42. Ibid.; Marilyn Schwartz, "JFK Commission seeks Depository," *Dallas Morning News,* August 21, 1971.

43. "Kennedy Memorial plan garroted," September 16, 1970.

44. Schwartz, "JFK Commission seeks Depository."

45. Marilyn Schwartz, "Take over Depository, McKool requests state," *Dallas Morning News,* July 29, 1971.

46. Schwartz, "JFK Commission seeks Depository." The commission could also accept the building as a donation from Mayhew, but that scenario was highly unlikely (see Mike Kingston, "A state-owned Kennedy Museum?" *Dallas Morning News,* August 17, 1971).

47. Kingston, "A state-owned Kennedy Museum?"

48. Maryln Schwartz, "The mysterious Mr. Mayhew," *Dallas Morning News,* August 29, 1971.

49. Kingston, "A state-owned Kennedy Museum?"

50. Schwartz, "The mysterious Mr. Mayhew."

51. Ibid.; Hugh Aynesworth, "Depository controversy lingers," *Dallas Morning News,* November 18, 1971.

52. Don Mason, "Old Depository in money trouble," *Dallas Morning News,* July 7, 1972.

53. Terry Kliewer, "Old memories of Depository being revived," *Dallas Morning News,* September 14, 1975.

54. Henry Tatum, "Depository bid denied," *Dallas Morning News,* March 24, 1973.

55. Ibid.

56. Incomplete newspaper clipping, *Dallas Times Herald,* March 25, 1973, IA/SFMDP.

57. Tony Castro, "For sale: a historic landmark," *Dallas Morning News,* March 15, 1973. Echoing the nonchalant attitude toward the building that preceded its sale at public auction in 1970, Byrd's spokesman, Warner Lewis, said simply: "The building is just sitting there. . . . Something needs to be done." Neither Byrd nor Lewis commented on the alleged deal that Byrd mentioned when he reclaimed ownership in the summer of 1972, though Lewis indicated that "the stage of serious negotiations" had not been reached with any interested party.

58. "For sale or lease: famous historic Dallas landmark," advertisement, *Dallas Times Herald,* September 12, 1975.

59. Dave McNeely, "Depository: historic site or assassin's monument," *Dallas Morning News,* April 27, 1973.

60. Shook interview, August 13, 1992, transcription p. 5.

61. Holt interview, June 26, 2008, transcription p. 4, OHC/SFMDP; "Fire hazards infest Dallas, speaker warns," *Dallas Morning News,* May 9, 1941.

62. Shook interview, August 13, 1992, transcription p. 8.

63. Castro, "For sale: a historic landmark."

64. Shook interview August 13, 1992, transcription p. 9.

65. Henry Tatum, "Media flooding Dallas for re-cap of tragedy," *Dallas Morning News,* November 19, 1973. On Saturday, November 23, 1963, Wise was assigned to retrace the steps of accused assassin Lee Harvey Oswald. In Dealey Plaza Wise encountered a distraught Jack Ruby—the colorful nightclub owner whom Wise knew casually, as did many reporters and law enforcement officials in Dallas. Ruby told Wise that he hated to think "that Mrs. Kennedy [was] going to have to come back [to Dallas] to testify" in a murder trial. Tears came to Ruby's eyes when Wise mentioned having photographed the western saddles that were to be presented to President Kennedy for his children at the Trade Mart luncheon. This brief exchange gained significance after Ruby fatally shot Oswald the following day, and Wise was called to testify at Ruby's 1964 trial (Wise interview, January 25, 1993, transcription p. 12, OHC/SFMDP).

66. Tatum, "Media flooding Dallas for re-cap of tragedy."

67. Ibid.; "Past Winners of the All-America City Award."

68. "Turnout urged at JFK service," *Dallas Morning News,* November 20, 1973.

69. Dotty Griffith, "Memories clear as Dallas skies," *Dallas Morning News,* November 23, 1973.

70. Wes Wise, interview by Stephen Fagin, September 22, 2005, transcription pp. 21, 25, OHC/SFMDP.

71. Jim Wright, interview by Wes Wise with Bob Porter, February 22, 1996, transcription pp. 21, 30, OHC/SFMDP.

72. "Former mayor Cabell invites businessmen to enter politics—if they can stand the gaff," *Dallas Morning News,* March 21, 1964.

73. Shook Interview, August 13, 1992, transcription p. 10; Hunt, "Lecture 2 of 13," transcription p. 3.

74. Seib, *Dallas: Chasing the Urban Dream,* p. 3.

75. Payne, *Big D,* pp. 370–71.

76. Ibid., pp. 371–72; Seib, *Dallas: Chasing the Urban Dream,* p. 4. Describing this dramatically altered skyline of Dallas, columnist Philip Seib wrote: "The once scattered strands of glass and steel are becoming forests. For the city watcher, Dallas's exuberance is fascinating" (ibid., p. 3).

77. "County eyes Depository building," *Dallas Morning News,* September 16, 1975.

78. Carolyn Barta, "Dallas planning historic district," *Dallas Morning News,* March 9, 1975; Hunt, "Lecture 13 of 13," transcription p. 4. In early 1973 the City Plan Commission proposed an ordinance that would permit "zoned historic landmarks" for entire neighborhoods or individual buildings within the Dallas city limits (Jan Hamill, "Historic designation law readied," *Dallas Morning News,* January 8, 1973).

79. Jeanne Barnes, "Cumberland rejuvenation wins citation," *Dallas Morning News,* November 2, 1971; Shook interview, August 13, 1992, transcription p. 11; Rodger Burson, interview by Arlinda Abbot with Stephen Fagin, February 13, 2002, transcription p. 3, OHC/SFMDP.

80. Shook interview, August 13, 1992, transcription p. 12; Hendricks interview, September 19, 2008, transcription pp. 6–8.

81. Hendricks interview, September 19, 2008, transcription pp. 6–8.

82. "County eyes Depository building"; "County checking out Depository purchase," *Dallas Morning News,* September 27, 1975.

83. "County checking out Depository purchase."

84. Hunt, "Lecture 2 of 13," transcription p. 4.

85. Ibid.; "County ends bid to buy Depository," *Dallas Morning News,* October 3, 1975; Sam Attlesey, "County shopping for office space," *Dallas Morning News,* April 9, 1976; Sam Attlesey, "County gains book building option," *Dallas Morning News,* April 20, 1976.

86. Sam Attlesey, "County may acquire matching funds for Schoolbook Depository purchase," *Dallas Morning News,* April 24, 1976.

87. Attlesey, "County gains book building option."

88. Attlesey, "County may acquire matching funds for Schoolbook Depository purchase."

89. Ibid.; "Looking to the future," *Dallas Morning News,* May 21, 1976.

90. Sam Attlesey, "Schoolbook Depository 1900s restoration urged," *Dallas Morning News,* April 30, 1976.

91. Ibid.

92. Sam Attlesey, "Commissioners indicate county to buy building," *Dallas Morning News,* May 21, 1976.

93. "Looking to the future."

94. Sam Attlesey, "County has eye on two buildings," *Dallas Morning News,* May 28, 1976.

95. Doug Domeier, "Lack of volunteers, funds plague civic organizations," *Dallas Morning News,* June 6, 1976; Sam Attlesey, "Commissioners expected to make decision on bonds," *Dallas Morning News,* February 11, 1977.

96. Attlesey, "Commissioners expected to make decision on bonds."

97. Ann Atterberry, "Years have passed, but not the sorrow," *Dallas Morning News,* November 23, 1976. After Folsom's decision Ron Kessler, chair of the Dallas County Democratic Party, organized his own ten-minute ceremony at the Kennedy Memorial on November 22, 1976. Approximately four hundred individuals gathered for the brief service; Mayor Folsom did not attend.

98. Ibid.; Hugh Aynesworth, "Depository controversy lingers," *Dallas Morning News,* November 18, 1971.

99. Sam Attlesey, "Bond vote shows signs of reviving," *Dallas Morning News,* August 12, 1976; Sam Attlesey, "County revises bond plan; 5c tax rate hike expected," *Dallas Morning News,* August 31, 1977; Mike Kingston, "Planning void costs money," *Dallas Morning News,* March 31, 1977; Sam Attlesey, "$170,000 county loss seen if purchase options lapse," *Dallas Morning News,* June 2, 1977; Sam Attlesey, "Commissioners try to stay solid on downtown site," *Dallas Morning News,* July 6, 1977.

100. Attlesey, "County revises bond plan; 5c tax rate hike expected"; "County bond election to offer voters five propositions," *Dallas Morning News,* September 2, 1977; "County bond election to offer voters five propositions," *Dallas Morning News,* September 2, 1977. Proposition No. 3's capital improvements included funds to renovate the sheriff's department crime lab as well as the county's juvenile detention center and some courthouses, including the Old Red Courthouse in Dealey Plaza. It also provided for the construction of a new mental health center and a county-wide "fire prevention and safety program" (Attlesey, "County revises bond plan; 5c tax rate hike expected"; "County bond election to offer voters five propositions").

101. Mrs. Edward Oliver, "Letters: yes vote urged for Proposition 3," *Dallas Morning News,* November 3, 1977.

102. "County bond election to offer voters five propositions."

103 Ibid.; Sam Attlesey, "Sheriff supports bond election," *Dallas Morning News,* September 16, 1977.

104. Sam Attlesey, "Dallas County voters approve bond plan," *Dallas Morning News,* November 9, 1977.

105. Sam Attlesey, "Commissioners quickly decide on list of projects to get bond funding," *Dallas Morning News,* November 11, 1977.

106. Shook interview, August 13, 1992, transcription pp. 9, 21.

Chapter 3. A Site of Reflection

1. Shook interview August 13, 1992, transcription pp. 8–9.

2. Philip Wuntch, "Martin Jurow, 1911–2004—Movie producer, stars' agent," *Dallas Morning News,* February 13, 2004.

3. Martin Jurow, interview by Bob Porter, May 12, 1993, transcription p. 4, OHC/SFMDP.

4. Lindalyn Adams, interview by Wes Wise with Bob Porter, March 14, 1997, transcription pp. 17–18, OHC/SFMDP; Hunt, "Lecture 2 of 13," transcription p. 5.

5. Adams interview, March 14, 1997, transcription p. 19. Adams frowned upon extremist acts from either end of the political spectrum and remained disturbed by some of the more radical right-wing demonstrations that took place in the city at the time. Although she recalled feeling "just sick" after John F. Kennedy's election in 1960, she was deeply grieved following his assassination. "I never cried as much in my whole life ever—even [after] losing my father. . . . I [will] never forget the grief and the trauma, and then . . . add to that the way Dallas was being blamed and maligned" (transcription pp. 9, 12–13).

6. Ibid., transcription pp. 15–17.

7. Ibid., transcription p. 22.

8. Burson interview February 13, 2002, transcription p. 5.

9. Dr. David L. Vanderwerken, "NEH project focuses on Dallas building with a tragic past," *Texas Humanist,* May 1979; Martha Heimberg, "County grapples with appropriate handling," *Dallas Downtown News,* February 13, 1978.

10. Vanderwerken, "NEH project focuses on Dallas building with a tragic past"; Shook interview, August 13, 1992, transcription p. 18.

11. Judson Shook, memorandum, telephone conversation with Ford's Theater curator, December 7, 1979, IA/SFMDP. Three years after the opening of The Sixth Floor exhibit Shook continued to reflect upon the history of Ford's Theater. Emphasizing the century that passed before the theater was renovated and reopened, he said: "Our community has done the same thing in a period of twenty-five or thirty years. And I hope the people a hundred years from now look at this and take into account that we were able, as a community, to collectively do this" (Shook interview, August 13, 1992, transcription p. 18).

12. U.S. Representative James M. Collins, letter to Mr. Judson Shook, January 20, 1978, IA/SFMDP.

13. Sam Attlesey, "'Oswald shrine' opposed," *Dallas Morning News,* January 27, 1978. Nonplussed by his criticism, the Commissioners Court dismissed Collins's public proposal as "ridiculous."

14. Philip Bacon, letter to Mr. Judson Shook, March 1, 1978, IA/SFMDP.

15. Eileen Keerdoja et al., "The Book Depository," *Newsweek Magazine* 91, no. 9, February 27, 1978; Judson Shook, memorandum, National Park Service Involvement in Texas School Book Depository, January 27, 1978, IA/SFMDP. The National Park Service official also told Shook that individuals often overrated the significance of sites in their own communities—an ironic statement considering the Dallas reaction to previous attempts to save the building. The official added that, while an adaptive reuse of the Depository would be challenging, without it the building would exist only to "satisfy the morbid curiosity of the public." Shook wrote in his notes that the Park Service displayed "courtesy without interest."

16. Norman Redlich, letter to Judson Shook, March 8, 1978, IA/SFMDP.

17. Norman Redlich, letter to Editor, *Dallas Morning News,* March 21, 1978, IA/SFMDP.

18. Rev. Lyle Barnett, letter to Judson Shook, March 7, 1978, IA/SFMDP; Hunt, "Lecture 2 of 13," transcription p. 4.

19. Bacon letter, March 1, 1978.

20. Director Louis F. Gorr, Dallas County Heritage Society, Inc., letter to Judson Shook, March 6, 1978, IA/SFMDP.

21. Ibid.; Hunt interview, March 26, 2003, transcription pp. 2–3; The Center for American History, "A Guide to the Lonn Taylor Papers." By one account, the Texas Historical Foundation—the sister organization of the Texas Historical Commission, established in 1965 as the commission's fund-raising arm but more recently engaged in independent preservation projects—provided Adams with $500 to hire an advisor to consult on the project prior to the county renovations (see Texas Historical Foundation, "Our Mission, Our History, Our People"; Hunt, "Lecture 2 of 13," transcription p. 5).

22. Conover Hunt, e-mail to author, January 8, 2009; Hunt interview, March 26, 2003, transcription pp. 28–29. Onassis, whom Hunt described as "very reserved," took the book project to Viking Press and served as its editor. Although Hunt spent years as project director for The Sixth Floor exhibit, she deliberately refrained from mentioning her connection to the former First Lady to any of her colleagues until after Onassis's death in 1994. Hunt recalled: "I certainly never contacted her [about The Sixth Floor project]. I had her address in New York, but . . . it would have been terribly inappropriate to involve her in this."

23. Hunt, "Lecture 2 of 13," transcription pp. 5–6, 3.

24. Conover Hunt, "Lecture 4 of 13," interview by Jeff West with Bob Porter et al., February 22, 1994, transcription pp. 11–12, OHC/SFMDP.

25. Hunt, "Lecture 2 of 13," transcription p. 6; Adams interview, March 14, 1997, transcription p. 22.

26. Adams interview, March 14, 1997, transcription p. 22; Conover Hunt-Jones, memorandum to Jack W. Robinson, City of Dallas, Consultant Commitment, April 13, 1979, IA/SFMDP.

27. Shook interview, August 13, 1992, transcription p. 13. This was something of a pet project for Shook, so he went to great lengths to ensure that the renovation of the space went according to plan, involving himself with the architects at every possible juncture.

28. Hunt, "Lecture 2 of 13," transcription p. 5; Don Mason, "Depository renovation planned," *Dallas Morning News,* November 5, 1977.

29. Hunt, "Lecture 2 of 13," transcription p. 5.

30. Hendricks interview, September 19, 2008, transcription pp. 6–7; Burson interview, February 13, 2002, transcription p. 4; The Spaghetti Warehouse Restaurant, "About Us."

31. Burson interview, February 13, 2002, transcription p. 5; Hendricks interview, September 19, 2008, transcription p. 8; Shook interview, August 13, 1992, transcription p. 12. Rodger Burson interviewed six structural engineers before selecting Thomas Taylor of Datum Engineers in Dallas to solve the problem of the window arches. Examples of the concrete screen on the Depository's exterior were saved for historical purposes.

32. Sam Attlesey, "Schoolbook Depository 1900s restoration urged," *Dallas Morning News,* April 30, 1976.

33. Hunt interview, March 26, 2003, transcription p. 4.

34. Burson interview, February 13, 2002, transcription p. 5; Hendricks interview, September 19, 2008, transcription p. 8.

35. Hendricks interview, September 19, 2008, transcription pp. 10, 7, 11, 33–34.

36. Ibid., transcription p. 8.

37. James L. Hendricks, interview by Stephen Fagin, December 1, 2008, transcription p. 5, OHC/SFMDP.

38. "County to let ABC film book Depository," *Dallas Morning News,* May 24, 1977; Tom Belden, "Spectators flashback," *Dallas Morning News,* July 4, 1977.

39. Eric Miller, "Nov. 22 re-enacted," *Dallas Morning News,* August 21, 1978. Lindalyn Adams, who watched from the sixth floor during these acoustical tests, recorded by one dozen microphones in Dealey Plaza, recalled that "there were forty or so shots [fired] from up there, and it was just deafening" (Adams interview, March 14, 1997, transcription p. 36).

40. Hunt interview, March 26, 2003, transcription p. 3.

41. Doug Domeier, "Advisor wants to know how many see JFK site," *Dallas Morning News,* September 9, 1978.

42. Hunt interview, March 26, 2003, transcription p. 3.

43. "Pedestrian Survey Results—Texas School Book Depository," 1978, IA/SFMDP; Domeier, "Advisor wants to know how many see JFK site."

44. Hunt, "Lecture 2 of 13," transcription p. 9.

45. Ibid., transcription p. 6.

46. Domeier, "Advisor wants to know how many see JFK site."

47. Scott Parks, "Depository revamp planned," *Dallas Morning News,* ca. April 1979, IA/SFMDP; Director Ramon Eduardo Ruiz, Division of Public Programs, letter to Judson Shook, May 31, 1979, IA/SFMDP.

48. Hunt interview, March 26, 2003, transcription p. 4.

49. Hunt, "Lecture 2 of 13," transcription p. 7.

50. Ibid.; Adams interview, March 14, 1997, transcription p. 24; Alexander Architectural Archive, *Walter Eugene George, Jr.*; Eugene George, interview by Stephen Fagin, September 11, 2008, transcription pp. 3–4, OHC/SFMDP.

51. George interview, September 11, 2008, transcription pp. 2–5.

52. Hunt, "Lecture 2 of 13," transcription p. 7. Lindalyn Adams recalled, "My sister lived in Singapore . . . [and] she called home and she said, 'Lindalyn, your name is in the paper.'" Via the wire service, news of the planning meeting had reached the *Singapore Straits Times* among other international newspapers (Adams interview, March 14, 1997, transcription p. 35).

53. Gary Shultz, "Committee plans Texas School Book Depository museum," *Dallas Times Herald,* April 13, 1979.

54. Adams interview, March 14, 1997, transcription p. 25.

55. Shultz, "Committee plans Texas School Book Depository museum."

56. Ibid.; Nicola Longford et al., "Founders Luncheon," February 16, 2009, transcription p. 11, OHC/SFMDP.

57. Hunt, *Dealey Plaza National Historic Landmark.* The House Select Committee on Assassinations published its delayed final report in July 1979 after the planning meeting in Dallas.

58. Scott Parks, "Depository revamp planned," *Dallas Morning News,* ca. April 1979, IA/SFMDP.

59. Longford et al., "Founders Luncheon," transcription p. 11.

60. Ibid., transcription p. 10.

61. Hunt, "Lecture 2 of 13," transcription p. 10.

62. Shultz, "Committee plans Texas School Book Depository museum."

63. Hunt, "Lecture 2 of 13," transcription p. 8.

64. Shultz, "Committee plans Texas School Book Depository museum."

65. Parks, "Depository revamp planned."

66. Hunt, "Lecture 2 of 13," transcription p. 7; George D. Akins, memorandum to Mr. Rodger Burson and Mr. Jay Beeman, April 16, 1979, IA/SFMDP. Eugene George had originally hoped to save an entire panel of the first-floor concrete screen. When that proved impractical, county architect George D. Akins recommended that, in addition to photographs and drawings, a total of only four blocks be saved "for duplication in future restorations."

67. Akins, memorandum to Mr. Rodger Burson and Mr. Jay Beeman, April 16, 1979.

68. *Hearings,* vol. 3, p. 250. Baker later testified that by the time he got to a place where he could see the suspect, Oswald "was walking . . . about 20 feet away from [Baker] in the lunchroom." Pistol in hand, Baker called out to Oswald, who turned around

and walked over. By that time Depository building manager Roy Truly, who had been leading Baker upstairs, came back to the second floor and saw Oswald standing "just inside the lunchroom door." Baker asked, "This man work here?" Once Truly informed Baker that he did, Baker was satisfied and left Oswald to hurry up the staircase (ibid., vol. 3, pp. 225, 252).

69. Ibid., vol. 3, p. 225.

70. Akins, memorandum to Mr. Rodger Burson and Mr. Jay Beeman, April 16, 1979; "Pedestrian Survey Results—Texas School Book Depository." Hunt's pedestrian survey in Dealey Plaza from the year before specifically asked about the lunchroom: 68 percent agreed that it should "be preserved in another area of the building."

71. Darryl Conine, interview by Gary Mack with Stephen Fagin and Arlinda Abbott, January 15, 2002, transcription p. 6, OHC/SFMDP.

72. Adams interview, March 14, 1997, transcription p. 26.

73. Hunt interview, March 26, 2003, transcription p. 4.

74. Adams interview, March 14, 1997, transcription pp. 26-27.

75. Hunt, "Lecture 2 of 13," transcription p. 7; Hendricks interview, September 19, 2008, transcription p. 8.

76. Hunt interview, March 26, 2003, transcription p. 6.

77. Shook interview, August 13, 1992, transcription p. 23.

78. "Sign atop Depository due removal," *Dallas Morning News,* November 22, 1977.

79. Judson Shook, letter to Dr. S. Dillon Ripley, Secretary, Smithsonian Institution, March 7, 1978, IA/SFMDP; Judson Shook, letter to Mr. William T. Alderson, Director, American Association of State and Local History, March 7, 1978, IA/ SFMDP; Judson Shook, memorandum to Dallas County Commissioners Court, June 19, 1978, IA/SFMDP.

80. William T. Alderson, Director, American Association for State and Local History, letter to Judson Shook, Director of Public Works, Dallas County Department of Public Works, March 9, 1978, IA/SFMDP.

81. Jim Lewis, "Hertz calls 'time out' on roof sign," *Dallas Morning News,* December 12, 1973; Hunt interview, March 26, 2003, transcription p. 7; Shook, memorandum to Dallas County Commissioners Court, June 19, 1978.

82. Hunt interview, March 26, 2003, transcription p. 6; "Sign atop Depository due removal"; Adams interview, March 14, 1997, transcription pp. 24-25. Hunt remembered the immediate removal of the Hertz sign as the first decision made by the planning committee, though Adams recalled that it took a great deal of discussion. "Historians felt that [it] should stay," she recalled, "that we would really be criticized if we took that down, [because it] had the clock on it that had the time of the assassination—12:30 P.M."

83. "It's all history now," *Dallas Morning News,* May 23, 1979; "Candidates for Senate seat speak," *Dallas Morning News,* October 31, 1967.

84. Longford et al., "Founders Luncheon," transcription pp. 7-8.

85. Hunt interview, March 26, 2003, transcription pp. 3-4; Dr. David L. Vanderwerken, "NEH project focuses on Dallas building with a tragic past," *Texas Humanist,* May

1979, IA/SFMDP; Conover Hunt, "Lecture 6 of 13," interview by Jeff West with Bob Porter et al., March 1, 1994, transcription p. 3, OHC/SFMDP; Hunt, "Lecture 2 of 13," transcription p. 7. "We lost the paint color war," Hunt said in 2003, "but there is original paint underneath any number of the windows on the sixth floor."

86. Hunt, "Lecture 2 of 13," transcription p. 8.

87. Shook interview, August 13, 1992, transcription p. 18.

88. Judson Shook, memorandum, National Park Service Involvement in Texas School Book Depository, January 27, 1978.

89. Ibid.

90. Adams interview, March 14, 1997, transcription p. 31.

91. Shook interview, August 13, 1992, transcription p. 20.

92. Adams interview, March 14, 1997, transcription p. 30; Shook interview, August 13, 1992, transcription p. 20.

93. Shook interview, August 13, 1992, transcription p. 21.

94. Burson interview, February 13, 2002, transcription p. 4.

95. Shook interview, August 13, 1992, transcription p. 21; Adams interview, March 14, 1997, transcription p. 30.

96. Shook, memorandum to Dallas County Commissioners Court, June 19, 1978.

97. The Texas School Book Depository was, however, recognized that year for its use as a warehouse as part of the West End Historic District.

98. National Register of Historic Places, "TEXAS—Dallas County." The Texas Theatre in Oak Cliff where Lee Harvey Oswald was arrested was added to the register in 2003.

99. Judson Shook, memorandum to Dallas County Commissioners Court, November 15, 1979, IA/SFMDP.

100. Conover Hunt, interview by Stephen Fagin, February 16, 2009, video recording, OHC/SFMDP.

101. "Dallas rejects Book Depository restoration," *Washington Post,* April 23, 1980.

102. Ibid.; "Background Summary of Project," ca. 1983, IA/SFMDP.

103. Hunt, "Lecture 2 of 13," transcription p. 9.

104. Joseph P. Treaster, "A life that started out with much promise took reclusive and hostile path," *New York Times,* April 1, 1981. News of the shooting hit Lindalyn Adams particularly hard because Hinckley grew up in her own neighborhood of Highland Park and had even attended school with her son (Adams interview, March 14, 1997, transcription p. 37).

105. Philip Taubman, "Suspect got idea some time ago, investigators say," *New York Times.* April 2, 1981.

106. Hunt interview, March 26, 2003, transcription p. 10; Hunt, "Lecture 2 of 13," transcription p. 9.

107. Texas Historical Commission, "Formerly the Texas School Book Depository building."

108. Ibid.; Longford et al., "Founders Luncheon," transcription p. 9.

109. Marjie Mugno, "Judson Shook making 'functional' history," *Dallas Downtown News*, November 26, 1979; Adams interview, March 14, 1997, transcription p. 40.

110. Adams interview, March 14, 1997, transcription p. 29.

111. Shook interview, August 13, 1992, transcription p. 16.

112. Adams interview, March 14, 1997, transcription p. 32. John Sissom's reasoning behind the awkward timing of his meeting with Adams remains unclear, although it reflects a desire to take advantage of a year-end tax deduction by making a donation to the nonprofit historical foundation.

113. Elna Christopher, "Kennedy museum to close in January," *Dallas Morning News*, October 30, 1981; Winston Churchill, "We Shall Fight on the Beaches."

114. Jeffry S. Unger, "Looking for a home," *Dallas Times Herald*, November 22, 1981.

115. "JFK Museum to tell reaction to tragedy," *Dallas Morning News*, July 6, 1970; Christopher, "Kennedy museum to close in January"; Vanderwerken, "NEH project focuses on Dallas building with a tragic past."

116. Dan Piller, "Kennedy museum losing its lease," *Dallas Times Herald*, October 29, 1981.

117. 501 Elm Street—known as the Dal-Tex building at the time of the assassination—did play into at least one conspiracy theory, situating a gunman on the second floor; in 1963 it also housed the dress manufacturing company co-owned by Abraham Zapruder, who famously filmed the assassination with his home movie camera.

118. Vanderwerken, "NEH project focuses on Dallas building with a tragic past"; Unger, "Looking for a home."

119. Unger, "Looking for a home."

120. Ibid.; Piller, "Kennedy museum losing its lease."

121. Adams interview, March 14, 1997, transcription p. 32. Nothing from the John F. Kennedy Museum made its way into the finished exhibition on the sixth floor that opened in 1989. In fact, following the 1984 arson attempt, Lindalyn Adams noted that she was unconcerned about whether the fire had damaged "things . . . from the old Kennedy museum" because they were "not anything we could use and without any intrinsic value" (Barry Boesch, "Fire breaks out at Book Depository," *Dallas Morning News*, August 23, 1984).

122. Christy Hoppe, "Tourists find door shut on history," *Dallas Morning News*, May 20, 1982. With his office located on the first floor, Aldo Hill, an employee in the county's budget office, became the building's "heavy"—so named by the *Dallas Morning News*—who frequently explained to tourists that the sixth floor was closed to the public. Another county employee said that, even though the elevators only went up to the second floor following phase one of the renovation, individuals still tried to access the sixth floor by pushing the nonfunctioning fifth floor button. Explained secretary Sylvia Martinez, "The [elevator] doors will open and shut and open and shut. I tell them there's no way up—and they look a little embarrassed."

123. Laura Miller, "Making peace with the past," *Dallas Morning News*, November 22, 1985.

124. George interview, September 11, 2008, transcription p. 24.

125. Adams interview, March 14, 1997, transcription p. 33. During this period Adams notably gave a tour to historian and author William Seale and Shirley Payne Low of Colonial Williamsburg. Adams later recalled that they did not have warm feelings toward the space and "just couldn't quite understand" the project.

126. Robert Staples and Barbara Charles, interview by Bob Porter, August 30, 1994, transcription p. 3, OHC/SFMDP; Adams interview, March 14, 1997, transcription p. 33; Staples and Charles, Ltd., "Online Portfolio"; "Exhibitions from the Past," *Archives/Corcoran Gallery of Art Online*; Conover Hunt, e-mail to author, January 8, 2009.

127. Hunt interview, February 16, 2009; Staples and Charles interview, August 30, 1994, transcription p. 3.

128. Staples and Charles, Ltd., "Online Portfolio."

129. Adams interview, March 14, 1997, transcription p. 33; Longford et al., "Founders Luncheon," transcription p. 8.

130. Barbara Charles, letter to Mrs. Reuben H. Adams, Chairman, Dallas County Historical Commission, December 3, 1980, IA/SFMDP.

131. Staples and Charles interview, August 30, 1994, transcription p. 4.

132. Mrs. Reuben H. Adams, letter to Barbara Charles, Staples and Charles Ltd., January 8, 1981, IA/SFMDP.

133. Hunt interview, March 26, 2003, transcription p. 9; Hunt interview, February 16, 2009. Barbara Charles has suggested that Hunt told Adams about the design firm, instigating their first contact at the Dallas Historical Society. Adams maintains that it was John Crain, then director of the society, who recommended that she consider the designers for The Sixth Floor project (Longford et al., "Founders Luncheon," transcription p. 8).

134. Adams interview, March 14, 1997, transcription p. 34; Dallas County Commissioners Court, Order No. 821269, State of Texas, Dallas County, August 9, 1982, IA/SFMDP.

135. Burson, Hendricks, and Walls, Conference Record, "Project: School Book 6th Floor, Project No. 8210," May 27, 1982, IA/SFMDP.

136. Burson interview, February 13, 2002, transcription p. 10.

137. Burson, Hendricks, and Walls, Conference Record, "Project: School Book 6th Floor, Project No. 8210."

138. Hendricks interview, September 19, 2008, transcription p. 13.

139. Hendricks interview, December 1, 2008, transcription p. 8.

140. Staples and Charles, Ltd, "Sixth Floor—Texas School Book Depository—Dallas," Exhibit Layout Sketch, 1982, IA/SFMDP; Laura Miller, "Panel unveils plans for JFK museum," *Dallas Morning News,* April 20, 1983.

141. Hendricks interview, September 19, 2008, transcription p. 14.

142. Ibid., transcription pp. 16, 39.

143. Hunt, "Lecture 6 of 13," March 1, 1994, transcription p. 17. Hendricks explained, "I'm walking into the space and here's the brick envelope and here is all . . . the woodwork, the beaded board ceiling. . . . We didn't want to walk into just a new

contemporary look or a new retail store look" (Hendricks interview, September 19, 2008, transcription p. 18).

144. George interview, September 11, 2008, transcription p. 6.

145. Ibid., transcription pp. 14, 7.

146. Staples and Charles interview, August 30, 1994, transcription p. 5.

147. Ibid., transcription p. 6.

148. Staples and Charles, Ltd, "Sixth Floor—Texas School Book Depository—Dallas."

149. Ibid.

150. Ibid.

151. Hunt, "Lecture 2 of 13," transcription p. 11.

152. Jeff Brown, "Proposed JFK exhibit could cost $3 million," *Dallas Times Herald,* April 20, 1983.

153. Lindalyn Adams, handwritten notes, April 19, 1983, IA/SFMDP.

154. Brown, "Proposed JFK exhibit could cost $3 million."

155. Shirley Caldwell, Chairman, Dallas County Historical Commission, letter to James L. Hendricks, April 21, 1983, IA/SFMDP.

156. Miller, "Panel unveils plans for JFK museum."

157. "Kennedy won't speak in Dallas, Fraser says," *Dallas Morning News,* April 20, 1983.

158. Wayne King, "Dallas mayor-elect says he will chart an international course for his city," *New York Times,* May 1, 1983.

159. Ibid.; Clifton Caldwell, letter to Kevin M. Leather, ca. May 1983, IA/SFMDP.

160. Kevin M. Leather, letter to Mayor A. Starke Taylor, Jr., May 4, 1983, IA/SFMDP.

161. C. Carole Monteau, letter to Dallas County Historical Commission c/o Mayor's Office, Dallas, Texas, July 24, 1983, IA/SFMDP.

162. Joe Oppermann, Deputy Preservation Officer, Texas Historical Commission, letter to Mrs. Clifton Caldwell, Chairman, Dallas County Historical Commission, April 19, 1983; Leis Sandberg, Senior Planner, Department of Planning and Development, Dallas, Texas, letter to Shirley Caldwell, Chairman, Dallas County Historical Commission, May 19, 1983, IA/SFMDP.

163. Sally Yerkovich, National Endowment for the Humanities, letter to Sharon Westmoreland, Dallas County Historical Commission, June 2, 1983, IA/SFMDP.

164. Hunt interview, March 26, 2003, transcription pp. 10–11.

165. Staples and Charles Ltd., "Sixth Floor—Texas School Book Depository—Dallas," Exhibit Layout Sketch, 1982.

166. Dallas County Historical Commission, "The 6th Floor: An Exhibition at the Former Texas School Book Depository," draft text for promotional and fund-raising packet, 1983, IA/SFMDP.

167. Ibid.

168. Ibid.

169. Ibid.

170. Hunt, "Lecture 2 of 13," transcription p. 13.

Chapter 4. A Site of Conflict

1. Hunt interview, March 26, 2003, transcription p. 7.
2. "Individuals and Groups Briefed on Exhibit Plans," ca. 1983, IA/SFMDP. Specifically targeted for these community briefings were representatives from the King Foundation and Hoblitzelle Foundation in Dallas.
3. Lindalyn Adams, handwritten notes, June 7, 1983, IA/SFMDP.
4. Hunt interview, March 26, 2003, transcription p. 8.
5. Marcus interview July 11, 1995, transcription p. 17.
6. Ibid., transcription pp. 18, 20.
7. Stanley Marcus Collection, "The JFK Assassination: 40 Years Later—Stanley Marcus Letter."
8. Longford et al., "Founders Luncheon," transcription p. 9.
9. Hunt interview, March 26, 2003, transcription p. 8.
10. Marcus interview, July 7, 1995, transcription p. 22.
11. Joe Simnacher, "John M. Stemmons dies at 92—Dallas family helped control Trinity River," *Dallas Morning News*, July 22, 2001; Hunt interview, March 26, 2003, transcription p. 8. Stemmons was best remembered locally as the businessman who straightened the main channel of Dallas's Trinity River, thus enabling the construction of a ten-lane freeway and an industrial district.
12. John Stemmons, interview by Wes Wise with Bob Porter, August 11, 1992, transcription p. 10, OHC/SFMDP.
13. Hunt interview, March 26, 2003, transcription p. 8.
14. Adams interview, March 14, 1997, transcription p. 39.
15. Stemmons interview, August 11, 1992, transcription p. 12.
16. Hunt, "Lecture 2 of 13," transcription p. 12.
17. Hunt interview, March 26, 2003, transcription pp. 4–9. Old City Park is now known as Dallas Heritage Village.
18. Conover Hunt, "Lecture 1 of 13," interview by Jeff West with Bob Porter et al., February 1, 1994, transcription p. 3, OHC/SFMDP.
19. Richard Lewis, Administrator, Dallas County Commissioners Court, letter to Mrs. Reuben H. Adams, September 27, 1983, IA/SFMDP.
20. Hunt, "Lecture 1 of 13," transcription p. 3.
21. Lewis, Letter to Mrs. Reuben H. Adams, September 27, 1983. The charter granted by the Texas secretary of state was number 640470-1.
22. Lindalyn Adams, handwritten notes, April 19, 26, 30, 1983, IA/SFMDP.
23. Hunt, "Lecture 2 of 13," transcription p. 12.
24. George V. Charlton, letter to Mrs. Reuben Adams, July 5, 1983, IA/SFMDP; John Field Scovell, letter to Commissioner Nancy Judge, April 28, 1983, IA/SFMDP.
25. Hunt, "Lecture 2 of 13," transcription p. 12.
26. "Change of mounts," *Dallas Morning News*, November 9, 1961.
27. Hunt, *Dealey Plaza National Historic Landmark*, p. 26.

28. Joe M. Dealey, interview by Wes Wise and Bob Porter, May 19, 1994, transcription p. 6, OHC/SFMDP; Manchester, *The Death of a President,* p. 110.

29. Adams interview, March 14, 1997, transcription p. 39; "Dallas County Historical Foundation," Current Members/Original Appointment/Term Expires, ca. 1983, IA/ SFMDP; Lucero, "Mayors Reflect on Fight to Build Texas Stadium."

30. Adams interview, March 14, 1997, transcription p. 39; "Dallas County Historical Foundation."

31. "Schedule for Completion of Exhibit," information packet, Dallas County Historical Foundation, ca. 1983, IA/SFMDP.

32. Adams interview, March 14, 1997, transcription p. 39.

33. Hunt, "Lecture 2 of 13," transcription p. 13. Adams's 1983 meeting notes provide some insight into the quality of individual being sought for participation in the project. After her meeting with Jess Hay, she carefully described his tasteful, lavish office space—with "scarlet velvet used extensively on walls, sofa, etc."—and his mannerisms, including having someone from his staff carry the hefty slide projector and model back to Adams's car after the meeting. "Mr. Hay," wrote Adams, "received us cordially, listened well—remarked that exhibit needed to highlight Kennedy and reasons he was such a charismatic leader." Adams wrote that Major General Robinson, whose office was also "tastefully furnished and filled with perfectly gorgeous works of art," listened attentively and readily agreed to serve on the board. Robinson, too, helped carry the ladies' equipment back to their car (Adams, handwritten notes, August 23, 1983).

34. "Hoblitzelle Foundation Home Page."

35. Mrs. Reuben H. Adams, letter to Mr. Robert Lynn Harris, Hoblitzelle Foundation, September 14, 1983, IA/SFMDP.

36. "Schedule for Completion of Exhibit."

37. Adams, letter to Mr. Robert Lynn Harris, September 14, 1983; Adams interview, March 14, 1997, transcription p. 41–42.

38. Dealey interview, May 19, 1994, transcription p. 11.

39. Adams interview, March 14, 1997, transcription p. 42.

40. "Press Interviews, Sixth Floor. Period from late July, 1983 through November 22, 1983," ca. 1983, IA/SFMDP.

41. Adams interview, March 14, 1997, transcription p. 52.

42. Shiffler and Hampton, "20 years later . . . , p. 23.

43. Hunt interview, February 16, 2009.

44. Dallas County Historical Foundation, Board Meeting Minutes, February 15, 1984, IA/SFMDP.

45. Adams, handwritten notes, June 7, 1983.

46. Conover Hunt, "Lecture 3 of 13," interview by Jeff West with Bob Porter et al., February 18, 1994, transcription p. 3, OHC/SFMDP; Maureen Dowd, "A city tour: trauma as legend," *New York Times,* August 22, 1984.

47. Dowd, "A city tour: trauma as legend."

48. Haynes Johnson, "Landmark fire kindles city's grimmest memory," *Washington Post,* August 24, 1984.

49. Adams interview, March 14, 1997, transcription p. 53; Hunt, "Lecture 3 of 13," transcription p. 3.

50. Adams interview, March 14, 1997, transcription p. 53.

51. Barry Boesch, "Fire breaks out at Book Depository," *Dallas Morning News,* August 23, 1984.

52. Walter Borges, "Depository fire was set, officials say," *Dallas Morning News,* August 24, 1984.

53. Wayne King, "Building that hid Oswald hit by fire," *New York Times,* August 24, 1984; John Crewdson, "Site of JFK slaying set afire," *Chicago Tribune,* August 24, 1984.

54. Johnson, "Landmark fire kindles city's grimmest memory."

55. King, "Building that hid Oswald hit by fire"; Alison Muscatine, "Arson ruled in blaze at historic site," *Washington Post,* August 24, 1984.

56. Adams interview, March 14, 1997, transcription p. 54.

57. Mrs. Reuben Adams, memorandum to Board of Directors, Dallas County Historical Foundation, August 27, 1984, IA/SFMDP.

58. Ibid.

59. Christi Harlan, "County approves $92,000 for Depository fire cleanup," *Dallas Morning News,* August 28, 1984.

60. "Anniversary of Kennedy's death is noted quietly at Dealey Plaza," *New York Times,* November 23, 1984.

61. Adams interview, March 14, 1997, transcription p. 44.

62. "Schedule for Completion of Exhibit."

63. Christopher Semos, interview by Bob Porter with Stephen Fagin, February 9, 2001, transcription p. 13, OHC/SFMDP.

64. Judge Lee F. Jackson, interview by Bob Porter with Stephen Fagin, January 12, 2001, transcription p. 9, OHC/SFMDP.

65. Bert L. Rohrer, "County to sell $41 million in bonds," *Dallas Morning News,* May 7, 1985. As far back as December 1979, Judson Shook had encouraged the county to move forward with phase two of the Depository renovation in order to "minimize distraction" once the building was occupied by county commissioners. Proposing that the county allocate funds from the same 1977 bond package that enabled the Depository purchase, Shook estimated at the time that finishing the third and fourth floors would cost just over $1 million (Judson Shook, memorandum to Commissioners Court, December 4, 1979, IA/SFMDP).

66. Hendricks interview, September 19, 2008, transcription p. 34.

67. Mrs. Reuben H. Adams, letter to Ross Perot, December 16, 1985, IA/SFMDP.

68. Laura Miller, "Making peace with the past," *Dallas Morning News,* November 22, 1985.

69. Henry Tatum, "Old wounds are hard to heal," *Dallas Morning News,* December 1, 1985.

70. "History of Sixth Floor Museum News Compilation, 1978–1989," provided to author by Gary Mack.

71. Ibid.; Adams, letter to Ross Perot, December 16, 1985.

72. Miller, "Making peace with the past"; Adams interview, March 14, 1997, transcription p. 41.

73. "History of Sixth Floor Museum News Compilation, 1978–1989."

74. Miller, "Making peace with the past."

75. Adams interview, March 14, 1997, transcription p. 44.

76. John Kirkpatrick, "Kennedy museum remains on hold," *Dallas Morning News,* November 22, 1986.

77. Mrs. Reuben H. Adams, letter to Paul Kahn, December 18, 1984, IA/SFMDP; Mrs. Reuben H. Adams, letter to Gene Peterson, December 18, 1984, IA/SFMDP.

78. Larry R. Powell, "Dart recognized for efforts to be uniformly better," *Dallas Morning News,* September 29, 1986; Ed Bark, "Lawyers in Oswald 'trial' spar," *Dallas Morning News,* October 1, 1986. The Dallas County Clerk's office had cooperated with the producers by "providing the names of 80 potential jurors . . . [while] a marketing firm chose the final 12." The event reaffirmed that emotions still ran high; defense attorney Spence said that an employee at Dallas/Fort Worth International Airport, upon learning what role Spence played in the trial, said, "I hope . . . that nobody ever assassinates you."

79. David Dillon, "Preserving a painful past," *Dallas Morning News,* August 16, 1987.

80. "History of Sixth Floor Museum News Compilation, 1978–1989."

81. Longford et al., "Founders Luncheon," transcription p. 7.

82. Jackson interview, January 12, 2001, transcription p. 9; Kevin Merida, "Jackson may seek new post," *Dallas Morning News,* December 13, 1985.

83. Jackson interview, January 12, 2001, transcription p. 10; Allen Pusey, "Jackson elected county judge," *Dallas Morning News,* November 5, 1986.

84. Jackson interview, January 12, 2001, transcription pp. 9–10. By comparison, Jackson's predecessor as county judge, David G. Fox, stepped down in January 1987 at the age of sixty-three and had already been chair and chief executive officer of the home building firm Fox and Jacobs, Inc., for fourteen years at the time of the assassination (see "Fox, David Gregory," paid obituary, *Dallas Morning News,* December 28, 2003).

85. Adams interview, March 14, 1997, transcription p. 45.

86. Lillian Bradshaw, interview by Bob Porter, May 1, 1998, transcription pp. 12–13, OHC/SFMDP

87. Nancy Cheney, interview by Wes Wise with Bob Porter, December 1, 1994, transcription pp. 9–10, OHC/SFMDP.

88. Ibid., transcription pp. 25–26.

89. Ibid., transcription p. 27; Adams interview, March 14, 1997, transcription p. 56.

90. Cheney interview, December 1, 1994, transcription p. 28.

91. Ibid., transcription pp. 29–30.

92. Adams interview, March 14, 1997, transcription pp. 47, 44.

93. Hunt, "Lecture 3 of 13," transcription p. 4.

94. Richard Sellars, "Memorial can confront a tragedy," *Dallas Morning News,* June 1, 1987.

95. Hunt, "Lecture 3 of 13," transcription pp. 4–5.

96. Lindalyn Adams, letter to Conover Hunt, ca. 1985–86, IA/SFMDP; Hunt, "Lecture 3 of 13," February 18, 1994, transcription p. 4.

97. Steve Brown, "Arbor begins renovation of buildings in West End," *Dallas Morning News,* April 10, 1985.

98. Ibid.; Lindalyn Adams, letter to Conover Hunt, May 19, 1987, IA/SFMDP; Lindalyn Adams, letter to Conover Hunt, April 19, 1984, IA/SFMDP. The northwest corner of the Depository building was mistakenly constructed on railroad property; upon learning this, the contractor trimmed the building's corner off along the property line so that "the Depository does not actually sit on railroad property, it just hangs over it." When it purchased the building, Dallas County entered into a contract with the Missouri Pacific Railroad to rent the land at a nominal price; Judson Shook said at the time that otherwise the county would simply acquire the property through eminent domain ("History of Sixth Floor Museum News Compilation, 1978–1989").

99. Conover Hunt, letter to G. Robert Blakey, July 25, 1987, IA/SFMDP.

100. Conover Hunt, letter to Bud Fensterwald, Assassination Archives & Research Center, Washington, D.C., August 19, 1987, IA/SFMDP.

101. Hunt, "Lecture 3 of 13," transcription p. 5.

102. Ibid., transcription p. 9.

103. Chris Kelley, "Dart route called threat to JFK site," *Dallas Morning News,* January 13, 1988.

104. Conover Hunt, memorandum to Historical Foundation Board, RE: Arguments about DART Alignments, September 11, 1987, IA/SFMDP.

105. Hunt, "Lecture 3 of 13," transcription p. 9; Conover Hunt, memorandum to Lindalyn Adams, Judge Lee Jackson, and Lillian Bradshaw, RE: Issues relating to DART alignments and Tower access, August 29, 1987, IA/SFMDP; Lawrence E. Young, "Dart lines near JFK assassination site opposed," *Dallas Morning News,* July 1, 1987.

106. Young, "Dart lines near JFK assassination site opposed."

107. G. Robert Blakey, letter to Chuck Anderson, Executive Director, DART, August 12, 1987, IA/SFMDP.

108. Ibid.; Hunt, letter to G. Robert Blakey, July 25, 1987.

109. Blakey, letter to Chuck Anderson, August 12, 1987.

110. Gary Mack, interview with author, March 18, 2009.

111. Terry Maxon, "Elm Line urged for subway," *Dallas Morning News,* August 2, 1987; Lawrence R. Good, letter to Richard Knight, Dallas City Manager, July 29, 1987, IA/SFMDP; Terry Maxon, "Dart board approves route for first rail line," *Dallas*

Morning News, December 16, 1987; Hunt, memorandum to Lindalyn Adams, Judge Lee Jackson, and Lillian Bradshaw, August 29, 1987.

112. Adams interview, March 14, 1997, transcription p. 48.

113. Chris Kelley, "Dart route called threat to JFK site," *Dallas Morning News,* January 13, 1988.

114. Charles A. Briggs, interview by Stephen Fagin, February 16, 2009, transcription pp. 7–8, OHC/SFMDP. One supporter of the portal was unconvinced that the limited intrusion at the site outweighed the cost of altering the subway's route, while DART board member Richard Smith cracked that he would lend his support if the foundation wanted to cover the $5 million required to move the subway line (Kelley, "Dart route called threat to JFK site").

115. "Dart route," *Dallas Morning News,* January 14, 1988.

116. Chris Kelley, "Dart panel urged to set June 4 vote," *Dallas Morning News,* February 24, 1988; Chris Kelley, "DART delays decision on subway line," *Dallas Morning News,* April 27, 1988.

117. Chris Kelley, "DART to put subway under Pacific Avenue," *Dallas Morning News,* May 11, 1988.

118. Chris Kelley, "Voters derail DART plan," *Dallas Morning News,* June 26, 1988; Chris Kelley, "Business groups back transit mall," *Dallas Morning News,* June 14, 1989.

119. Dillon, "Preserving a painful past."

120. Ibid.

121. Robert C. Wurmstedt, "Dallas' debate over Depository tower reflects city's confusion," *Fort Worth Star-Telegram,* August 31, 1987.

122. Lee F. Jackson et al., letter to Curtis Tunnel, Executive Director, Texas Historical Commission, June 29, 1987, IA/SFMDP; Mrs. Reuben H. Adams, letter to Curtis Tunnel, Executive Director, Texas Historical Commission, June 19, 1987, IA/SFMDP; Hunt, "Lecture 3 of 13," February 18, 1994, transcription p. 6.

123. Dillon, "Preserving a painful past."

124. Tony Callaway, letter to Leif Sandberg, Senior Planner, City of Dallas, August 5, 1987, IA/SFMDP; David Dillon, "Tower OK'd for former Depository," *Dallas Morning News,* August 12, 1987; Hunt, "Lecture 3 of 13," transcription p. 7.

125. Ibid.; Sherry Jacobson, "Elevator tower design OK'd for JFK exhibit," *Dallas Morning News,* October 14, 1987.

126. Jacobson, "Elevator tower design OK'd for JFK exhibit"; Hunt, "Lecture 3 of 13," February 18, 1994, transcription p. 7; Conover Hunt, memorandum to Doug Farris, RE: Factors Relative to Exhibit Access, December 23, 1987, IA/SFMDP.

127. Hunt, "Lecture 3 of 13," transcription p. 5.

128. Robert C. Wurmstedt, "Dallas' debate over Depository tower reflects city's confusion," *Fort Worth Star-Telegram,* August 31, 1987.

129. Peter Applebome, "Dallas treads painfully toward opening Kennedy assassination exhibit," *New York Times,* August 18, 1987.

130. Dillon, "Preserving a painful past," *Dallas Morning News,* August 16, 1987.

131. John Bryant, letter to Mrs. Reuben H. Adams, President, Dallas County Historical Foundation, May 11, 1987, IA/SFMDP.

132. John Bryant and Ronald D. Coleman, letter to the Honorable William P. Horn, Department of the Interior, May 11, 1987, IA/SFMDP.

133. Hunt, "Lecture 3 of 13," transcription p. 8.

134. Jackson interview, January 12, 2001, transcription pp. 10–11.

135. Kara Kunkel, "$200,000 collected to help create exhibit on assassination of JFK," *Dallas Times Herald,* October 13, 1987; Adams interview, March 14, 1997, transcription p. 43; Dallas County Historical Foundation, memorandum to Betty Williams, January 4, 1989, IA/SFMDP.

136. Helen Holmes, "Judge Fox and Jess Hay to Head Fund Drive for the Sixth Floor," Press Release, Helen Holmes and Associates, Inc., October 7, 1987, IA/SFMDP; Lillian Bradshaw, interview by Bob Porter, May 1, 1998, transcription p. 15, OHC/SFMDP.

137. "Kennedy exhibit," *Dallas Morning News,* October 27, 1988; Adah Leah Wolf, interview by Stephen Fagin, May 11, 2009, video recording, OHC/SFMDP; Holmes, "Judge Fox and Jess Hay to Head Fund Drive for the Sixth Floor." Even the Dallas Convention and Visitors Bureau, which had no attendance information for Dealey Plaza to share with Conover Hunt a decade earlier, applauded the foundation's efforts, noting that the once vocal calls to tear down the Depository now seemed "foolish" ("Dallas set to turn Oswald's perch into 'a tourist draw,'" *Atlanta Journal and Constitution,* January 31, 1988).

138. Bradshaw interview, May 1, 1998, transcription p. 15.

139. As Conover Hunt had predicted, it was Dallas's responsibility to open The Sixth Floor, yet she and the planners were also determined to present the project in the best possible light for a national audience. Hunt told the *Chicago Tribune* that the community was "finally ready to handle it"; Judge Jackson explained to *Time* magazine that Dallas had "come to terms with worldwide curiosity." A popular statement, credited to David Fox in the fund-raising press release and repeated almost verbatim by Lee Jackson in an interview with the *New York Times,* was that The Sixth Floor was "simply a recognition that something important happened here that people still want[ed] to know more about" (Holmes, "Judge Fox and Jess Hay to Head Fund Drive for the Sixth Floor"; Peter Applebome, "Dallas treads painfully toward opening Kennedy assassination exhibit," *New York Times,* August 18, 1987; Paul Weingarten, "24 years later, city is planning to face Kennedy's slaying," *Chicago Tribune,* August 25, 1987; "Acknowledging the past," *Time* 130, no. 9, August 31, 1987).

140. Hunt interview, February 16, 2009.

141. "Dear Friend," letter from David G. Fox/Jess Hay, December 1, 1987, IA/SFMDP; "Dear Friend," letter from Lee Jackson, December 1, 1987, IA/SFMDP; "Dear Friend," letter from Annette Strauss, December 1, 1987, IA/SFMDP.

142. Bradshaw interview, May 1, 1998, transcription p. 16.

143. Ibid.; Jess Hay, interview by Bob Porter, February 22, 2001, transcription p. 12, OHC/SFMDP.

144. Jim Sullivan, "Society unveils plans for exhibit," *Dallas Times Herald,* April 11, 1988.

145. Memorandum to Betty Williams, January 4, 1989, IA/SFMDP.

146. Texas Historical Commission, "Antiquities Code of Texas."

147. Hunt, "Lecture 3 of 13," transcription pp. 9–10.

148. Ibid., transcription p. 10; Southern Methodist University Anthropology Department, "Dallas County Administration Building Archeological Project," May 6, 1996, p. 4, IA/SFMDP; Melinda Henneberger, "$75,000 archaeological study OK'd," *Dallas Morning News,* December 29, 1987; Connie Pryzant, "Archaeologists dig into Dallas' past," *Dallas Morning News,* February 24, 1988.

149. Pryzant, "Archaeologists dig into Dallas' past"; Hunt, "Lecture 3 of 13," transcription p. 10.

150. Kara Kunkel, "Downtown dig details the dawn of Dallas," *Dallas Times Herald,* February 24, 1988.

151. Southern Methodist University Anthropology Department, "Dallas County Administration Building Archeological Project," p. 3.

152. Hunt, "Lecture 3 of 13," transcription p. 10.

153. Kunkel, "Downtown dig details the dawn of Dallas."

154. Lawrence E. Young, "County OKs contract for Kennedy project," *Dallas Morning News,* March 1, 1988.

155. "Construction starts on JFK assassination exhibit," *Dallas Morning News,* March 9, 1988; Hendricks interview, September 19, 2008, transcription pp. 18–19.

156. Hunt interview, March 26, 2003, transcription p. 18.

157. Hendricks interview, September 19, 2008, transcription p. 19.

158. "Work on JFK exhibit is back on schedule, official says," August 2, 1988; Hunt interview, March 26, 2003, transcription p. 18.

159. Hunt interview, March 26, 2003, transcription p. 18.

160. Ibid.

161. "Work on JFK exhibit is back on schedule, official says," *Dallas Morning News,* August 2, 1988; JFK assassination exhibit to open downtown Feb. 20," *Dallas Morning News,* October 12, 1988.

162. Judy Howard, "Kennedy exhibit criticized," *Dallas Morning News,* June 1, 1988.

163. Allen and Cynthia Mondell, interview by Stephen Fagin, June 13, 2002, transcription p. 19, OHC/SFMDP.

164. Howard, "Kennedy exhibit criticized"; Cheney interview, December 1, 1994, transcription p. 30.

165. Howard, "Kennedy exhibit criticized"; Associated Press, "Sen. Kennedy says family disturbed by museum plan," *Dallas Times Herald,* June 2, 1988.

166. Charles U. Daly, letter to Mrs. Reuben H. Adams, President, Dallas County Historical Foundation, June 8, 1988, IA/SFMDP; Mrs. Reuben H. Adams, letter to Mr. Charles Daly, Director, The John F. Kennedy Library, June 1, 1988, IA/SFMDP.

167. Cheney interview, December 1, 1994, transcription p. 30.

168. Howard, "Kennedy exhibit criticized"; Associated Press, "Sen. Kennedy says family disturbed by museum plan."

169. "Kennedy exhibit," *Dallas Morning News,* June 2, 1988; "JFK exhibit will honor history," *Dallas Times Herald,* June 4, 1988.

170. "Kennedy exhibit."

171. Carl A. Henry, "Sixth floor," *Dallas Morning News,* June 20, 1988.

172. Lawrence E. Young, "Plans to charge fee for JFK exhibit, close aid office are criticized," *Dallas Morning News,* August 9, 1988.

173. "Handling infamy in Dallas," *New York Times,* October 16, 1988; Hunt, "Lecture 3 of 13," transcription p. 13; Adams interview, March 14, 1997, transcription p. 57. In September the foundation hired the Dallas office of Tracy-Locke Public Relations and retained their services through the exhibition's opening the following February. For a period of weeks Adams met with the PR firm every day, learning how to give media interviews. Hunt later said that Tracy-Locke did not so much spin the story as prevent the story from spinning out of control. In 1994 she said: "Remember that the entire process of conceiving, planning, building, [and] changing . . . The Sixth Floor exhibit was recorded by the media. There was virtually no privacy allowed for the eleven years that I worked on it and the twelve-plus that Lindalyn worked on it." This problematic relationship with journalists at least ensured that The Sixth Floor rarely fell off the national radar, while museums and nonprofit organizations around the country dreamed of such broad interest in their subject matter (Hunt, "Lecture 3 of 13," transcription p. 10).

174. Holmes, "Judge Fox and Jess Hay to Head Fund Drive for the Sixth Floor"; Applebome, "Dallas treads painfully toward opening Kennedy assassination exhibit."

175. Ibid.

176. From that moment through the release of Oliver Stone's controversial film *JFK* and its aftermath, Pennebaker served as the media's go-to academic for comments on the Kennedy assassination. "I was the only one with data," Pennebaker recalled in 2008. "It was really funny. . . . I suspect I'm one of the only academics ever to be on *Entertainment Tonight*" (Dr. James W. Pennebaker, interview by Stephen Fagin, October 17, 2008, transcription p. 15, OHC/SFMDP).

177. Pennebaker, *Opening Up,* p. 170.

178. Pennebaker interview, October 17, 2008, transcription p. 7.

179. Ibid., transcription pp. 7–9; James W. Pennebaker, "Schoolbook Depository Research Project," ca. 1988, Dr. James W. Pennebaker Collection/The Sixth Floor Museum at Dealey Plaza.

180. Pennebaker interview, October 17, 2008, transcription p. 9.

181. Ibid., transcription p. 12.

182. Ibid., transcription pp. 8, 12; Pennebaker, *Opening Up,* p. 170; Pennebaker, "Schoolbook Depository Research Project," pp. 4–6.

183. Pennebaker interview, October 17, 2008, transcription pp. 12, 15; Pennebaker, *Opening Up,* p. 170.

184. Jeff Collins, "'The Sixth Floor' provides a window to the past," *Dallas Times Herald,* November 22, 1988.

185. Steve McGonigle, "Survey: JFK's death still haunts Dallasites," *Dallas Morning News,* November 8, 1988.

186. Dr. Paul Geisel, interview by Stephen Fagin, September 5, 2008, transcription p. 19, OHC/SFMDP.

187. Blackie Sherrod, "Shadows—Dallas' dark journey," *Dallas Morning News,* November 20, 1988; "Dallas on trial: accusations and self-doubts torment the city," *Dallas Morning News,* November 20, 1988; Ed Timms, "JFK tragedy prompted soul-searching in city," *Dallas Morning News,* November 20, 1988; Steven R. Reed, "Memorials help Dallas deal with loss," *Dallas Morning News,* November 22, 1988.

188. Timms, "JFK tragedy prompted soul-searching in city."

189. Henry Tatum, "Dallas a quarter-century later," *Dallas Morning News,* November 16, 1988.

190. Lindalyn Adams, "Opening of Sixth Floor to fulfill a historic responsibility," *Dallas Times Herald,* November 22, 1988; Jeff Collins, "'The Sixth Floor' provides a window to the past," *Dallas Times Herald,* November 22, 1988.

191. Collins, "'The Sixth Floor' provides a window to the past." The exhibition received significant local news coverage. The *Morning News* carried personal viewpoints by Conover Hunt and former county judge David Fox, who had by then taken over from Lindalyn Adams as the foundation's president, while Adams retained her position of board chair. Hunt succinctly answered frequently asked questions about The Sixth Floor, including what artifacts would be on display—specifically whether or not the Mannlicher-Carcano rifle was to be included—and what The Sixth Floor's conclusions regarding either a lone gunman or a conspiracy would be. Fox—whose article was scripted with the help of Timothy Palmer at Tracey-Locke—represented the establishment viewpoint, acknowledging that he and many in the community felt that, after dedicating the Kennedy Memorial in 1970 and saving the Depository for use as county office space, "we'd made our peace and done our part." For the thousands who visit Dealey Plaza, however, the city now had an obligation to address its history in a straightforward manner. The Sixth Floor signified that Dallas had "finally emerged from the long shadow of the assassination." Lindalyn Adams, meanwhile, lent her name to an article in the *Dallas Times Herald* summarizing the project's long development. The same day as Adams's commentary, the *Times Herald* printed a large graphic showing the exhibition's layout, alongside two additional articles covering both The Sixth Floor and Dealey Plaza (Conover Hunt, "Answers about JFK exhibit," *Dallas Morning News,* November 22, 1988; David Fox, "The Sixth Floor," *Dallas Morning News,* November 20, 1988; Mrs. Reuben H. Adams, letter to Mr. Timothy J. Palmer, Editorial Supervisor, Tracy-Locke Public Relations, December 1, 1988, IA/SFMDP).

192. William Murchison, "Let's stop grieving about the tragedy of Nov. 22, 1963," *Dallas Morning News,* November 16, 1988.

193. Peter Applebome, "25 years after the death of Kennedy, Dallas looks at its changed image," *New York Times,* November 21, 1988.

194. Michael Etzkin, "That November day in 1963 . . . ," *Washington Post,* November 27, 1988.

195. Sherrod, "Shadows—Dallas' dark journey."

196. Lawrence E. Young and Monique Boulze, "Thousands gather to remember JFK," *Dallas Morning News,* November 23, 1988.

197. Mondell and Mondell interview, June 13, 2002, transcription p. 40; Adams interview, March 14, 1997, transcription p. 58; Mrs. Reuben H. Adams, letter to Mrs. Jodie Corley Hughes, Vice President, Tracy-Locke Public Relations, November 30, 1988.

198. "County historical group hands out awards," *Dallas Morning News,* November 18, 1988.

Chapter 5. A Site of History

1. Hunt interview, February 16, 2009.

2. Mack interview, March 18, 2009.

3. Jurow interview, May 12, 1993, transcription p. 7.

4. Hunt interview, March 26, 2003, transcription p. 9.

5. Staples and Charles interview, August 30, 1994, transcription p. 9.

6. Briggs interview, February 16, 2009, transcription p. 5.

7. Hunt interview, March 26, 2003, transcription p. 14.

8. Ibid.; Briggs interview, February 16, 2009, transcription pp. 5, 8.

9. Staples and Charles interview, August 30, 1994, transcription pp. 8–9.

10. Briggs interview, February 16, 2009, transcription p. 7.

11. Ibid.; Hunt interview, February 16, 2009.

12. Hunt, "Lecture 4 of 13," transcription p. 14; Geisel, interview, September 5, 2008, transcription p. 10.

13. Conover Hunt, memorandum to Dave Fox, September 30, 1988, IA/SFMDP; Wolf interview, May 11, 2009.

14. Hunt, "Lecture 4 of 13," transcription p. 14.

15. Mack interview, March 18, 2009.

16. Ibid.; Hunt, "Lecture 4 of 13," transcription p. 14; Conover Hunt, e-mail to author, March 23, 2012.

17. Malcolm Kilduff, interview by Bob Porter, April 16, 1993, transcription p. 25, OHC/SFMDP.

18. Bugliosi, *Reclaiming History: The Assassination of President John F. Kennedy,* p. 989.

19. Krajicek, "The Assassination of John F. Kennedy: Introduction."

20. Hunt, e-mail to author, March 23, 2012.

21. Mack interview, April 5, 2012.
22. Jim Moore, interview by Stephen Fagin, September 21, 2011, transcription pp. 5–6, OHC/SFMDP.
23. Hunt interview, March 26, 2003, transcription p. 14.
24. Ibid., transcription p. 13.
25. Hunt, "Lecture 6 of 13," transcription p. 8; Hunt interview, March 26, 2003, transcription p. 7.
26. Hunt interview, March 26, 2003, transcription p. 7.
27. Hunt, "Lecture 6 of 13," transcription p. 9.
28. Hunt, e-mail to author, April 5, 2012.
29. Linden interview August 4, 1997, transcription p. 12.
30. Hunt, e-mail to author, March 23, 2012.
31. Hunt, "Lecture 1 of 13," transcription p. 16; Hunt, e-mail to author, April 5, 2012. Several museum founders referenced the Texas Theatre chair as an example when discussing how the foundation determined appropriate artifacts for the exhibition. In reality, the chair was not offered to the Dallas County Historical Foundation until May 1989, three months after the exhibit opened to the public. It was subsequently evaluated, declined for exhibition, and returned to the Texas Theatre in Oak Cliff (see Tracy Everbach, "Oswald's chair gets new home," *Dallas Morning News,* May 25, 1989).
32. Mrs. Reuben H. Adams, letter to Dr. Don W. Wilson, Archivist of the United States, February 3, 1988, IA/SFMDP.
33. Hunt, "Lecture 6 of 13," transcription p. 13.
34. Hunt, "Lecture 4 of 13," transcription p. 11.
35. Mack interview, March 18, 2009.
36. Zapruder Film, The Sixth Floor Museum at Dealey Plaza.
37. Hunt, "Lecture 4 of 13," transcription p. 11.
38. Mack interview, March 18, 2009.
39. Hunt, "Lecture 6 of 13," transcription p. 5.
40. Staples and Charles interview, August 30, 1994, transcription p. 15.
41. Ibid.; Adah Leah Wolf, memorandum to file, June 17, 1988, IA/SFMDP.
42. Hunt, "Lecture 6 of 13," transcription p. 5.
43. Linden interview, June 9, 2008, transcription p. 8.
44. This panel was included in the finished exhibit but not found in the concept designs from the early 1980s.
45. Dr. Thomas H. Smith, interview by Stephen Fagin, January 24, 2008, transcription p. 9, OHC/SFMDP; Conover Hunt, memorandum to Allen Clemson, December 22, 1988, IA/SFMDP; Cheney interview, December 1, 1994, transcription p. 35.
46. Hunt, "Lecture 4 of 13," transcription pp. 8–10.
47. Hunt interview, March 26, 2003, transcription p. 7.
48. Conover Hunt, Sixth Floor Exhibition Outline, ca. 1987, IA/SFMDP.
49. Hunt, "Lecture 6 of 13," transcription p. 15.

50. Hunt interview, February 16, 2009, video recording; Staples and Charles interview, August 30, 1994, transcription p. 8.
51. Hunt, "Lecture 4 of 13," transcription p. 9.
52. Hunt interview, March 26, 2003, transcription p. 9.
53. Hunt, "Lecture 6 of 13," transcription p. 3.
54. Hunt, "Lecture 4 of 13," transcription p. 6.
55. Staples and Charles interview, August 30, 1994, transcription pp. 9–10; Hunt, "Lecture 6 of 13," transcription p. 4.
56. Hunt, "Lecture 6 of 13," transcription p. 3.
57. Hunt, "Lecture 4 of 13," transcription p. 10. For a number of years no digital word-processing file of the exhibition text was known to exist. When the full text of the exhibition panels was newly transcribed into a Microsoft Word document in 2003—single-spaced in Times New Roman twelve-point type—it was 17,344 words long (forty-one pages). This total did not include photograph or artifact captions or the text of the multipanel assassination weekend timeline (see The Sixth Floor Museum at Dealey Plaza, "John F. Kennedy and the Memory of a Nation," exhibition text, ca. 1989, IA/SFMDP).
58. Staples and Charles interview, August 30, 1994, transcription p. 7.
59. Hunt, "Lecture 6 of 13," transcription p. 5.
60. Staples and Charles interview, August 30, 1994, transcription p. 11.
61. Hunt, Sixth Floor Exhibition Outline.
62. The Sixth Floor Museum at Dealey Plaza, "John F. Kennedy and the Memory of a Nation"; Hunt, *Dealey Plaza National Historic Landmark,* p. 13.
63. Hunt, Sixth Floor Exhibition Outline.
64. Ibid.; Hunt, "Lecture 6 of 13," transcription pp. 8–9; Hunt, Sixth Floor Exhibition Outline.
65. Hunt, Sixth Floor Exhibition Outline; Hunt, *Dealey Plaza National Historic Landmark,* p. 13.
66. Ibid.
67. Mack interview, March 18, 2009.
68. Hunt, Sixth Floor Exhibition Outline; Hunt, "Lecture 6 of 13," transcription p. 13; The Sixth Floor Museum at Dealey Plaza, "John F. Kennedy and the Memory of a Nation"; Hunt, *Dealey Plaza National Historic Landmark,* p. 13.
69. Hunt, "Lecture 6 of 13," transcription p. 14. As of 2013 the section on "Conspiracy?" remains as it was in 1989. Hunt noted in 1994 that a future board of the Dallas County Historical Foundation "might become more balanced in its view of presenting both sides of the issue through equal allocations of space," because the area covering the government investigations remains one of the floor's largest (ibid., transcription p. 15).
70. Ibid., transcription p. 15.
71. The Sixth Floor Museum at Dealey Plaza, "John F. Kennedy and the Memory of a Nation."

72. Ibid., p. 41.

73. Staples and Charles interview, August 30, 1994, transcription p. 13.

74. Hunt, Sixth Floor Exhibition Outline.

75. Conover Hunt, memorandum to Powers That Be, October 25, 1988, IA/SFMDP.

76. Longford et al., "Founders Luncheon," transcription p. 10.

77. Hunt interview, February 16, 2009.

78. Hunt interview, March 26, 2003, transcription p. 9.

79. Hunt, "Lecture 6 of 13," transcription p. 6.

80. Hunt interview, February 16, 2009; Hunt interview, March 26, 2003, transcription p. 11; Staples and Charles interview, August 30, 1994, transcription p. 11; Hunt, memorandum to Allen Clemson, December 22, 1988.

81. Mondell and Mondell interview June 13, 2002, transcription pp. 5–6, 8–10; Media Projects, Inc., "About Us."

82. Mondell and Mondell interview, June 13, 2002, transcription p. 10; Hunt, "Lecture 6 of 13," transcription p. 6.

83. Media Projects, Inc., "Proposal for the Six Documentaries That Will Be Integrated into the Sixth Floor Exhibit," ca. 1988, IA/SFMDP.

84. Hunt interview, February 16, 2009.

85. Jurow interview, May 12, 1993, transcription p. 7.

86. Ibid.; Mondell and Mondell interview, June 13, 2002, transcription p. 7.

87. Mondell and Mondell interview, June 13, 2002, transcription p. 15.

88. Hunt interview, February 16, 2009; Hunt, "Lecture 6 of 13," transcription p. 13.

89. Hunt interview, February 16, 2009.

90. Mondell and Mondell interview, June 13, 2002, transcription pp. 18–21; Hunt, "Lecture 6 of 13," transcription p. 13; Mack interview, March 18, 2009.

91. Mondell and Mondell interview, June 13, 2002, transcription pp. 29, 33.

92. Robert S. Strauss, letter to Walter Cronkite, September 26, 1988, IA/SFMDP.

93. David G. Fox, letter to Mr. Robert S. Strauss, January 4, 1988, IA/SFMDP; Robert Strauss, draft letter template to blank, ca. 1988, IA/SFMDP.

94. Media Projects, Inc., "Proposal for the Six Documentaries That Will Be Integrated into the Sixth Floor Exhibit." The Mondells included Walter Cronkite in their original written proposal, though they envisioned him hosting a three-minute "newscast" as the exhibit's first video presentation to examine the major events of the early 1960s.

95. Linden interview, August 4, 1997, transcription p. 10; Cheney interview, December 1, 1994, transcription p. 30; Mrs. Reuben H. Adams, letter to Mr. Robert Strauss, July 8, 1988, IA/SFMDP.

96. Adams and Jurow both mailed Strauss personal letters. Adams's correspondence was dated four days prior to Jurow's letter (Adams, letter to Strauss, July 8, 1988; Martin Jurow, letter to Mr. Robert Strauss, July 12, 1988, IA/SFMDP).

97. Mrs. Reuben H. Adams, Letter to Mr. Robert S. Strauss, August 9, 1988, IA/SFMDP.

98. Strauss, letter to Walter Cronkite, September 26, 1988; Mrs. Reuben Adams, letter to Mr. Robert S. Strauss, September 13, 1988, IA/SFMDP.

99. Mondell and Mondell interview, June 13, 2002, transcription p. 37.

100. The Sixth Floor Exhibit, *Legacy* film, Working Script, May 26, 1988, IA/SFMDP.

101. Mondell and Mondell interview, June 13, 2002, transcription, p. 38. Allen Mondell's script did not necessarily reflect the personal viewpoint of Cronkite. In *The Legacy* film, Cronkite describes the crucial role played by broadcast news over the assassination weekend, acknowledging that "television had come of age." When asked in 2004 if the assassination was the moment when television came of age, however, Cronkite replied, "Not entirely. We were edging up to that anyway. . . . Television wasn't new to us" (Walter Cronkite, interview by Vicki Daitch and Stephen Fagin, April 14, 2004, transcription p. 23, OHC/SFMDP; Allen Mondell and Cynthia Mondell, *Films from The Sixth Floor*, video recording, ca. 1989, Video Library/The Sixth Floor Museum at Dealey Plaza).

102. The Sixth Floor Exhibit, *Legacy* film.

103. Mondell and Mondell, *Films from the Sixth Floor*.

104. Hunt, "Lecture 6 of 13," transcription p. 15.

105. Ibid.; The Sixth Floor Exhibit, *Legacy* film.

106. Hunt, "Lecture 6 of 13," transcription p. 15.

107. John F. Kennedy, "Inaugural Address."

108. Jurow interview, May 12, 1993, transcription p. 7.

109. Hunt, "Lecture 4 of 13," transcription p. 15; Hunt, "Lecture 6 of 13," transcription p. 17.

110. Hunt, "Lecture 4 of 13," transcription p. 15.

111. Antenna Audio Tours, "Audio Tour Script: The Sixth Floor: John F. Kennedy and the Memory of a Nation," ca. 1989, IA/SFMDP.

112. Hunt, "Lecture 4 of 13," transcription p. 15.

113. Conover Hunt, memorandum to Judge Lee Jackson, March 2, 1988, IA/SFMDP; Gene George, memorandum to Jim Hendricks, Dan Brautner, Conover Hunt, October 19, 1988, IA/SFMDP; Conover Hunt, memorandum to Chris Tellis, Antenna Audio Tours, December 31, 1988, IA/SFMDP.

114. Hunt, "Lecture 4 of 13," transcription p. 5.

115. Moore, "Open Window to History," p. 23.

116. Hunt, "Lecture 6 of 13," transcription pp. 4, 17.

117. George interview, September 11, 2008, transcription p. 12.

118. Hunt, "Lecture 4 of 13," transcription p. 13; Moore, "Open Window to History," p. 24.

119. Hunt, "Lecture 4 of 13," transcription p. 7 (quotation); Staples and Charles interview, August 30, 1994, transcription p. 7.

120. Hunt, "Lecture 4 of 13," transcription p. 7.

121. Hunt, "Lecture 6 of 13," transcription p. 11; Hunt, "Lecture 4 of 13," transcription p. 5. Thus only two small holes, less than one inch wide, were drilled into each side of the wooden columns.

122. Hunt, "Lecture 6 of 13," transcription p. 11; Hunt, memorandum to Allen Clemson, December 22, 1988.

123. Hunt, "Lecture 6 of 13," transcription p. 12.
124. Hunt interview, March 26, 2003, transcription p. 16; George, memorandum to Jim Hendricks, Dan Brautner, Conover Hunt, October 19, 1988.
125. Hunt interview, March 26, 2003, transcription p. 16.
126. Hunt, "Lecture 4 of 13," transcription p. 7.
127. Rick Lane, interview by Stephen Fagin, June 26, 2009, transcription p. 10, OHC/SFMDP.
128. Hunt, "Lecture 6 of 13," transcription pp. 10–11; Mack interview, March 18, 2009; Moore interview, September 21, 2011, transcription p. 5.
129. Hunt interview, March 26, 2003, transcription p. 18.
130. Hendricks interview, September 19, 2008, transcription p. 23.
131. Hunt interview, February 16, 2009.
132. Hunt, "Lecture 6 of 13," transcription p. 15.
133. Hunt interview, March 26, 2003, transcription p. 19; "Key Staff Assignments for 2/13–2/20," Schedule of Events for the Opening of The Sixth Floor, ca. 1989, IA/SFMDP.
134. Carl Henry, interview by Bob Porter, February 11, 1998, transcription p. 36, OHC/SFMDP.
135. "Key Staff Assignments for 2/13–2/20."
136. Ibid.; Adams interview, March 14, 1997, transcription p. 15.
137. Hunt, "Lecture 3 of 13," transcription p. 14.
138. Lawrence E. Young, "Exhibit contracts approved," *Dallas Morning News,* December 28, 1988.
139. Henry Tatum, "Sixth floor's fragile memories," *Dallas Morning News,* February 15, 1989.
140. Steve Blow, "Sixth floor opens, and a circle closes," *Dallas Morning News,* February 17, 1989.
141. Greene, "The Sixth Floor: A Personal View."
142. Tom Kennedy, "Book depository exhibit 'special,'" *Houston Post,* February 16, 1989.
143. Elizabeth Hudson, "The sniper's nest," *New York Times,* February 20, 1989; "Museum on Kennedy opens in Dallas," *New York Times,* February 21, 1989; Hunt interview, March 26, 2003, transcription p. 19.
144. Hunt interview, March 26, 2003, transcription p. 19.
145. "See Oswald's Lair—for $4."
146. Paul Weingarten, "JFK exhibit helps Dallas face its past," *Chicago Tribune,* February 21, 1989.
147. Scott Sunde and David Fritze, "'Today we stand whole again,'" *Dallas Times Herald,* February 20, 1989.
148. Tracy-Locke Public Relations, "Content Analysis: The Sixth Floor," March 9, 1989, IA/SFMDP.
149. Kathy Jackson, "1,700 attend as sixth floor opens," *Dallas Morning News,* February 21, 1989.

150. "The Sixth Floor Opening Ceremony," schedule of events, February 20, 1989, IA/SFMDP.

151. Judge Lee F. Jackson, Opening Ceremony Remarks, February 20, 1989, IA/SFMDP.

152. "The Sixth Floor Opening Ceremony."

153. J. Jackson Walter, Opening Ceremony Remarks, February 20, 1989, IA/SFMDP.

154. "JFK remembered," *Dallas Morning News,* February 18, 1989; "JFK history well served," *Dallas Times Herald,* February 17, 1989.

155. Memory Books, The Sixth Floor Exhibit, February 1989, IA/SFMDP.

156. Associated Press, "Planned JFK exhibit in Dallas criticized," *Houston Chronicle,* April 17, 1989; "Metro report," *Dallas Morning News,* June 20, 1989; Chip Brown, "Visitors share view of JFK's assassin," *Houston Chronicle,* November 22, 1989.

157. Hunt interview, March 26, 2003, transcription p. 19; "Metro report," *Dallas Morning News,* August 4, 1989.

158. Conover Hunt, letter to Sixth Floor Staff, July 28, 1989, IA/SFMDP.

159. Conover Hunt, e-mail to author, January 8, 2009.

160. Hunt interview, March 26, 2003, transcription p. 20; Bob Hays, interview by Bob Porter with Wes Wise, March 25, 1993, transcription pp. 2–4, 13, OHC/SFMDP; "Metro report," *Dallas Morning News,* May 23, 1989.

161. Hays interview, March 25, 1993, transcription p. 6.

162. Ibid., transcription pp. 13–14; Rugg et al., "Critiquing Museum Exhibitions XIII: Interpreting Community," transcription by author, p. 10.

163. J. Gary Shaw, interview by Stephen Fagin, July 23, 2007, transcription pp. 11/–12, OHC/SFMDP.

164. "About the Assassination Archives and Research Center."

165. Associated Press, "Planned JFK exhibit in Dallas criticized."

166. Shaw interview, July 23, 2007, transcription p. 13.

167. David Flick, "Market forces conspire to move alternative JFK site," *Dallas Morning News,* December 5, 2006.

168. Robin Doussard, "A painful walk through history," *Austin American-Statesman,* March 11, 1990.

169. Marcus C. Stewart III, "Hundreds mark anniversary of Kennedy's assassination," *Austin American-Statesman,* November 23, 1990.

170. Ibid., transcription p. 15.

171. Adams interview, March 14, 1997, transcription pp. 60–61.

172. Linden interview, August 4, 1997, transcription p. 19.

173. Paul Weingarten, "A painful memory," *Austin American-Statesman,* March 5, 1991.

174. "Movie site," *Dallas Morning News,* February 26, 1991; Pete Slover, "6th Floor exhibit sought as film set," *Dallas Morning News,* February 28, 1991.

175. Semos interview, February 9, 2001, transcription p. 17.

176. Judge Lee F. Jackson interview by Bob Porter with Stephen Fagin, January 12, 2001, transcription p. 16, OHC/SFMDP.

177. Weingarten, "A painful memory." Dallas County had permitted a film crew working

on the ABC television movie *The Trial of Lee Harvey Oswald* to shoot some scenes inside the Depository building in 1977, but Oliver Stone's request was the first time a production company wanted access to the building after it had been renovated as a county office building. Immediately after *JFK* finished its Dallas filming, LAVA Films, Inc., requested similar access for a feature film on Jack Ruby. Exterior but no interior filming took place at the Depository for the lower-budget *Ruby* movie starring Danny Aiello in the title role, and some bricks on one side of the building were permanently discolored by spray paint. As a result, Dallas County kept $15,000 worth of the production company's security deposit (see "County to let ABC film book depository," *Dallas Morning News,* May 24, 1977; Anne Belli, "Use of county buildings sought for movie on Ruby," *Dallas Morning News,* May 22, 1991; Anne Belli, "Film crews accused of harming building," *Dallas Morning News,* January 23, 1992).

178. "6th Floor exhibit sought as film set," 1991; Weingarten, "A painful memory"; Pete Slover, "County OKs contract for JFK film," *Dallas Morning News,* March 13, 1991.

179. "6th Floor exhibit sought as film set."

180. Jane Sumner, "Foundation backs Stone's request to use sixth floor for JFK movie," *Dallas Morning News,* March 21, 1991.

181. Adams interview, March 14, 1997, transcription p. 61.

182. Meg Read, interview by Bob Porter, May 3, 1995, transcription p. 10, OHC/SFMDP.

183. Sumner, "Foundation backs Stone's request to use sixth floor for JFK movie."

184. Semos interview, February 9, 2001, transcription p. 17; Adams interview, March 14, 1997, transcription p. 62.

185. Adams interview, March 14, 1997, transcription pp. 61–62; Hunt interview, March 26, 2003, transcription p. 21.

186. Lori Stahl, "Filming to reroute 21,000 drivers a day," *Dallas Morning News,* April 9, 1991.

187. Linden interview, August 4, 1997, transcription p. 20.

188. Hunt interview, March 26, 2003, transcription p. 21.

189. Linden interview, August 4, 1997, transcription p. 19; Mankiewicz, "About the Debate"; "JFK."

190. Cronkite interview, April 14, 2004, transcription p. 24.

191. Tunheim, *Final Report of the Kennedy Assassination Records Review Board,* p. xxiii.

192. McAdams, "Assassination Records Review Board Testimony."

193. Adriane Wilson, "Film piques interest in Kennedy exhibit," *Dallas Morning News,* January 27, 1992.

194. Dan R. Barber, "Attendance at Sixth Floor hits record high," *Dallas Morning News,* April 19, 1992; Beth Silver, "JFK exhibit logs millionth visitor," *Dallas Morning News,* June 25, 1992.

195. Shermakaye Bass, "Window into our souls," *Dallas Morning News,* February 18, 1993.

196. Rugg et al., "Critiquing Museum Exhibitions XIII: Interpreting Community," transcription by author, p. 10; Jeff West, interview by James K. Lambert, ca. 2003, video recording, courtesy of James K. Lambert.

197. Hays interview, March 25, 1993, transcription p. 15.

198. Linden interview, August 4, 2008, transcription p. 14; Jerome Weeks, "Moving to a new stage in his career," *Dallas Morning News,* September 21, 1993.

199. West interview, ca. 2003.

200. Rugg et al., "Critiquing Museum Exhibitions XIII: Interpreting Community," p. 6.

201. Conover Hunt, e-mail to author, April 26, 2009; Wolf interview, May 11, 2009.

202. Rugg et al., "Critiquing Museum Exhibitions XIII: Interpreting Community," p. 11.

203. Hunt, e-mail to author, April 26, 2009.

204. Hunt interview, March 26, 2003, transcription p. 24.

205. Ibid.; Al Brumley, "Dealey Plaza is recognized," *Dallas Morning News,* October 13, 1993.

206. Read interview, May 3, 1995, transcription p. 12.

207. Hunt interview, March 26, 2003, transcription p. 24.

208. Read interview, May 3, 1995, transcription p. 12.

209. Hunt interview, March 26, 2003, transcription p. 24.

210. Steven R. Reed, "Thousands honor JFK during Dallas ceremony," *Houston Chronicle,* November 23, 1993.

211. Hunt interview, March 26, 2003, transcription p. 26.

212. Hunt, "Lecture 1 of 13," transcription p. 9.

213. Ibid., transcription p. 19.

214. Ibid., transcription p. 18.

215. "About the Collections."

216. Hunt interview, March 26, 2003, transcription p. 20.

217. Rugg et al., "Critiquing Museum Exhibitions XIII: Interpreting Community," p. 4; West interview, ca. 2003.

218. "History of the John F. Kennedy Memorial Plaza."

219. Ibid.; Ballinger, et al., *The Rededication of the John Fitzgerald Kennedy Memorial.*

220. "History of 411 Elm Street."

221. Rugg et al., "Critiquing Museum Exhibitions XIII: Interpreting Community," p. 6.

222. "Historical group plans to expand JFK exhibits," *Austin American-Statesman,* November 22, 1995; Richard Stolley, interview by Jeff West, November 22, 1996, transcription p. 15, OHC/SFMDP.

223. West interview, ca. 2003.

224. Collections Management Policy, The Sixth Floor Museum at Dealey Plaza, revised 2009, IA/SFMDP; Nicola Longford, interview with author, April 28, 2009.

225. Clark Baack, e-mail to author, September 30, 2007.

226. Robert Miller, "Director's path mirrors the nation's history," *Dallas Morning News,* August 28, 2005.

227. Longford interview, April 28, 2009.

228. Ibid.

229. West interview, ca. 2003.

230. "Museum Café + Store Main Page."

231. Longford interview, April 28, 2009.

232. Ibid.

233. Ibid.

234. Mrs. L. A. Mote, "Demolish Depository," letter to editor, *Dallas Morning News,* September 10, 1972.

Conclusion

1. Adams interview, March 14, 1997, transcription p. 59.

2. Longford et al., "Founders Luncheon," transcription pp. 2, 6.

3. Ibid., transcription pp. 10, 12.

4. Ibid., transcription p. 4.

5. Foote, *Shadowed Ground: America's Landscapes of Violence and Tragedy.*

6. Woods, "On the Road to Civil Rights: Memphis."

Epilogue

1. Gallup, "Presidential Approval Ratings—Gallup Historical Statistics and Trends."

2. Nicola Longford, interview with author, April 6, 2012.

3. Ibid.

4. Sharron Conrad et al., "Meet the Museum: Teaching about the President," public program, April 13, 2012, video recording, OHC/SFMDP.

5. Mack interview, April 5, 2012.

6. Longford interview, April 6, 2012.

7. Edward Linenthal, e-mail to author, April 10, 2012.

BIBLIOGRAPHY

Primary Sources

Oral History Collection, The Sixth Floor Museum at Dealey Plaza (OHC/SFMDP)

Adams, Lindalyn. Interview by Wes Wise with Bob Porter, March 14, 1997.

Bosworth, Warren. Interview by Bob Porter, September 24, 1997.

Bradshaw, Lillian. Interview by Bob Porter, May 1, 1998.

Briggs, Charles A. Interview by Stephen Fagin, February 16, 2009.

Burson, Rodger. Interview by Arlinda Abbot with Stephen Fagin, February 13, 2002.

Bush, Dorothy M. Interview by Stephen Fagin with Al Maddox, September 11, 2003.

Castleberry, Vivian. Interview by Stephen Fagin, August 19, 2004.

Chambers, James. Interview by Wes Wise with Bob Porter, June 10, 1994.

Cheney, Nancy. Interview by Wes Wise with Bob Porter, December 1, 1994.

Conine, Darryl. Interview by Gary Mack with Stephen Fagin and Arlinda Abbott, January 15, 2002.

Conrad, Sharron, et al. "Meet the Museum: Teaching about the President." Public program. April 13, 2012. The Sixth Floor Museum at Dealey Plaza Public Program.

Cronkite, Walter. Interview by Vicki Daitch and Stephen Fagin, April 14, 2004.

Dealey, Joe M. Interview by Wes Wise and Bob Porter, May 19, 1994.

Dillard, Tom. Interview by Wes Wise with Bob Porter, July 19, 1993.

Elwonger, Charles. Interview by Stephen Fagin, May 5, 2003.

Frazier, Buell Wesley. Interview by Gary Mack with Stephen Fagin and Dave Perry, June 19, 2002.

Gatlin, Glen. Interview by Stephen Fagin, April 17, 2003.

Geisel, Dr. Paul. Interview by Stephen Fagin, September 5, 2008.

George, Eugene. Interview by Stephen Fagin, September 11, 2008.

Godbold, Bryghte. Interview by Stephen Fagin, October 11, 2007.

Harkness, D. V. Interview by Stephen Fagin, June 29, 2006.

Hay, Jess. Interview by Bob Porter, February 22, 2001.

Hays, Bob. Interview by Bob Porter with Wes Wise, March 25, 1993.

Hendricks, James L. Interviews by Stephen Fagin, September 19, 2008, and December 1, 2008.

Henry, Carl. Interview by Bob Porter, February 11, 1998.

Holmes, Bert. Interview by Wes Wise with Bob Porter, August 3, 1993

Holmes, Helen. Interview by Wes Wise with Bob Porter, May 3, 1993.

Holmes, Rev. William A. Interview by Stephen Fagin, March 2, 2007.

Holt, Bill. Interview by Stephen Fagin, June 26, 2008.

Hunt, Conover. Interview by Stephen Fagin with Gary Mack, March 26, 2003.

———. Interview by Stephen Fagin, February 16, 2009.

———. "Lecture 1 of 13." Interview by Jeff West with Bob Porter et al., February 1, 1994.

———. "Lecture 2 of 13." Interview by Jeff West with Bob Porter et al., February 11, 1994.

———. "Lecture 3 of 13." Interview by Jeff West with Bob Porter et al., February 18, 1994.

———. "Lecture 4 of 13." Interview by Jeff West with Bob Porter et al., February 22, 1994.

———. "Lecture 6 of 13." Interview by Jeff West with Bob Porter et al., March 1, 1994.

———. "Lecture 13 of 13." Interview by Jeff West with Bob Porter et al., July 29, 1994.

Irons, Shelia. Interview by Stephen Fagin, March 19, 2009.

Jackson, Judge Lee F. Interview by Bob Porter with Stephen Fagin, January 12, 2001.

Jefferies, George. Interview by Stephen Fagin, March 5, 2007.

Jernigan, Dr. A. Jack. Interview by Stephen Fagin, August 16, 2007.

Jonsson, Erik. Interviews by Wes Wise with Bob Porter, June 30, 1992, and August 17, 1992.

Jurow, Martin. Interview by Bob Porter, May 12, 1993.

Kilduff, Malcolm. Interview by Bob Porter, April 16, 1993.

Koenig, David. Interview by Stephen Fagin, August 7, 2007.

Landry, Tom. Interview by Wes Wise with Bob Porter, April 14, 1996.

Lane, Rick. Interview by Stephen Fagin, June 26, 2009.

Linden, Dr. Glenn M. Interview by Bob Porter with Ray Langston, August 4, 1997.

———. Interview by Stephen Fagin, June 9, 2008.

Longford, Nicola, et al. "Founders Luncheon," February 16, 2009.

MacNeil, Robert. Interview by Stephen Fagin, April 16, 2004.

Marcus, Stanley. Interview by Wes Wise with Bob Porter, July 11, 1995.

Martin, Murphy. Interview by Bob Porter with Stephen Fagin, June 22, 2001.

McDonald, Maurice "Nick." Interview by Stephen Fagin, November 20, 2003.

McKnight, Felix. Interview by Bob Porter, March 9, 1995.

Mondell, Allen, and Cynthia Mondell. Interview by Stephen Fagin, June 13, 2002.

Mooney, Luke. Interview by Gary Mack with Stephen Fagin, December 4, 2002.

Moore, Jim. Interview by Stephen Fagin, September 21, 2011.

Pappas, Ike. Interview by Wes Wise with Conover Hunt and Bob Porter, March 1, 1993.

Pelou, François. Interview by Stephen Fagin, July 22, 2005.

Pennebaker, Dr. James W. Interview by Stephen Fagin, October 17, 2008.

Peters, Evadeane. Interview by Stephen Fagin, April 12, 2005.

Read, Meg. Interview by Bob Porter, May 3, 1995.

Rugg, Ruth Ann, et al. "Critiquing Museum Exhibitions XIII: Interpreting Community." American Association of Museums Annual Meeting and Museum Expo 2002, May 16, 2002.

Russell, Tom. Interview by Stephen Fagin, March 16, 2004.

Semos, Christopher. Interview by Bob Porter with Stephen Fagin, February 9, 2001.

Shaw, J. Gary. Interview by Stephen Fagin, July 23, 2007.

Shipp, Bert. Interview by Wes Wise with Bob Porter, November 17, 1992.

Shook, C. Judson. Interview by Wes Wise with Bob Porter, August 13, 1992.

Smith, Dr. Thomas H. Interview by Stephen Fagin, January 24, 2008.

Staples, Robert, and Barbara Charles. Interview by Bob Porter, August 30, 1994.

Stemmons, John. Interview by Wes Wise with Bob Porter, August 11, 1992.

Stolley, Richard. Interview by Jeff West, November 22, 1996.

Terry, Marshall. Interview by Stephen Fagin, June 18, 2003.

Thompson, Josiah. Interview by Bob Porter, November 21, 1998.

Valenti, Jack. Interview by Stephen Fagin, February 24, 2004.

Wise, Wes. Interview by Bob Porter, January 25, 1993.

———. Interview by Stephen Fagin, September 22, 2005.

Wolf, Adah Leah. Interview by Stephen Fagin, May 11, 2009.

Wright, Jim. Interview by Wes Wise with Bob Porter, February 22, 1996.

Tape and Video Recordings

"History of Sixth Floor Museum News Compilation, 1978–1989." Video recording, Gary Mack Collection, Dallas, Texas.

KRLD-TV Videotape. November 22–23, 1963, and March 14, 1964. KRLD-TV/
KDFW Collection/The Sixth Floor Museum at Dealey Plaza.

Mondell, Allen, and Cynthia Mondell. *Films from The Sixth Floor.* Video
recording, ca. 1989. Video Library/The Sixth Floor Museum at Dealey
Plaza.

West, Jeff. Interview by James K. Lambert. ca. 2003, video recording, James K.
Lambert Collection, Minneapolis, Minnesota.

WFAA Radio Recording. November 22, 1963. WFAA Collection/The Sixth
Floor Museum at Dealey Plaza.

Other Archival Collections

Alger, Bruce. Keynote Address at Dallas County Republican Convention, May
14, 1960, Box 8, Folder 19, Bruce Alger Collection, Dallas Public Library.

"Earle Cabell Mayoral Correspondence, Kennedy Assassination, November 24,
1963." Box 11, Folder 1, Earle Cabell Papers, DeGolyer Special Collections
Library, Southern Methodist University, Dallas, Texas.

Pennebaker, James W. "Schoolbook Depository Research Project," ca. 1988. Dr.
James W. Pennebaker Collection/The Sixth Floor Museum at Dealey Plaza.

Texas Historical Commission. "Formerly The Texas School Book Depository
Building." Historic Marker Text, Recorded Texas Historic Landmark 1980.

Author Interviews

Longford, Nicola. Interviews with author, April 28, 2009; April 6, 2012.

Mack, Gary. Interviews with author, October 17, 2008; March 18, 2009; April 5,
2012.

Secondary Sources
Books

Ballinger, Lacie, et al. *The Rededication of the John Fitzgerald Kennedy
Memorial: June 24, 2000.* Dallas: The Sixth Floor Museum at Dealey Plaza,
2000.

Belli, Melvin, and Maurice C. Carroll. *Dallas Justice.* New York: David McKay,
1964.

Bishop, Marsha Brock, and David P. Polk, eds. *And the Angels Wept.* St. Louis:
Chalice Press, 1995.

Blow, Steve, and Sam Attlesey. "The Tenor of the Times." In *November 22: The
Day Remembered,* 1–5. Dallas: Taylor Publishing, 1990.

Bugliosi, Vincent. *Reclaiming History: The Assassination of President John F. Kennedy*. New York: W. W. Norton, 2007.

Catton, Bruce, ed. *Four Days*. New York: American Heritage, 1964.

Connally, Nellie, and Mickey Herskowitz. *From Love Field*. New York: Rugged Land, 2003.

Dempsey, John Mark, ed. *The Jack Ruby Trial Revisited*. Denton: University of North Texas Press, 2000.

Foote, Kenneth E. *Shadowed Ground: America's Landscapes of Violence and Tragedy*. Austin: University of Texas Press, 2003.

Hearings before the President's Commission on the Assassination of President John F. Kennedy. 26 vols. Washington, D.C.: GPO, 1964.

Holloway, Diane, ed. *Dallas and the Jack Ruby Trial: Memoir of Judge Joe B. Brown, Sr.* San Jose, Calif.: Authors Choice, 2001.

Huffaker, Bob, Bill Mercer, et al. *When the News Went Live: Dallas 1963*. New York: Taylor Trade, 2004.

Hunt, Conover. *Dealey Plaza National Historic Landmark*. Dallas: The Sixth Floor Museum at Dealey Plaza, 1997.

———. *JFK for a New Generation*. Dallas: The Sixth Floor Museum at Dealey Plaza and Southern Methodist University Press, 1996.

Leslie, Warren. *Dallas Public and Private*. Dallas: Southern Methodist University Press, 1964.

MacNeil, Robert, ed. *The Way We Were*. New York: Carroll and Graf, 1988.

Manchester, William. *The Death of a President*. New York: Harper and Row, 1967.

Mankiewicz, Frank. "About the Debate." In *JFK: The Book of the Film*, edited by Oliver Stone and Zachary Sklar. New York: Applause Books, 1992.

Payne, Darwin. *Big D*. Dallas: Three Forks Press, 2000.

Pennebaker, James W. *Opening Up*. New York: Avon Books, 1990.

Posner, Gerald. *Case Closed*. New York: Anchor Books, 1993.

Segura, Judith Garrett. *BELO: From Newspapers to New Media*. Austin: University of Texas Press, 2008.

Seib, Philip. *Dallas: Chasing the Urban Dream*. Dallas: Pressworks, 1986.

The Warren Commission Report: Report of the President's Commission on the Assassination of President John F. Kennedy. New York: St. Martin's Press, 1964.

Wright, Lawrence. *In The New World*. New York: Vintage Books, 1989.

Articles in Magazines and Other Periodicals

Fagin, Stephen. "American Biography: Lee Harvey Oswald." *American History Magazine* 38, no. 5 (Dec. 2003): 18–20, 22, 70, 72.

———. "Dallas Police vs. the World Press: November 1963." *Legacies: A History Journal for Dallas and North Central Texas* 18, no. 2 (Fall 2006): 36–48.

Greene, A. C. "The Sixth Floor: A Personal View." *Southwestern Historical Quarterly* 94, no. 1 (July 1990): 171–77.

Keerdoja, Eileen, et al. "The Book Depository." *Newsweek* 91, no. 9 (Feb. 27, 1978): 12.

Moore, Jonathan. "Open Window to History." *Texas Architect* (Nov./Dec. 2008): 22–25.

"See Oswald's Lair—for $4." *Time* 133, no. 9 (Feb. 27, 1989): 25.

"The Shame of Dallas, Texas." *Saturday Evening Post* 237, no. 14 (April 11, 1964): 82.

Shiffler, D. Ann, and Jeff Hampton. "20 Years Later . . . " *Dallas: The Business Perspective* 62, no. 1 (Nov. 1983): 23.

Vanderwerken, Dr. David L. "NEH Project Focuses on Dallas Building with a Tragic Past." *Texas Humanist* (May 1979): 1, 10–11.

West, Jeff. "Wiser Heads Prevailed." *American History Magazine* 38, no. 5 (Dec. 2003): 60–65.

Newspapers

Atlanta Journal and Constitution
Austin American-Statesman
Chicago Tribune
Dallas Downtown News
Dallas Morning News
Dallas Observer
Dallas Times Herald
Fort Worth Star-Telegram
Houston Chronicle
Houston Post
New York Times
Washington Post

Websites

"About the Assassination Archives and Research Center." AARC Online. http://www.aarclibrary.org/aarc.htm (accessed April 18, 2009).

"About the Collections." *The Sixth Floor Museum at Dealey Plaza*, 2009. http://www.jfk.org/go/collections/about (accessed April 17, 2009).

Alexander Architectural Archive. *Walter Eugene George, Jr.* http://www.lib.utexas.edu/taro/utaaa/00009/00009-P.html (accessed February 13, 2009).

"Bryghte Godbold Inducted into Alabama Hall of Fame." Samuel Ginn College of Electrical and Computer Engineering, Auburn University. Fall 2003 Newsletter, Vol. 4, No. 1. http://eng.auburn.edu/files/file148.pdf (accessed May 13, 2009).

The Center for American History. "A Guide to the Lonn Taylor Papers." *Texas Archival Resources Online*. http://www.lib.utexas.edu/taro/utcah/00506 /cah-00506.html (accessed February 15, 2009).

Churchill, Winston. "We Shall Fight on the Beaches." *The Churchill Centre and Museum Online*, 2009. http://www.winstonchurchill.org (accessed April 29, 2009).

"Exhibitions from the Past." *Archives/Corcoran Gallery of Art Online*, 2008. http://www.corcoran.org/exhibitions/past-exhibitions/archives/1980 (accessed April 13, 2012).

Gallup. "Presidential Approval Ratings—Gallup Historical Statistics and Trends." Gallup Inc., 2012. http://www.gallup.com/poll/116677 /Presidential-Approval-Ratings-Gallup-Historical-Statistics-Trends.aspx (accessed April 13, 2012).

"History of the John F. Kennedy Memorial Plaza." *The Sixth Floor Museum at Dealey Plaza*, 2009. http://www.jfk.org/go/about/history-of-the-john-f-kennedy-memorial-plaza (accessed April 17, 2009).

"Hoblitzelle Foundation Home Page." *The Hoblitzelle Foundation Online*. http:// www.hoblitzelle.org/home.html (accessed April 27, 2009).

"JFK." *The Internet Movie Database*, IMDb.com, Inc., 2009. http://www.imdb .com/title/tt0102138/ (accessed April 24, 2009).

John Birch Society. "About the John Birch Society," 2009. http://www.jbs.org /about-jbs/history (accessed April 13, 2012).

Kennedy, John F. "Inaugural Address." The American Presidency Project, 2009. http://www.presidency.ucsb.edu/ws/index.php?pid=8032YBrowser.HTML\ Shell\Open\Command (accessed March 13, 2009).

Krajicek, David. "The Assassination of John F. Kennedy: Introduction." TruTV Crime Library, Turner Entertainment Networks, Inc., 2012. http://www .trutv.com/library/crime/terrorists_spies/assassins/jfk/1.html (accessed April 5, 2012).

Lucero, Stephanie. "Mayors Reflect on Fight to Build Texas Stadium." *CBS 11 News,* December 18, 2008 http://cbs11tv.com/cowboys/fight .to.build.2.890749.html (accessed April 28, 2009).

McAdams, John C. "Assassination Records Review Board Testimony." *The Kennedy Assassination Home Page.* http://mcadams.posc.mu.edu/arrb/ (accessed April 25, 2009).

Media Projects, Inc. "About Us." Media Projects, Inc. Online. http://www
    .mediaprojects.org/about/ (accessed April 17, 2012).
"Museum Café + Store Main Page." *The Sixth Floor Museum at Dealey Plaza*,
    2010. http://www.jfk.org/go/store/store-cafe (accessed April 5, 2012).
National Register of Historic Places. "TEXAS—Dallas County." *National
    Register of Historic Places Online.*http://www.nationalregisterofhistoric
    places.com/tx/Dallas/state.html (accessed April 29, 2009).
Organ, Jerry. "Murder Perch to Museum." *The Kennedy Assassination Home
    Page,* Dr. John McAdams website, 2008: http://mcadams.posc.mu.edu/
    organ4.htm (accessed May 6, 2009).
"Past Winners of the All-America City Award." National Civic League, 2007.
    http://www.ncl.org/index.php?option=com_content&view=article&id=130
    &Itemid=186 (accessed April 17, 2012).
The Sixth Floor Museum at Dealey Plaza. *The Sixth Floor Museum at Dealey
    Plaza Online*, 2009. http://www.jfk.org (accessed April 27, 2009).
The Spaghetti Warehouse Restaurant. "About Us." *The Spaghetti Warehouse
    Restaurant Online*, 2007. http://www.meatballs.com/aboutus/about_his
    tory.html. (accessed April 17, 2012).
Stanley Marcus Collection. "The JFK Assassination: 40 Years Later—Stanley
    Marcus Letter." *DeGolyer Library Online*, Southern Methodist University.
    http://smu.edu/jfk/marcus.asp (accessed April 30, 2009).
Staples and Charles, Ltd. "Online Portfolio." PDF File, 2009.http://www.staple
    sandcharles.com/wp-content/uploads/2012/05/SC-Portfolio.pdf (accessed
    April 17, 2012).
Texas Historical Commission. "Antiquities Code of Texas." Amended
    September 1, 1997. http://www.thc.state.tx.us/rulesregs/RulesRegsPDF
    /AntiqCode.pdf (accessed March 3, 2009).
Texas Historical Foundation. "Our Mission, Our History, Our People." *Texas
    Historical Foundation Online.* http://www.texashistoricalfoundation.org
    /abouthf (accessed April 17, 2012).
Texas State Historical Association. "First Baptist Church, Dallas." *The
    Handbook of Texas Online*, April 2009. www.tshaonline.org/handbook
    /online/articles/WW/ivf1.html. (accessed May 15, 2009).
———. "Walker, Edwin A." *The Handbook of Texas Online*, April 2009. www
    .tshaonline.org/handbook/online/articles/WW/fwaaf.html (accessed May
    15, 2009).
Tunheim, John R. *Final Report of the Kennedy Assassination Records Review
    Board.* Google Book Search. http://books.google.com
    /books?id=OibCmEpOqDwC (accessed April 30, 2009).

Woods, Keith. "On the Road to Civil Rights: Memphis." Poynter Online, April 4, 1997. http://www.poynterextra.org/extra/king/memphis.html (accessed May 1, 2009).

Zapruder Film. The Sixth Floor Museum at Dealey Plaza. http://www.jfk.org /go/collections/about/zapruder-film-chronology (accessed April 17, 2012).

INDEX

References to illustrations appear in italic type.

AARC. *See* Assassination Archives and Research Center (AARC)
ABC. *See* American Broadcasting Company (ABC)
A. H. Belo Corporation, 107, 139
Adams, Lindalyn, 67, 70, 72, 75, 95, 150, 152, 153, 165, 166, 190n5, 191n21, 193n52, 194n82, 195n104, 208n191; and Commissioners Court, 78–79; and Dallas County Historical Foundation, 91–92, 93; Dealey Plaza model, 127–28; on exhibit design, 83–84; exhibit planning team, 66, 71, 73, 77–78; exhibit preview, 146–47; exhibit promotion, 88, 89–90, 98, 99, 100, 104, 110, 114; and Sixth Floor, 59–60, 61, 62, 94, 109, 111, 192n39, 197n125
Adams, Reuben, 75
Adaptive reuse, 53–54, 63, 71, 142–44
Adolphus Hotel, Democratic rally at, 22–23
Akins, George D., Jr., 66–67, 193n66
Alderson, William T., 70
Alexander, Bill, 27
Alexander, D. B., 50
Alger, Bruce, 20–21, 22, 24, 31
Allman, Pierce, 13, 142
Altgens, James, 142
Alyea, Tom, 15
Ambassador Hotel, 46

American Broadcasting Company (ABC), 13, 64, 139, 215–16n177
Anderson, Charles, 103
Anderson, Win, 41, 42
Antenna Tours, 142
Antiquities Code of Texas, 107
Arbor Development Corporation, 77, 101
Archaeology, 107–108
Armstrong, Bob, 158
Arson, at Book Depository, 41, 42, 94–95, 184n206
Artifacts, 210n31; Sixth Floor Museum, 127–29, 159
Ash, Mary Kay, 94
Assassination, John F. Kennedy's, 7–8, *116*; as Dallas's "secret," 50th anniversary of, 171; 111–12; second investigation of, 67–68; 10th anniversary, 51–52; 25th anniversary, 110–11, 112–14
Assassination Archives and Research Center (AARC), 152
Assassination attempt, on Ronald Reagan, 73–74, 75
Assassination Records Review Board, 155
Atsugi Air Base, Oswald at, 5–6
Audiocassette tour, 142

Baker, Marion, 10, 83, 193–94n68
Bannister, Guy, 7
Beal, William, 23
Belin, David, 142
Bell, Audrey, 142
Belli, Melvin, and Ruby trial, 27, *28*, 29–31

Belo Corporation. *See* A. H. Belo
    Corporation
Bickley, Alex, 44
Blakey, G. Robert, 66, 68, 102–103,
    124–25
Blow, Steve, 148
Bookstore, 129
Boone, Eugene, 142
Boyd, Elmer, 5
Bradshaw, Lillian, 98–99, 106–107, 129
Briggs, Charles A., 103, 123–24, 165
Bright, H. R. "Bum," 25
Brown, E. B., 78, 100
Brown, Joe B., 27, 28
Bryan, John Neely, 107, 108
Bryant, John, 106
Bryant, Megan, 158
Bugliosi, Vincent, 97–98
Burke, Roger, 153
Burleson, Phil, 27
Burson, Rodger, 54, 60, 63, 66, 72, 79,
    192n31
Bush, Dorothy, 5
Bush, George H. W., 155
Byrd, D. Harold, 40, 51, 54, 183n181;
    ownership of Book Depository, 37,
    41–42, 47, 49–50, 187n57

Cabell, Earle, 18, 32, 33, 52–53
Caldwell, Shirley, 74, 77, 84, 92
Call to Action exhibit, 161–62
Camelot Productions, 154–55
Castleberry, Vivian, 9–10
Castro, Fidel, 7
CBS Evening News, 26
CBS News, 139
Cecil and Ida Green Foundation, 107
Cell phone walking tour, 162
Central Intelligence Agency (CIA), 124
Challenge grants, Hoblitzelle Foundation,
    93, 97
Chambers, James F., 17, 18, 21

Charles, Barbara, 100, *119*, 124, 147, 165,
    197n133; exhibit design, 77, 78, 79,
    81–83, 85–87, 123, 128, 129, 130–
    31, 136, 139, 142–43; exhibit model,
    83–84
Cheney, Allison, 99
Cheney, Nancy, 98, 99–100, 110, 129, 165
Citizens Council, 25; and Dallas's image,
    31–32
City of Dallas Landmark Commission,
    104
Clergy, response to assassination, 26–27
Clinton, Bill, 155
Coggins, Paul, 166
Collins, James M., 61, 191n13
Collins, William E., 92
Color Place of Dallas, 143
Columbia Broadcasting System (CBS),
    10, 139
Commercial exploitation, 153–54
Committee for Kennedy Assassination
    Site Memorial, 35
Communism, Oswald's interest in, 4–5
Conceptual design, 78–79
Conde, Carlos, 35
Connally, John B., 7, 23, 25, 52, 152
Connally, Nellie, 7, 26, 158
Conservatism, in Dallas, 19–25, 31–32
Conspiracy Museum, 152
Conspiracy of One (Moore), 146
Conspiracy theories, 125, 126, 128,
    151–52
Cooper, William, 92
Crain, John, 66, 93, 197n133
Criswell, W. A., 20
Cronkite, Walter, 139–40, 155, 212n94,
    213n101
Crowley, Frank, 84
Cuba, 7
Cullum, Bob, 31
Curry, Jesse, 25

Dallas, 52, 108; conservatism of, 19–25, 190n5; criticisms of, 26–27; exhibit approval, 84–85; growth and development of, 53, 90, 188n76; impact on of assassination, 9–10, *11*, 111–14; memorials in, 33–36; opposition to Kennedy, 21–22, 24–25; rehabilitating image of, 31–33; as Republican town, 18–19; right-wing activism in, 30–32; Ruby trial, 27–30, *30*; as scapegoat, 17–18

Dallas Area Rapid Transit (DART), 204n114; subway portal plants, 101–104

Dallas Chamber of Commerce, antiharassment ordinance, 24–25

Dallas City Council, preservation of Book Depository, 43, 44

Dallas Convention Center, 94

Dallas County, 93; acquisition of Book Depository building, 45, 53, 54–58, 203n98; building renovation, 62–64, 69–71, 74–75; revenue bonds, 105–106; Sixth Floor exhibit planning, 65–66

Dallas County Administration Building, dedication of, *74–75*

Dallas County Commissioners Court, 33, 55, 58, 96, 108, 114, 191n13; and historic preservation, 60, 73; and Oliver Stone movie, 153, 154; on Sixth Floor exhibit, 68, 71, 78–79, 83–84, 91–92

Dallas County Commissioners Courtroom, in Book Depository, 53, 64, *74*

Dallas County Democratic Party, 96

Dallas County Heritage Society, 60, 61, 66, 92

Dallas County Historical Commission, 73, 77, 91, 92, 114

Dallas County Historical Foundation, 91, 100, 103, 138, 157, 211n69; exhibit development, 127, 129; fund-raising, 95, 96, 97, 99, 106–107; members of, 92–93; and Oliver Stone movie, 153, 154–55; research team, 124–25

Dallas Convention and Visitors Bureau, 65

Dallas Cowboys, 10

Dallas District Attorney's office, 96

Dallas Historical Society, 60, 61, 66

Dallas Justice (Belli), 30–31

Dallas Morning News, 21, 36, 43, 92; on Sixth Floor exhibit, 147–48; on 25th anniversary, 112–14

Dallas Morning News–WFAA Foundation, 93

Dallas Onward, 44, 45

Dallas Park Board, 35

Dallas Park Department, 62

Dallas Police Crime Scene Search Unit, 14–15

Dallas Police Department, 12, 13, 17, 25, 95, 182n170

Dallas Symphony Orchestra, 160

Dallas Times Herald, 17, 21, 23–24, 104

Dallas Welcoming Committee, 94

Daly, Charles, on Sixth Floor Museum, 109–10, 129

DART. *See* Dallas Area Rapid Transit (DART)

Dealey, E. M. "Ted," 21, 25, 92

Dealey, George Bannerman, 92

Dealey, Joe M., 19, 92, 93, 95, 96

Dealey Plaza, 34–35, 47, 111, 114, *116, 117, 118, 122,* 155, 162, 189n100, 192n39; commercial exploitation of, 153–54; and DART subway plans, 101–102; FBI model of, 127–28, 159; as memorial, 35–36; as National Historic Landmark District, 73, 151, 157–58; tourists at, 56, 65, 77, 100

Decker, Bill, 25

Democratic Party: Johnson campaign and, 22–23; in Texas, 18–19, 25, 47

Demolition, 70

Dillard, Tom, 26

Dillon, David, 104

Doussard, Robin, 152

Drew, Robert, 139

Eisenhower, Dwight D., 18

Elevator shaft, 106; designs for, 104–105

Exhibit: design of, 81–83, 84–85; development of, 126–32, 142; funding for, 73, 95, 96, 97; installation of, 142–46; model of, 83–84, 120; opening of, 149–51; planning for, 78–81; planning team, 64, 66–67, 68, 71, 77–78, 100, 101; previews of, 146–49; promotion of, 89, 90–91; revisions to, 85–88; staff, 158–59

Fair play for Cuba Committee, 7

Federal Bureau of Investigation (FBI), 6

Fensterwald, Bud, 152

Ferrell, Mary, 125

Filmmakers, for Sixth Floor Exhibit, 137–41

Films, 125, 215–16n177; Oliver Stone's, 153–55; Zapruder, 83, 116, 128, 152, 159

Films from The Sixth Floor, 138

Flach, Jeff, 154

Folsom, Robert, 56, 77, 189n97

Ford's Theater, 46, 60, 61, 190n11

Fort Worth, Oswalds in, 6–7

Foster, James, 167

Fox, David G., 106, 146, 154, 202n84, 205n139, 208n191

Frazier, Buell Wesley, 3, 4

Fritz, Will, 5

Fund-raising. See under Sixth Floor Museum

Funeral, Kennedy's, 8, 10

Garrison, Jim, 7, 83, 153

Geisel, Paul, 124

George, Eugene, 66–67, 78, 79, 100, 119, 123, 165, 193n66; adaptive reuse of Sixth Floor, 142–44; exhibit planning, 80–81

Givens, Charles, 10

Goals for Dallas program, 32, 33

Godbold, Bryghte, 32

Golman, Joe, 49

Gorr, Louis F., 66

Grants: challenge, 93, 97; NEH planning, 62, 65–66, 85

Grassy knoll scenario, 68, 83, 103, 128

Greenberg, Bob, 96

Greene, A. C., 148

Grieving process, national, 8

Groden, Robert, 125, 126

Haley, J. Evetts, 20

Hall, Ralph, 48

Hargis, Bobby, 142

Harman, Michael, 61

Hay, Jess, 92, 106, 200n33

Hays, Bob, 151, 152–53, 156

HCRS. See Heritage, Conservation, and Recreation Service (HCRS)

Helvarg, David, 142

Hendricks, Burson, and Wells: adaptive reuse, 53–54; conversion of Book Depository, 62–63; Sixth Floor conceptual exhibit design, 78–79

Hendricks, James L., 40, 53, 84, 119, 165; building renovations, 63–64, 96, 100; Sixth Floor Visitors Center design, 79–80, 104–105, 143, 197–98n143

Hendricks and Callaway, 96

Henry, Carl, 110, 125, 146

Heritage, Conservation, and Recreation Service (HCRS), meeting with, 72–73

Heritage Display, 143

Hertz Billboard, 70–71, 95, 118, 193n82

Hill, Robert M., 41

Hinckley, John, 73, 195n104
Historic buildings, adaptive reuse of, 53–54
Historic preservation, 53, 60, 188n78
Historic sites, National Park Service policies regarding, 71–72
Hoblitzelle Foundation, 93, 106
Holmes, Bert, 31
Holmes, Helen, 25, 29
Holmes, William A., 26–27
Holt, Bill, 36–37
House Select Committee on Assassinations, 66, 127, 130
Houston Post, exhibit preview, 148
Howard, Larry, 152
"Hundred Days of Love, A," 27
Hunt, Conover, 46, 61–62, 76, 78, 85, 94, 100, 105, 108, 111, 114, *119*, 138, 142, 144, 146, *147*, 150, 151, 155, 166–67, 197n133, 200n33, 205n139, 208n191, 211n69; on building preservation, 42, 43; and Commissioners Court, 71, 73; on DART plans, 102–103; on Dealey Plaza as National Historic Landmark, 157–58; exhibit development and, 126–27, 128, 129–30; exhibit planning team and, 65–67, 71, 101; exhibit promotion and, 88, 89–90, 107; exhibit text, 136–37; on Kennedy legacy, 135–36; and research team, 123, 124, 125–26
Hunt, H. L., 20
Hunt, Nelson Bunker, 20
Hutchinson, Kay Bailey, 158

Interviews, archived, 159
Irving, Texas, Marina Oswald in, 7

Jackie paintings (Warhol's), 161
Jackson, Bob, 161
Jackson, Jim, 55

Jackson, Lee F., 106, 108, 142, 150, 153, 158, 162, 166, 205n139; promotion of Sixth Floor exhibit, 98, *99*
Jefferies, George, 18
Jenkins, M. T., 142
JFK (film), 153–55, 156, 207n176, 215–16n177
JFK Assassination Information Center, 151–52
JFK for a New Generation, 151
John Birch Society, 19, 20
John F. Kennedy and the Memory of a Nation, previews, 146–49
Johnson, Lady Bird, 22
Johnson, Lyndon, 10, 89, 125; presidential campaign, 21–22
Johnson, Philip, 35, 111, 160; Kennedy Memorial design, 33, 48
Jonsson, J. Erik, 31, 32
Jurow, Martin, 59, 123, 141, 212n96; *Films from The Sixth Floor*, 138

Katy Building, 152
Kennedy, Edward M., 84, 99, 100, 110
Kennedy, Jacqueline. *See* Onassis, Jacqueline Kennedy
Kennedy, John F., *115*, *116*; Dallas's opposition to, 21–22, 24–25; legacy of, 135–36; memorializing, 33–35, 47–48; portrayal in Sixth Floor Exhibit, 129–30; trip to Dallas, 7–8, 25–26
Kennedy, Robert, 18, 19, 46
Kennedy, Tom, 148
Kennedy Center for the Performing Arts, 160
Kennedy Citizens Memorial Committee, John F., 33
Kennedy Memorial, 33–34, *34*, 35, 48, 181–82n161, 189n97
Kennedy Memorial Book Fund, John F., 34, 47

Kennedy Memorial Center, John F., 49

Kennedy Memorial Commission, John F., 47, 48; recommendations of, 49–51

Kennedy Museum, John F., 75–77, 196n121

Kennedy Presidential Library, John F., 138–39

Kilduff, Malcolm, 125

King, Martin Luther, Jr., 18, 46

KLIF, 13

Landry, Tom, 10, 113

Lane, Rick, 145

Lane Container Company, 145

Langley, Martina, on memorializing Kennedy, 34–35

Leavelle, James, 142

Legacy, The (film), 139–41, 213n101

Leo, Jack, 68–69

Lesar, James, 152

Light rail system. *See* Dallas Area Rapid Transit (DART)

Lincoln, Abraham, 96, 135; and Ford's Theater, 35, 46, 60, 101

Linden, Glenn, 129, 153, 155, 157, 165

London Weekend Television, 97

Longford, Nicola, 136, 162, 163, 166, 171

Loss and Renewal: Transforming Tragic Sites, 159

Love Field, 8; reception at, 25–26, *115*

Lowe, Jacques, 161

Lunchroom, 193–94n68, 194n70; and building renovation, 69–70; and Sixth Floor Exhibit, 83, 130

Mack, Gary, 40, 42, 103, 123, 125, 126, 128, 136, 139, 159, 162, 172

MacNeil, Robert, 13

Marcus, Stanley, 23, 27, 89–90

Marx, Karl, 4–5

Mayhew, Aubrey, *39*, 42, 49; and Book Depository building, 37–38, 184nn206, 212, 213; museum plans

of, 40–41; National Register of Historic Places application, 46–47

McAdams, John, 125

McDermott Foundation, Eugene, 107

McDonald, M. N., 10, 177n31

McElhaney, Jackie, 124

McGehee, Frank, 20, 23

McIntire, Mel, 127

McKnight, Felix, 17

McKool, Mike, 43, 47, 48

McNeely, Dave, 50

Media, 94, 95; exhibit previews, 146, 147–48; photographs, 126–27; on 10th anniversary, 51–52

Media Projects, Inc., videos produced by, 137–41

Melde, Craig, 104–105

Melton, Bill, 150

Memorials: Book Depository as, 36–37; Dealey Plaza as, 35–36; for Kennedy, 33–35, 47–48

Memory, of tragedies, 168–69, 170–73

Memory Books, 136, 150

Meredith, James, 19

Mexico City, Oswald in, 7

Miller, Laura, 84, 97

Miller, Melody, 100, 110

Missouri Pacific Railroad, 101

Mondell, Allen, 114, *119*, 212n94, 213n101; video production, 137–41

Mondell, Cynthia, 114, *119*, 212n94; video production, 137–41

Montgomery, Marian Ann, 158

Mooney, Luke, 14, 15

Moore, Jim, 125, 145; *Conspiracy of One*, 146

Moreno, Samuel, 92, 94

Morton H. Meyerson Symphony Center, 160

Morton's of Chicago, 107

Motorcade, 7–8, *9*, 26

Mourning, national, 8–9

Murchison, William, 113

Murtagh, William, 72
Museum Café + Store, 162–63
Museum of the Moving Image, 161

Nasher, Raymond D., 48, 49
National Academy of Science, grassy knoll
    scenario refutation, 68
National Broadcasting Company (NBC),
    13, 139
National day of mourning, 8
National Endowment for the Humanities
    (NEH), 85; planning grant, 62, 65–66
National Historic Landmark District,
    Dealey Plaza as, 73, 151, 157–58
National Historic Preservation Act, 43,
    103
National Historic Sites Commission, 44
National Indignation Convention, 20, 23
National Park Service: on historic preser-
    vation, 61, 191n15; and Kennedy his-
    toric sites, 71–72; and Sixth Floor
    Museum, 100, 129
National Register of Historic Places, 43,
    53, 195n98; application to, 46–47, 50,
    72–73
NEH. See National Endowment for the
    Humanities (NEH)
Newman, Bill, 142, 168
Newman, Gayle, 142
New Orleans, Oswald in, 7
News coverage, 18, 26, 28; of anti-UN
    protest, 23–24; and Book Depository,
    13, 15, 17
New York Times, 17, 148
Nixon, Richard, 19
North Texas film commission, 153

Oak Cliff, Texas Theatre in, 10, 12, 155,
    195n98
Onassis, Jacqueline Kennedy, 7, 62, 100,
    191n22
One November Day (film), 97

On Trial: Lee Harvey Oswald (television
    program), 97–98
Oppermann, Joe, 84
Oral History Project and Collection, 159,
    160, 161, 171
Orr, Roy, 55, 56, 78–79
Osborne, Kevin, 131
Oswald, June, 7
Oswald, Lee Harvey, 20, 112, 146; arrest
    of, 10, 12, 177n31; employment at
    Book Depository, 3–4; exhibit treat-
    ment of, 83, 87; life of, 4–7; in lunch-
    room, 69, 193–94n68; murder of,
    12–13, 187n65
Oswald, Marguerite, 4
Oswald, Marina Prusakova, 3, 6, 7

Paine, Ruth, 3, 7
Pappas, Ike, 36, 142
Parking garages, 101
Parkland Memorial Hospital, 8, 13
Payne, Darwin, 31, 33–34
Pelou, François, 17
Pennebaker, James, 111–12, 124, 207n176
Perot, H. Ross, 97
Phoenix I Restoration and Construction,
    Ltd., 160
Photographic archive, 127
Pickett, David, 54
Porter, Abigail, 123, 124
Powell, Boone, Sr., 92
Power, Becky, 92
Power, Robert, 92
Powers, David, 142
President John F. Kennedy Records
    Collection Act, 155
Press, criticism of Dallas, 17–18
Price, John Wiley, 108, 154
Protests: by Republicans, 22–23; against
    United Nations, 23–24
Proto Productions, silk-screening by, 143
Purse Building, 55, 57

Radio stations, 13
Rapoport, Bernard, 49
Rawlings, Mike, 171
Ray, James Earl, 46
Read, Meg, 154, 157
Reagan, Ronald, attempted assassination of, 73–74, 75
Redlich, Norman, 61
Renovation, 77; of Book Depository, 62–64, 69–71, 74–75, 96, 100, 193n66; of Sixth Floor, 142–44, 194–95n85
Republican National Convention (1984), 94–95
Republican Party, and Dallas, 18–19, 21–22
Research team, 123–26
Revenue bonds, 105–106
Rhodes, Thomas B., 45, 55–56
Right-wing activism, Dallas and, 19–20, 30–32
Robinson, Hugh G., 92–93, 200n33
Rookstool, Farris, 125
Ross, David, 66
Rozelle, Pete, 10
Ruby, Jack, 12, 17, 187n65; trial of, 27–31
Russell, Richard, 37, 182n170
Russell, Tom, 19, 36

Saturday Evening Post, 17
Security, 68–69
Sellars, Richard, 100, 101, 103, 106, 157
Semos, Chris, 96, 153
September 11, 2001, 161
Sexton Building. See Texas School Book Depository building
Shaw, Clay, 7
Shaw, J. Gary, 151–52
Shelley, Bill, 4
Sherrell, Cindy, 61
Sherrod, Blackie, 113–14
Shipp, Bert, 15

Shook, Judson, 42, 45, 51, 52, 53, 54, 56, 57, 58, 66, 74, 166, 190nn11, 15, 192n27, 201n65; on renovation of Book Depository, 62–63, 70, 75; on Sixth Floor museum, 59, 60–61, 72
Showtime Network, 97
Sims, Richard, 5
Sissom, Estelle, 75–76
Sissom, John, 162, 196n112; John F. Kennedy Museum, 75–76
Sixth Floor Museum at Dealey Plaza, 71, 120, 168–69, 194–95n85; artifacts in, 127–29; building restoration and exhibit installation, 142–46; collections and exhibit staff, 158–59; Daly, Charles, on, 109–110; entrance fees/admission prices, 96, 110; exhibit design and development, 78–79, 126–32, 132, 142; exhibit planning team, 64–67, 100, 101; exhibit previews, 146–49; expansion of, 162–63; exterior elevator shaft for, 104–105; fund-raising, 74, 85, 93, 95, 96, 97, 99, 105–107, 196n112, 205n139; George, Eugene, and, 80–81; layout of, 133–37; management of, 91–92; opening of, 149–51; operations of, 152–53; origins of, 59–60, 61–62; planning for, 77–78, 84–88; potential impacts of, 111–12; programming for, 161–62; promotion of, 89, 93–94, 98–100, 114; relevancy of, 171–72; research team, 123–26; security, 68–69; seventh floor expansion, 160–61; sniper's perch in, 144–45; Shook, Judson, and, 60–61; Oliver Stone's use of, 153–55; twentieth anniversary, 165–67; videos produced for, 137–41; visitation, 150–52, 155–56; visitors to, 163–64
Smith, Preston, 48
Smith, Russell, 43, 44

Smith, Stephen, 33, 100
Smith, Thomas H., 93, 129
"Sniper's perch/nest," 69, 100, 112; as
    dominant element, 81, 134; news
    coverage of, 14–17; re-creation of,
    144–45
Solon, John J., 41
Sorensen, Ted, 48
Southern Methodist University (SMU),
    Archaeology Research Program,
    137–38
Southfork Ranch, as tourist destination,
    65, 94, 111
Southland Corporation, 93
Southwestern Historical Quarterly, exhibit
    review, 148
Souvenir hunters, 69
Soviet Union, Oswald in, 6
Spence, Gerry, 97–98, 202n78
Staples, Robert, 100, 165; exhibit design,
    77, 78, 79, 81–83, 85–87, 124, 129,
    130–31, 139, 142–43; exhibit model,
    83–84
Stemmons, John, 90, 199n11
Sterrett, Lew, 33
Stevenson, Adlai, 23–*24*, 89
St. Joe Brick Works, 108
Stone, Oliver, *JFK,* 152, 153–55, 207n176,
    215–16n177
Strauss, Annette, 106
Strauss, Robert, 139, 140, 212n96
Strickman, Evelyn, 4
Strong, Jack, 48
Subway, DART plans for, 101–104,
    204n114

"Tag Day," 21–22
Tames, George, 148
Tatum, Henry, 113, 148
Tax Reform Act (1986), 97
Taylor, A. Starke, 84
Taylor, Lon, 61

Television, 64; news broadcasts, 12, 13; *On
    Trial: Lee Harvey Oswald,* 97–98
Terry, Marshall, 20
Texas Historical Commission, 46, 61, 66,
    191n21; Sixth Floor exhibit design,
    84–85, 104, 105
Texas Historical Foundation, 60, 191n21
Texas House of Representatives, 48
Texas School Book Depository build-
    ing, *117, 118, 122,* 183n182, 195n97,
    196n122; arson fires at, 42, 94–95,
    184n206; commercial exploitation,
    153–54; Dallas County acquisition
    of, 49–50, 54–58, 203n98; as Dallas
    County Administration Building,
    74, 74–75; HCRS meeting on, 72–73;
    history of, 13–14; Mayhew's owner-
    ship of, 37–38, 184nn206, 212, 213;
    as memorial, 35, 36–37; as museum,
    40–41; National Register of Historic
    Places application, 46–47, 50; opposi-
    tion to saving, 45–46, 52–53, 185n18;
    preservation of, 43, 44–45, 50–51;
    proposed acquisition of, 47–48; ren-
    ovation of, 62–64, 69–71, 74–75,
    96, 100; Oliver Stone's movie and,
    153–55
Texas School Book Depository Company,
    Oswald's employment at, 3–4
Texas Senate, 48
Texas Theatre, 10, 12, 155, 195n98,
    210n31
Thomas, Carl, 57
Thomas J. Hayman Construction
    Company, 108
Thompson, Josiah, 142
Thornton, R. L., 33
Ticket revenue, 106
Timms, Ed, 113
Tippit, J. D., 10, 12
Tonahill, Joe, 27, *28*
Toppel, Louis, 37, 70–71

Tourism, 53; Book Depository and, 36–37, 51, 64, 98–99, 196n122; Dealey Plaza, 56, 65, 100; Kennedy Memorial and, 33–34; Kennedy Museum, 76–77

Tracy-Locke Public Relations, 111, 148–49, 207n173

Tragedies, remembering, 168–69, 170–73

Tretick, Stanley, 161

Trial of Lee Harvey Oswald, The, filming of, 64, 215–16n177

Truly, Roy, 10, 14, 193–94n68

Tyson, Jim, 55, 57, 79

Unfinished Business: Kennedy and Cuba (exhibit), 160

United Nations, protests against, 23–24

United Nations Day, 23

University of Texas tower, 46

U.S. House Select Committee on Assassinations, 67–68

U.S. Marine Corps, Oswald in, 5–6

U.S. Transportation Department, 103–104

Video presentations, 137

Visitors Center, 101, 102, 106, *121, 149*; construction of, 108–109, 143; exterior elevator shaft, 104–105; Hendricks's design of, 79–80; rotating exhibits, 159–60

Visual media, 125

Wade, Henry, 27, *30*, 57

Walker, Edwin A., 7, 19–20, 23

Walter, J. Jackson, 150

Walters, G. C., 37

Warhol, Andy, *Jackie* paintings of, 161

Warren, Earl, 10, 20

Warren Commission, 10, 18, 67, 83, 87, 125, 126, 127

Washington Post, 95

Weber, Garry, 78–79; building preservation, 42–43, 44–45

Weber, Harriet, 92

Weingarten, Paul, 153–54

Weiss, Bart, 138

West, Jeff, 156, 157, 158, 160

West End Historic District, 53, 85, 101, 104, 152, 195n97; building renovation in, 63–64

West End Marketplace, 151–52

West End Task Force, 84–85

WFAA, 13, 139

Whitman, Charles, 46

Whittington, John, 54, 55, 56

Wilson, Don, 127

Wilson, Will, 22

Wise, Wes, 45, 50, 51–52, 187n65

WNEW, 36

Wolf, Adah Leah, 124, 157, 165–66

Woods, Char, 142

Wright, Jim, 25, 52

Yarborough, Ralph, 25

Zapruder, Abraham, 126, 196n117; home movie, 83, *116*, 128, 152, 159

Zeder, Fred M., 43, 44, 46